A Place of Power

Blind indeed are those who do not see the sweep of a movement whose orbit infinitely transcends the natural sciences and has successfully invaded and conquered the surrounding territory — chemistry, physics, sociology, and even mathematics and the history of religions. One after the other all the fields of human knowledge have been shaken and carried away by the same underwater current in the direction of the study of some *development*. Is evolution a theory, a system, or a hypothesis? It is much more; it is a general condition to which all theories, all hypotheses, all systems must bow and which they must satisfy henceforward if they are to be thinkable and true. Evolution is a light illuminating all facts, a curve that all lines must follow.

PIERRE TEILHARD DE CHARDIN,
The Phenomenon of Man

Man is not a passive receiver of stimuli coming from an external world, but in a very concrete sense *creates* his universe.

LUDWIG VON BERTALANFFY,
General Systems Theory

A Place of Power
THE AMERICAN EPISODE IN HUMAN EVOLUTION

Walt Anderson

Goodyear Publishing Company, Inc.
Santa Monica, California

Library of Congress Cataloging in Publication Data

Anderson, Walt, 1933–
   A place of power.

   Includes index.
   1. United States – Politics and government.
2. Human ecology – United States. 3. Natural history –
United States. I. Title.
JK39.A54   301.5'92'0973   76-12809
ISBN 0-87620-080-3
ISBN 0-87620-079-X pbk.

ISBN: 0-87620-080-3 (case)   0-87620-079-X (paper)
Y-0803-0 (case)   Y-079X-4 (paper)

iv

Interior and Cover Design: John Isely
Photo Research: Genoa Caldwell
Copy and Developmental Editing: Victoria Pasternack
Supervising Production Editor: Sue MacLaurin
Layout and Art Production: Sally Collins and Andy Lucas

Current Printing (last number): 10 9 8 7 6 5 4 3 2 1
Printed in the United States of America

Acknowledgements

The two people whose efforts and encouragement have been most important to me are my wife, Maurica, and my editor, Dave Grady. Maurica typed manuscripts, wrote letters, researched, and shared my fascination with bits and pieces of ecological history. Dave contributed many things to the work, including an unfailing conviction that the project was exciting and worthwhile.

The manuscript was sent out for readings to James Danielson (North Texas State University), Dan Nimmo (University of Tennessee), and Philippa Strum (Queens College). Many of their comments, criticisms, and suggestions were taken into account in the final revision. Dan Nimmo's two reviews at different stages of the book's development were especially helpful.

I am grateful to Bill Press, now director of the Office of Planning and Research, State of California, for a careful reading of Chapter Three, and to many other friends and associates — among them Elizabeth Campbell, Jack Drach, Rachel Norstrand, Maurica Osborne, M. Samvedana, Richard Wilson, and Bill and Lois Wilcoxen — who read parts of the manuscript and helped out along the way. Sue MacLaurin and Pam Tully steered us through all the prepublication details, and the final product owes a great deal to the photo research of Genoa Caldwell, the manuscript and developmental editing of Victoria Pasternack, and the graphic design of John Isely.

I would also like to acknowledge my debt to two writers who, in different ways, contributed immeasurably to my own thinking. One of them is Lewis Mumford, whose works I have been reading for well over twenty years with great admiration for the breadth and depth of his vision of human life. It is amazing to me that in a materialistic society we have produced so few people who pay close attention to how material things — such as food and tools and houses and machines — shape and express the quality of our daily lives. Lewis Mumford does just that, and does it brilliantly. The other writer is Thomas Landon Thorson. His *Biopolitics* is cited only once in the following pages, but I am sure that if I had not read it six years ago, I would not have written this book.

Contents

Preface

This is chiefly a book about American political history, and in it the reader will encounter many of the people and subjects expected to appear in such a work: Christopher Columbus, the Pilgrims, the United States Constitution, Thomas Jefferson, Benjamin Franklin, Andrew Jackson, slavery, Abraham Lincoln, immigration, the Westward Movement, buffaloes, Indians, Johnny Appleseed, Teddy Roosevelt, John D. Rockefeller, multinational corporations, the energy crisis, air pollution, Richard Nixon, and other family favorites.

The reader will also encounter, perhaps with some uncertainty about what it is doing here, a good deal of material about plants and animals and soil and waterways, material of the sort that is usually set apart as "natural history." I include such material in an attempt to show that our political history is also natural history, that government is a biological and evolutionary phenomenon.

So this book is both a look at American politics, past and present, and an exposition of a different way of looking at politics. My approach could be called a theory, but I prefer to think of it as a perspective: if you take this perspective, look at the American experience from the point of view it suggests, then certain things that you have more or less known about before — such as the fact that not only people but also plants and animals came to America from other parts of the world — take on a new significance, and the unity of political and natural history becomes apparent.

The perspective should come clear in the first chapter. I do not plan to try to summarize it here, but it might be helpful if I state a couple of things that it is *not* in order to avoid any misconceptions.

First, it is not a revival of Social Darwinism, that school of philosophy-cum-political ideology that flourished in America in the late eighteenth and early nineteenth centuries. Social Darwinism was a rather calculated misreading of evolutionary theory that fastened its teeth into one fragment of Darwinian thought — the idea of the survival of the fittest — and made it the basis of a new political ideology. The basic message of that ideology was that greed and imperialism do the work of nature by perpetuating the strongest and best societies and individuals while eliminating the weakest (I refer to it hopefully in the past tense, although it still lives on in the hearts of some). I do not want to dismiss Social Darwinism entirely. There was some truth in it, and it served a historical purpose: it did, at least, start people thinking about politics in evolutionary terms. Its most obvious shortcomings were that it was ethically shallow — Social Darwinists never got very far in their thinking about what evolutionary responsibilities come with power — and it drew some hasty conclusions about what constituted fitness to survive. Today we cannot be so confident that Western industrialized society is all that fit.

Second, the perspective is not an exercise in searching out biological or instinctual explanations for what "really" motivates us to do the things we do — explaining political behavior in terms of instinctive aggressiveness, for example. The trouble with explanations of this sort is that they overemphasize the role of instinctive drives and underestimate the dimension of culture, language, symbolic systems of meaning and communication. Nothing human is fully explained without reference to that dimension. Ludwig von Bertalanffy, the father of general systems theory, insisted that human behavior could not be reduced to prehuman terms:

Symbolic behavior, the "secondary process," cannot be "reduced" or "resolved into" primary processes, innate action schemes or simple learning processes. On the other hand, primary motivation goes right through all behavioral levels. . . . Human warfare cannot be reduced to man's aggressive drive; war and so-called essential aggression in the great scourges of mankind from Tamerlane to contemporaries presuppose not only bloodthirsty and belligerent instincts but an elaborate symbolic framework, an ideology. . . . But, by the same token, war would be biologically impossible except for the instinctual possibility of intra-specific aggression.[1]

Since I have mentioned systems theory I should also state, mainly for the benefit of political scientists, that the perspective I work from has little in common with the "systems" approach that is commonly employed in political science. General systems theory as originally outlined by von Bertalanffy and others was solidly grounded in biology and evolution. But a funny thing happened to it on its way over to

x

---

[1]Ludwig von Bertalanffy, *Robots, Men and Minds* (New York: Braziller, 1967), pp. 34-35.

the social sciences: it lost that context and became highly mechanistic. The political order was sometimes likened to a huge factory, and frequently it was represented in drawings that looked rather like wiring diagrams for an old crystal radio set.[2] This was unfortunate because it encouraged the student to overlook the most interesting thing about the political system — the fact that it is alive.

To keep in touch with that important fact I frequently use the word *ecosystem* instead of simply *system*. Usually the word ecosystem has been used to denote smaller and nonhuman organizations of life, but its meaning — a community of beings and their environment, viewed as a whole — is equally applicable to a city or a nation. There are microecosystems and macroecosystems.

Finally, it would be good to keep in mind that, although it is useful to isolate ecosystems so we can study them as functioning wholes, no living system is truly closed; it is always connected to other systems and contained by larger systems. As John Muir observed, when we try to pick out anything by itself we find it hitched to everything else in the universe.

---

[2]See David Easton, *A Systems Analysis of Political Life* (New York: Wiley, 1965).

1

The End of Nature

All the processes of industrial production
that are the material end-products of
scientific technology have one characteristic
of overwhelming effect — their capability
of enormously magnifying human productivity
by endowing men with literally superhuman
abilities to control the physical and
chemical attributes of nature.
ROBERT L. HEILBRONER, *An Inquiry into the Human Prospect*

This land is your land, this land is my land,
This land was made for you and me.
WOODY GUTHRIE, Refrain from "This Land Is Your Land"

The Big Doomsday-Eve Parade

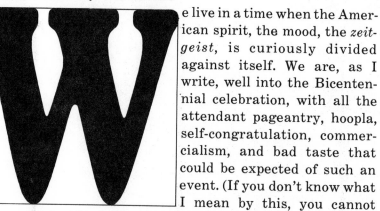 e live in a time when the American spirit, the mood, the *zeitgeist*, is curiously divided against itself. We are, as I write, well into the Bicentennial celebration, with all the attendant pageantry, hoopla, self-congratulation, commercialism, and bad taste that could be expected of such an event. (If you don't know what I mean by this, you cannot have walked with your child in the streets of Disneyland, as I have, and watched a plastic Mickey Mouse lead a parade of American heroes through the smog.) At the same time that this celebration, outwardly so muscular and confident, strides through our daily lives there is a pervasive sense of pessimism abroad in the land — a loss of hope for the future, a loss of faith in the system — so strong and recent that it seems as though the bottom has suddenly dropped without warning out of the American dreamboat.

There has always been a public argument between the pointers-with-pride and the viewers-with-alarm and a corresponding private tension within each of us between patriotic pride in the American accomplishment and shame of its vulgarities and inequities. This public dialogue, this inner conflict, is nothing new — yet something is new. The whole process has made a quantum leap in our time, so that it is now much more

2

intense and asks a cosmic and urgent question: Are we going to survive?

The question has to do with doomsday, and of course it is not so much a question as a vague set of images: the collapse of fundamental institutions, the drastic decline in American power, various kinds of ecological catastrophe, nuclear war, the total destruction of civilization, the extinction of the human species. I do not think that I have mentioned anything in this quick inventory of disaster that has not, at one time or another, loomed for most of us as a real future likelihood.

The human imagination has probably always known thoughts of this kind, but doomsday has become a more imminent and conceivable eventuality over the past few decades. The atomic bomb brought the first warning that the human species had attained an unprecedented capacity for destruction. As the stockpiles of atomic weapons built up, we had to come to friendly terms with the hideous possibilities of what might lie beyond a deliberate or accidental unleashing of those forces by the major international powers. That possibility has not faded, but the range of scenarios has expanded recently to include the potential for a different kind of nuclear showdown precipitated by some guerilla group or have-not nation that has — perhaps as a result of American programs to establish nuclear power facilities abroad — become capable of constructing and using an atomic weapon.

The nuclear holocaust scenarios have at least one reassuring facet: They haven't happened yet. They can be anticipated and thus perhaps prevented. But there is another class of potential disasters lacking even this consolation. I mean the various catastrophes that are, some say, inevitable — products of sequences of events already too far advanced to stop. The population issue is in this class. Here we are warned by Paul Ehrlich and others that the time for averting crisis has already passed, that the dynamics of growth are carrying us helplessly toward a time of famines. While Ehrlich and the population activists point to this crisis, others contemplate the oceans and tell us that here, too, we have set forces in motion that are well past the point of return.[1] The waters are already seriously contaminated and the sources of the contamination — industrial and agricultural wastes, human sewage — are steadily increasing their output. A similar message is contained in *The Limits to Growth*, whose authors report that supplies of many of the world's key nonrenewable resources are fast running out, while consumption of them continues to increase.[2] They offer the

3

---

[1]See, for example, Paul Ehrlich, *The Population Bomb* (New York: Ballantine Books, 1968), and Wesley Marx, *The Frail Ocean* (New York: Ballantine Books, 1969).
[2]Donella H. Meadows et al., *The Limits to Growth* (New York: Universe Books, 1972).

lily-pond riddle as a way of understanding these exponential-growth problems in which the rate of change changes. Imagine a pond in which a lily pad is growing and doubling its size each day, so that in thirty days it will completely cover the pond and kill everything in it. You observe the lily pad's growth and do not decide to cut it back until the day it covers half the pond. When is that? The answer is: the twenty-ninth day.

The shared characteristic of these exponential-growth catastrophes, as opposed to the nuclear explosion group, is that they do not await the act of some terrorist or misguided national leader; they are already happening. All we have to do is proceed with business as usual and the time of famines, the death of the seas, the exhaustion of the world's resources will arrive on schedule.

We must also confront the reality of a number of already evident problems — perhaps less apocalyptic than those mentioned above, but nonetheless serious and pressing. It takes no special statistical skill or sociological foresight to see that something is troubling our usual supplies of energy, that money becomes progressively less valuable, that many people are unemployed, that many of the people who *are* employed are caught up in meaningless drudgery at the service of huge institutions, that our nominally "democratic" governmental institutions frequently seem to operate as if the people they are supposed to serve were the enemy.

All of these present problems and potential disasters also share a common characteristic: they are the products of human action. Once people's fears focused chiefly on forces beyond human control. Look at ancient myths of the end of the world and you will find stories of upheavals caused by natural or divine powers — done perhaps in retribution for some human sin or folly, but still not directly brought about by human action. Yet today it is inescapable that the calamities we fear most are of our own doing, by-products of our ever-increasing control of natural forces. There have undoubtedly been times and places where famines resulted from purely natural causes, but the famines we fear today are the consequences of a human population explosion caused by our success in reducing the death rate. Famine may, in a sense, be a "natural" disaster; but nature has changed. If by "nature" we mean the old concept of something that proceeds without human interference or management, then there is scarcely any nature left in the world; certainly not in that segment of the world we call the United States of America.

This Land Was Made for You and Me

The whole thrust and purpose of the American experience has been in the direction of (1) bringing to this continent a vast number of people from other parts of the world, and (2) modifying this continent to make it suitable for the kind of social organization its new inhabitants wanted. Over the rather brief span of centuries that American history covers, we have built a huge, artificial ecosystem of farms and factories and cities, artificial waterways and sculptured land spaces. This is what we must now run — and keep it running, because it sustains our lives.

The American continent has been transformed; it is now an artificial ecosystem and it must be managed by human action. This cannot be stopped, now, nor can we return to a natural order untouched by human society. We are at the controls, whether we like it or not. If suddenly the human race were to disappear from the North American continent there would be a period of ecological chaos followed by the emergence of a new balance of nature. But it would have very little resemblance to the America that existed before Columbus arrived. And since we do not intend to disappear and do not know how to live in anything *but* an artificial ecosystem, we would do well to confront the fact that we have indeed created one and now must manage it. We must confront the fact that our "system" — the whole political/social/economic interaction — must govern the entire physical space of America, all its water and air and living creatures.

When the new political system we now call the United States of America was organized and put into operation, it became the legitimate government of its citizens. Following the recognized concept of the nation-state as a territorial entity, it assumed jurisdiction over the physical space itself, the land and water within its borders. Furthermore, it assumed governing power over all the other living creatures within that physical space. American history does not indicate that the birds, beasts, and flowers were ever consulted on this point, but nevertheless their lives came under the control of the new human civilization. There was, of course, no explicit discussion of this dimension of political power at the time. It was an implicit and unquestioned part of the consciousness of Western culture, as old as Genesis.

The system, the United States, is simultaneously a political system and a *biological* system of great complexity. It contains within it billions of identifiable ecosystems. Some of these, in mountain wildernesses and deserts and untouched coastal

> All biological subsystems of whatever kind are linked by the fact that their destinies are ultimately subject to the control of the species at the top of the system's hierarchy.

5

areas, carry on their life processes much as they did ages before the first white settlers came to America. Many ecosystems owe their existence entirely or in part to human activity. But all biological subsystems of whatever kind are linked by the fact that their destinies are ultimately subject to the control of the species at the top of the system's hierarchy. Consider your day's intake of food and the clothes you wear and you will begin to get some idea of how many life systems become inputs to your own. Look out the window and you can see that the environment has been shaped by human action. The political order is not merely a power system governing the lives of human beings. It also governs nature. It is itself an ecosystem.

Consider how political decisions steer ecology and evolution. Farm policies affect land use and all living things in and on the land. Agriculture generally favors the propagation of species that have commercial value and seeks to control or eliminate those that compete with or prey upon the favored species. Any policy that concerns pollution affects many ecosystems. Dam building and canal building alter water systems and all the life processes connected with them. Urbanization and highway building bulldoze and pave their ways through ancient natural habitats. The creation of wilderness areas and parks maintains existing ecosystems at the pleasure of public (human) policy. Income tax and welfare policies influence human population growth. Even seemingly unbiological matters such as inflation and depression leave their ecological marks, because economic conditions affect birthrates, and anything that affects the number of people affects the national ecology generally.

Growing human numbers, changing patterns of consumption, and the advances of technology have produced a tremendous increase in our demands on the environment and also in our ability to control it. Some dawning awareness of this was reflected in the conservation movement of the Theodore Roosevelt era at the beginning of the twentieth century and, more recently, in the surge of concern about population and ecology.

So it is generally understood now that the political system deals with some "environmental issues." But full realization of our situation has not yet shown up either in politics or in political science. Environmentalists are more clear-sighted about the matter than most people, but environmentalists tend to be (for good reasons) preoccupied with preventing things: stopping development projects, slowing population growth. Also, the whole mystique of ecology places a high value on the natural, on the "balance of nature." However attractive this may be, in a way it is deceptive because there no longer is any

such thing as a "balance of nature" in the United States of America.

So far our management of this artificial life system has been a rather hit-or-miss proposition characterized by an intensive effort to avoid recognizing the fact that we are in control. Nevertheless we are: the driver is still the driver, even when asleep at the wheel.

This is where we are now: at a place of power, of control over the environment and over the course of evolution.

Any policy that concerns pollution affects many ecosystems. Dam building and canal building alter water systems and all the life processes connected with them.

Evolutionary Politics

When I say that politics is an evolutionary process, I mean two things: first, that political institutions have evolved out of our cultural and genetic heritage and are the adaptive systems of the human species; second, that public policies — the deliberate actions of human beings — now share with nature the responsibility for determining the course of evolution. The first part of this is a familiar, although much neglected, item in our common stock of knowledge. It is at least as old as Aristotle, who found it sensible to be both a biologist and a political philosopher and to deal with the adaptive systems of organisms and the political systems of human beings as if they were all parts of the natural order of things. The second part of the proposition, our political responsibility for evolution, is just now forcing itself into our collective consciousness and being mightily resisted along the way. But the facts to support it are right before us all, and we must inevitably take them in and make them part of our understanding of who we are and what we do in the world.

First let us think about politics as adaptation. Any political order — a wandering tribe, a primitive agricultural society, a city-state, or a modern nation — is a body of people who have organized themselves in relation to each other within a given physical environment, and who share the aim of attaining some degree of satisfaction of what they believe to be their needs. That is what politics is. We usually define it according to its external manifestations such as elections and laws, but those are only some of the modern tools of the process.

Pay attention to the word *organize*. There is a profound connection between the words *organize, organ, organism,* and *organization.* They all come from a common root meaning "work" and "interaction." Every living thing organizes. Only a few species have developed role structures and systems of cooperation that human scientists are willing to call "societies," but in fact no living thing is solitary. The nineteenth-century French scientist Espinas saw this when he protested against the rigidity of the common idea of what constituted an animal society. He argued that social life is not "a restricted accidental condition found only among such privileged species as bees, ants, beavers, and men, but is in fact universal."[3]

Social life means "cooperative interaction" not only among members of the same species but also among different species. William Wheeler, an American entomologist, was speaking of this kind of social life when he wrote that "Even the so-called solitary species are necessarily more or less cooperative members of groups or associations of animals of different species."[4]

Everywhere in life we see patterns of interaction, systems of survival and growth within an environment. A tidepool with its community of beings of different species is one such pattern, a beehive is another. The beehive is a highly developed system of interaction among members of the same species, but it is also part of a larger life system that involves the reproduction of flowers and — if the beehive happens to belong to a farmer or get raided by a bear — the nourishment of other animal species. Human societies are also patterns of biological interaction; a nation, no less than a tidepool or a beehive, is a biological system.

Political orders are biological systems that have certain unique characteristics. An anthill has some things in common with a human society but is still a much different kind of

8

[3]Espinas, *Des Sociétés Animales* (Paris: Ballière, 1878).
[4] William Wheeler, *The Social Life Among the Insects* (New York: Harcourt Brace, 1923). This debate is reviewed in W. C. Allee, *The Social Life of Animals* (Boston: Beacon Press, 1958).

The child takes in, or internalizes, the knowledge and world view of its culture. This internalized knowledge shapes the individual's so- cial life no less than the genetically en- coded information inherited by an ant shapes its life — but the information is derived through learning symbolic material, not through the genes. The cul- ture itself becomes a part of the evolutio- nary process.

organization. One of the major differences is the way the system is perpetuated from one generation to the next. An ant functions within its system instinctively; the information it needs in order to know what to do is genetically encoded and immediately available at birth. But the human genetic heritage alone does not equip us to take a place in society; we must learn the rules of social behavior as we grow up.

I do not mean that learning is uniquely human. Most animals, especially those higher on the evolutionary ladder, have to learn things from others of their kind. We can see one example of this from the work of Robert Ardrey's South African naturalist who took an infant otter and an infant baboon and kept each apart from its own kind and its natural habitat for three years. When they were returned to their native environments the otter, which had never before seen a body of water, plunged into it after a few minutes' hesitation and soon caught a fish. But the baboon, a more intelligent animal, was helpless. It could not survive in its own natural environment. It had not learned how.[5]

Many animals learn, but they learn by trial and error or by imitation of other members of their own species. The human species is distinctive in *how much* it learns and also in *how* it learns. The human child takes in a tremendous amount of information and much of this is passed on by verbal communication. The child takes in, or internalizes, the knowledge and world view of its culture. This internalized knowledge shapes the individual's social life no less than the genetically encoded information inherited by an ant shapes its life — but the information is derived through learning symbolic material, not through the genes. The culture itself becomes a part of the evolutionary process. A number of biologists such as C. H. Waddington have written of this:

If one compares the Paleolithic population of scattered nomadic hunters with modern highly populous and complex societies, it is not the comparatively slight changes in bodily structure which differentiate us from Cromagnon man that makes the greatest impression. Human evolution has been in the first place a cultural evolution. Its achievements have been the bringing into being of societies in which contributions deriving from such sources as Magna Carta, Confucius, Newton and Shakespeare can be both perpetuated and utilized.[6]

10

---

[5]Robert Ardrey, *African Genesis* (New York: Atheneum, 1961), pp. 71-2.
[6]C. H. Waddington, *The Ethical Animal* (London: George Allen and Unwin, 1960), p. 103.

And Dobzhansky, among the most influential modern students of evolution, writes:

The appearance of culture signified the beginning of a hitherto non-existent type of evolutionary development — the evolution of culture, of human evolution proper. . . . Biological heredity is transmitted by genes; consequently it is handed down exclusively from parents to their children and other direct descendants. Culture is transmitted by teaching and learning. At least in principle, "the social legacy" can be transmitted by anyone to anyone, regardless of biological descent. Man may be said to have two heredities, a biological one and a cultural one; all other species have only the biological one.[7]

We may understand this better if we move beyond the culture/biology distinction and simply think of culture as a special, and *uniquely human*, biological process. Look at it this way.

Up to a certain stage in the earth's development, evolution was shaped by the forces we customarily think of as biological: mutation, natural selection, and the genetic transmission of information from one generation to the next. Then the human species perfected its powers of symbolic communication and added to its genetic heredity a cultural heredity. That is, knowledge about how to survive and satisfy human needs began to be passed on by a body of teaching and learning, which continually changed and grew. This was a new form of evolutionary development. In *Biopolitics*, Thomas Landon Thorson suggests the term "cultural DNA" as a way of understanding the biological function of culture:

Nature has found a way in the warm-blooded, mammalian primate passageway to increase the capacity to adapt by adding to instinct the capacity to learn, and finally not only the capacity to learn but the capacity to teach as well. While we certainly are not in a position to specify all of the precise details, the evidence is substantial that in the human passageway nature found a new method of information transfer, namely, that product of human learning and teaching that we call culture. And through this system of information transfer evolution has continued, giving man the ability to fly, to stay beneath the sea, and to modify his environment in thousands, perhaps millions of ways. It is from this perspective that we must see the phenomenon of politics,

11

[7]T. Dobzhansky, *The Biological Basis of Human Freedom* (New York: Columbia University Press, 1956), pp. 26, 27.

remembering always that ... the cultural system is basically a "socio-genetic" system, a system of information transmission.[8]

When Aristotle described *homo sapiens* as "the political animal," he was communicating his discovery that human beings, unlike other species, were capable of improvising many different kinds of adaptive structures — patterns of roles, laws, values, rituals, and symbols — and of adapting these to meet new conditions.

12

remembering always that ... the cultural system is basically a "socio-genetic" system, a system of information transmission.[8]

As the human species spread over the globe, adapting to different environments and undergoing different historical experiences, many patterns of culture developed; peoples became more distinct from one another culturally than genetically, and over time (as Waddington noted) went through cultural changes that were greater than the physical changes produced by mutation and natural selection. As cultures diversified, many different forms of human social organization emerged.

Any species, as we have noted, has some form of social organization, which is a way of functioning within its environment. But with very few exceptions, members of the same species organize the same way generation after generation. Some insect species have followed precisely the same pattern of social organization for billions of generations, and a group of them kept separately in an artificial environment will organize in precisely the same way as did their ancestors. If the environment is not suitable they may perish, but the social order will not change. Human societies, however, change.

One reason human societies change is that the "socio-genetic" system includes history. Other species pass on information from one generation to the next, but not verbalized conceptualizations of the whole sweep of evolution and the society's experience — not, we may assume, any idea that members of one generation will live their lives differently from the preceding generation — an idea so fundamental to contemporary human life that we scarcely discuss it.

Our cultural heritage includes recorded information about the past, and our knowledge of the past shapes the present in many ways. The United States Constitution, for example, is a distillation of history: it was constructed on the basis of certain precedents, models of government that the authors wanted to imitate, and also on the basis of things that had been written by political-philosophical theorists such as Locke and Montesquieu. The Constitution was constructed to *avoid* certain developments that had occurred in other countries, such as undue concentration of power in the executive branch. The Constitution's famous system of "checks and balances," for example, was set up as an obstacle to a certain kind of development that its authors knew of from history and were determined to prevent.

[8]Thomas Landon Thorson, *Biopolitics* (New York: Holt, Rinehart and Winston, 1970), pp. 110-11.

When Aristotle described *homo sapiens* as "the political animal," he was communicating his discovery that human beings, unlike other species, were capable of improvising many different kinds of adaptive structures — patterns of roles, laws, values, rituals, and symbols — and of adapting these to meet new conditions. Aristotle's purpose in studying the variations among these structures was to learn their strengths and weaknesses so that people could create more effective political institutions. His work and that of other political philosophers was recorded and passed on from generation to generation. The human species was beginning to acquire a body of information for use in evaluating and adjusting its own political systems, information distilled from experience.

We still have a long way to go in learning to evaluate and adjust our institutions, but the capacity to do so at all is distinctively human and is part of what is meant when we describe the species as political by nature. We have no evidence that any other species thinks abstractly about its social and adaptive patterns and consciously alters them as a result of such thinking.

Another dimension of human political orders, and here I return to my basic definition of politics, is that they involve patterns of interaction not only among human beings but also between the society and a given physical environment. Some students of behavior, notably Konrad Lorenz[9] and Robert Ardrey,[10] have placed great emphasis on "territoriality" or the attachment to a certain physical space, and have argued that this is a genetically inherited characteristic. It may well be, but it is also clearly mediated by symbolic learning. For example, instinctive territoriality can hardly be expected to account for an urge to defend a piece of land that one has never seen, but in 1941 millions of Americans reacted with rage to the Japanese bombing of Hawaii. Again, in the 1960s following the Communist revolution in Cuba, cars in California sported bumper stickers with the warning that "They're only 90 miles away," which may have been symbolically accurate but was several thousand miles off geographically. In earlier stages of history political groupings were set off either by conspicuous natural boundaries or by equally conspicuous artificial ones such as city walls. Modern political boundaries are likely to be visible only on a map.

A society's occupation of a territory carries with it the freedom to use its resources — agricultural lands, minerals, water,

[9]Konrad Lorenz, *On Aggression* (New York: Harcourt Brace, 1966).
[10]Robert Ardrey, *The Territorial Imperative* (New York: Atheneum, 1966).

13

Bureaucracies have a way of holding onto power once delegated, and bodies of experts often develop languages of their own, systems of symbolic communication that are not likely to be understood (and not meant to be understood) by the generalist.

15

and air — and this naturally becomes a source of power. In the nineteenth century the great nations of Europe and the United States relied heavily on coal; currently we are observing the new eminence of the oil-producing nations of the Near East. The geographical area occupied by the United States is one of the world's richest, lending itself to both agricultural and industrial productivity. We have energetically exploited this wealth — no other society in history has been able to attain such a high level of satisfaction of material needs.

This brings us to the final element in my basic definition of politics, which is that people go to the trouble of organizing themselves in relation to one another and to their physical environment to satisfy what they believe to be their needs. I added the word *believe* because there is no clear consensus from one culture to the next about what people need, what social and physical environments are necessary or desirable for human beings to live and grow in.

Nevertheless, some human needs may well be species-wide. Abraham Maslow's theory of human growth classified basic needs into a hierarchical system of five categories, ranging from basic physiological needs through safety needs, belongingness and love needs to esteem needs (self-respect and respect from others), and culminating with self-actualization needs. Maslow believed that although these needs might not be recognized in all societies, they are genetically inherited and a basic part of the makeup of every human being.[11]

One thing that becomes immediately apparent from a glance at Maslow's list of human needs is that they call for social interaction. Even the most fundamental of them — food, shelter, safety — are more efficiently taken care of through cooperation among a number of people, and satisfaction of the higher needs is scarcely conceivable except in a social context. Maslow's assertion that these needs are genetically inherited must be taken as a hypothesis, but there is a powerful amount of evidence to support the view that human beings are inherently social, that cooperative arrangements are entered into not only as a means toward efficiently obtaining the basic needs of the physical organism but also for their own sake.

Now let us look at another aspect of species adaptation. Any biological system is a modification of the environment. An ant society digs tunnels, builds rooms for special purposes such as food storage and egg hatching, and in the process creates about it the specialized environment we call an anthill. Any living thing is not only *in* its environment, it is in *interaction with*

[11]Abraham Maslow, *Motivation and Personality* (New York: Harper & Row, 1954).

its environment; an organism is actually an organism/environment field. This is true of the humblest spot of lichen on a rock, and it is also true of human societies. The United States of America is not simply a collection of people in a certain geographic space but a collection of people interacting with a geographic space that they have modified for their purposes. The space, America, has been re-created according to our culture's view of what is necessary to life. Our equivalents of ant tunnels and chambers are enormous clearings that were once forests, complex networks of roads and waterways, reservoirs and artificial lakes, domesticated animals and disappearing native species, cornfields on the plains that once held herds of buffalo, gigantic structures of steel and stone anchored in deep bedrock. All this is our organism/environment field. As our technology changes, our capacity to modify it grows.

Not only technology, but technological change, dominates American history. We have moved from horse-drawn carriages to supersonic jets in a little over a hundred years. Consider this summation: "In the last century, we have increased our speeds of communication by a factor cf 10^7; our speeds of travel by 10^2; our speeds of data handling by 10^6; our ability to control diseases by something like 10^2."[12]

Our tool-making and machine-making capacities have increased at such spectacular rates and have so dramatically altered the quality of human life and the condition of the natural environment that technological change sometimes seems to have a life of its own. We wonder whether we are using the tools or they are using us. A major theme in American culture has been praise for our technological capacities: "Yankee know-how" always saves the day, and change equals progress. Nowadays we are not so sure about all this and begin to suspect that technology is not our faithful servant, after all.

There would have been less confusion about this if we had understood all along that technological change is also social change. That information has been available. Karl Marx saw that the Industrial Revolution was a transformation of the social order; Max Weber wrote of the increasing bureaucratization and "rationalization" of human existence; Lewis Mumford showed that technological change is only one dimension of a reorganization of human society and consciousness that has been going on and gaining momentum for many centuries.

In American history we see this mainly as a process of industrialization: the emergence of mass production was a technological change and also a reorganizaion of society. What had

17

---
[12] John R. Platt, "What We Must Do," *Science*, 28 November 1969, p. 1115.

18

once been primarily a nation of scattered farmers rapidly became a unified network of production and consumption. The change incorporated new technologies of transportation, communication, mining, and manufacture, and it also created new power elites, absorbed a great segment of the European peasantry into the working ranks, and spurred the growth of cities. Today we are all part of the production-consumption network. Most of us work for pay and purchase all the things we need or can afford, and I doubt that even the most independent farm or uncompromising rural commune supports human life without resorting to the sale or purchase of goods.

The industrialization of America also had its impact on our political institutions. The Civil War was, in part, a conflict between the economic needs of an industrializing North and a South that was dependent on other sources for manufactured goods. Its outcome was a triumph for economic policies that cleared the way for the most rapid industrialization of any society in human history. Today we think of politics largely in relation to the competition of interest groups that represent different segments of the industrial order — the building industry, the aircraft industry, organized labor, and so forth. Agriculture is now an industry employing complex technologies and mass-production organizational methods; and our defense system is no longer a body of men prepared to go to war but rather a military-industrial complex developing ever more elaborate technologies of destruction.

Although we retain the basic framework of the governmental institutions created at the original writing of the United States Constitution, the actual processes and responsibilities of government have changed enormously with the transformation of America from a small and mainly agricultural nation to a large, densely populated, and heavily industrialized one. Along the way it has been necessary to deal with this growing complexity by improvising within the framework, notably by creating a body of bureaucratic agencies to regulate various operations that come within a certain field of specialization, resulting in such agencies as the Federal Communications Commission.

The basis for this transformation was solidly built into the original institutional structures. Even though the authors of the United States Constitution could not have anticipated the rate of technoloical change that lay ahead, they did know that they were in the process of creating a social organization that would protect private property, maintain a national monetary system, and in many ways facilitate trade and commerce both inside the national boundaries and with other nations.

Technology is power, and it requires decision making. We shall see more clearly as we go along that at the present level of human technological prowess, different lines of technological activity are actually different lines of evolutionary development for the human race and for the world's ecosystem. And technological decision making is done, sooner or later, through governmental processes. The institutional system devised to protect the rights of a rather small number of eighteenth-century artisans, farmers, and merchants is now ultimately responsible for charting the course of a technological capability undreamed of a century ago and still ceaselessly expanding. Now the governmental process is called on to determine whether the accumulation of freon gas from aerosol containers will increase skin cancer forty years hence. The government becomes the referee for such issues. Like it or not, government has become the decision maker, the cerebral cortex of technology.

Technological change has imposed some severe strains on the democratic process. Although our institutions have proved themselves flexible enough to accommodate enormous changes in the kind of society they were designed to govern, the nature of the government has also changed along the way. Complex technological issues do not seem to lend themselves to the traditional methods of representative democracy — the debate of issues, the determination of policies by a vote of elected representatives of the people. As the problems presented to government became more technologically complex it became necessary for Congress to delegate authority for specialized decision making to agencies that, presumably, had at their fingertips greater expertise. There has been a steady drift away from representative democracy toward "technocracy," or government by experts. Although elected representatives theoretically have the power to oversee technocratic decision making, this power is not always easily exercised. Bureaucracies have a way of holding onto power once delegated, and bodies of experts often develop languages of their own, systems of symbolic communication that are not likely to be understood (and not meant to be understood) by the generalist.

Thus we come to one of the great dilemmas of human progress. The human race has developed its symbolic and technological capacities to a degree that has made us unlike any other living species, and this in turn has enabled us to develop adaptive systems (of which the United States of America is an example) of unprecedented complexity. This progress was intended, of course, to increase the personal power of each individual. And yet we find that many of the decisions that affect the quality of our lives are remote and inaccessible — even incomprehensible — to most of us. Even those who are in positions of power seem to have a limited capacity to reach into all the corners of government. Presidents have often complained of the difficulty of influencing the various agencies that are theoretically under their command.

Yet the system does not move only of its own volition. It is guided by whatever degree of consensus we have about our needs and goals, by our commonly held beliefs and values. If we want to understand how we got into our present situation, it is this cultural consensus rater than the acts of this or that official that we must examine.

The Dominant Social Paradigm (DSP)

It was once generally believed that personality traits were passed on through the bloodlines, so that any normal citizen of a given nation could be expected to inherit genetically his or her "national character." In the day of Social Darwinism, the argument for America's "manifest destiny" to expand was based on the belief in inherent racial characteristics, the "strength" and "energy" of Anglo-Saxons. Even today racist thought in America is continually tormented by the fear that, as a result of intermarriage, the natural vigor of the Anglo-Saxons will be diluted by the more "languid" genetic heritage of blacks and Latins, and the strength of the nation will decline as a consequence.

Ideas of this sort represent one extreme position in the familiar "nature-nurture," or "heredity-environment," debate. This is the argument about how much of a person's character is determined by genetic heredity and how much by cultural heredity. The debate is still alive and will never be finally resolved, because there is no human being who is totally the product of genetic heredity unmodified by learning or socialization, nor is there anyone born into the world an instinctless *tabula rasa* to be molded entirely by the society. Each of us is an edifice of culture built on a foundation of genetic heredity or, to switch metaphors, a river of instinctual drives that flows as best it can through the dams and channels erected by society.

We are born with genetic characteristics that predispose us toward taking in the culture. One such characteristic is the rather long period during which the human infant is dependent on others for survival. Another that is shared with the young of many species is imitative behavior. Lion cubs learn to hunt this way, and human beings learn many things, including language, mainly by imitation. Human beings also appear to have an instinctive species-wide need for group membership, which expresses itself in a bewildering variety of ways. The course of early human genetic evolution produced a being ready to evolve in new ways by taking in the accumulated wisdom (and foolishness) of its society.

So, although we can never draw an absolutely distinct line between our two kinds of evolutionary heritage, it is clear that we do not, like some species, act out our patterns of social life simply according to genetic programming. We do the things we do as a society on the basis of values and beliefs we have acquired while growing up. Obviously there is diversity of values and beliefs within American society, but there is also consensus, without which no social action would be possible. If we keep this consensus in view the seemingly rudderless movements of the social system can be seen to have a purpose, and the frightening predicaments in which we now find ourselves can be seen to have resulted from quite respectable courses of action supported by nearly all of us.

This consensus has a rather elusive quality, partly because it is so obvious and omnipresent that we scarcely notice it and partly because it is rather hard to describe. Various terms are used to describe these values and beliefs: "political culture," "consciousness," "belief system," "national character." I plan to borrow the term used by Dennis Pirages and Paul Ehrlich: *dominant social paradigm*, or *DSP* for short. As they describe it the DSP is the end-product of socialization and education, the society's common stock of beliefs, habits, and values:

A DSP is a mental image of social reality that guides expectations in a society. A DSP is the socially relevant part of a total culture. Different societies have different DSPs. A social paradigm is important to society because it helps make sense of an otherwise incomprehensible universe and to make organized activity possible. It is an essential part of the cultural information that is passed from generation to generation as it guides the behavior and expectations of those born into it.[13]

First, the DSP includes beliefs about what is "real." The belief that the earth is round and revolves around the sun, for example, has been part of our DSP for a few hundred years. Second, the DSP includes value propositions about what is good or bad and prescribes ways of behaving. Some aspects of the American

---

[13]From *Ark II* by Dennis C. Pirages and Paul R. Ehrlich, Copyright © 1974 by Dennis Pirages and Paul R. Ehrlich. Reprinted by permission of The Viking Press.

DSP are shared with most of the modern world, some are common to industrialized societies, some to English-speaking countries, and some are uniquely American. Pirages and Ehrlich list as common to most industrialized societies the following beliefs:

A belief in progress, faith in the steady increase of material affluence (which unfortunately is often equated with progress), and belief in the necessity and goodness of growth. Other central features of the industrial DSP seemingly include high values placed on work, the nuclear family, and career-oriented formal education; a strong faith in the efficacy of science and technology (as opposed to religion) to solve problems; and a view of Nature as something to be subdued by mankind.[14]

In addition to these characteristics, Americans are generally people who value personal achievement and competition, egalitarianism, and materialism. Americans are seen as having relatively little respect for inherited social status and a compensating awe of material evidence of personal achievement; little sense of their own membership in a social class and a tendency to be dependent on the status conferred by individual achievement or (more common in today's organized society) by position in some institutional hierarchy. And Americans share with other peoples a strong strain of ethnocentrism — a belief in the natural superiority of their own way of doing things.

I have been stressing character-trait aspects of the DSP, but we should keep it in mind that the DSP is a *gestalt*, a holistic unit that includes not only the prevailing traits of the people in a society but also their image of reality. This image of reality can change. When Darwin's evolutionary theory exploded upon the Western world, it required a modification of society's perception of the world, and many social values altered as a result. The DSP is not merely handed down unchangingly from one generation to the next but is subject to modification; this is a fundamental part of cultural evolution. It means that a human society can change, even reorganize itself within a single generation — something that no species can do on the basis of genetic evolution alone. However, we can never complacently assume that at any given time people will readily let go of their cultural heritage and adopt a new set of basic beliefs and values. On the contrary, the mental sets we take in from cultural DNA appear to be capable of programming the human mind even more deeply and tenaciously than the instincts.

[14]Ibid., p. 44.

Americans are seen as having relatively little respect for inherited social status and a compensating awe of material evidence of personal achievement; little sense of their own membership in a social class and a tendency to be dependent on the status conferred by individual achievement or (more common in today's organized society) by position in some institutional hierarchy.

Internalization Some values, beliefs, and behavioral characteristics of the DSP are fairly easy to change or eliminate, and others are not. Anthropologists speak of the "onion peel" nature of acculturation, that culture is added layer by layer, and the layers formed first are the least likely to change.[15] This early learning is quite different from the later learning processes that are formally identified as education. "Much of early learning," notes another study of socialization, "takes place at a nonconscious level. . . . What we learn without being conscious that we *are* learning is likely to be accepted as a given — a 'fact of nature'."[16]

The same message comes to us from several different sources. The details differ, but the general proposition is that some portions of the DSP are so embedded in our consciousnesses that they become integral parts of the individual's personality. Anthropologists of the Sapir-Whorf persuasion tell us that when we learn to speak our native language, we learn not only a means of communication but also a structure of reality:

The forms of a person's thought are controlled by inexorable laws of pattern of which he is unconscious. These patterns are the unperceived intricate systematizations of his own language. . . . every language is a vast pattern-system, different from others, in which are culturally ordained the forms and categories by which the personality not only communicates, but also analyzes nature, notices or neglects types of relationships and phenomena, channels his reasoning, and builds the house of his consciousness.[17]

The Sapir-Whorf hypothesis is one way of saying that the culture is so deeply programmed into us that we experience it as part of ourselves, part of "reality." Psychoanalysis says essentially the same thing and comes a step or two closer to showing how this serves a political function.

In the past century Freudian and post-Freudian psychology has created a shift in perspective toward experiences previously not thought to be part of political education. It began to appear that the most significant part of training for citizenship takes place long before the young human being has any concept whatever of the state or of its laws. Freud was strongly influenced by Darwin's work and Freudian theory was built on

[15]Melford Spiro, "The Acculturation of American Ethnic Groups," *American Anthropologist* 57 (1955): 1230-52.
[16]Fred I. Greenstein, *Children and Politics*, rev. ed. (New Haven, Conn.: Yale University Press, 1969), p. 80.
[17]Benjamin Whorf, *Language, Thought and Reality* (New York: Wiley, 1956), p. 214.

"*Homo sapiens* trains his children for the roles they will fill as adults. This is as true of the Eskimo three-year-old who is encouraged to stick his little spear into a dead polar bear as it is of an American child of the same age who turns on TV to absorb commercials; the one will be a skilled hunter, the other a virtuoso consumer."

25

evolutionary concepts. It deals with inner conflict, mainly the conflict between the genetic and the cultural heritage. The genetic heritage includes powerful and (for Freud) essentially antisocial sexual and aggressive drives that the individual must learn to control in order to become "civilized." The cultural heritage, which is taken in by the individual and made a part of the psyche, serves to inhibit those animal drives. Freud saw this conflict as the source of all neurosis and also as the foundation of all social order.

Psychoanalytic theory was a fundamental revision of earlier notions of obedience, because it argued that (1) the experiences wherein the person internalizes the culture's inhibitions take place in early childhood, long before any explicit training in respect for social authority; and (2) the culture truly becomes a part of the psychological makeup of the individual, so that throughout life, respect for authority is more a matter of internal drive than external power. As Erich Fromm describes it:

In order that any society may function well, its members must acquire the kind of character which makes them want to act in the way they have to act as members of the society or of a special class within it. They have to desire what objectively is necessary for them to do. Outer force is replaced by inner compulsion, and by the particular kind of human energy which is channeled into character traits.[18]

The general idea we get from these statements is that some aspects of the DSP are built so solidly into us that they are highly resistant to change; we do not even recognize them as matters of opinion. This situation may appear highly satisfactory from a conservative's point of view, but rather bleak if you are standing by for an immediate transformation of the American consciousness.

Let us not lose sight of the fact that the internalization of culture starts with a relationship to nature — one's own. We become members of society by gaining some power over our genetically inherited drives. Wilhelm Reich made a strong case that family life, with its training in controlling natural urges (especially sexual ones), was basic training for future surrender to other forms of external authority.[19] If we accept this proposition, that initiation into the political order is essentially an act of conquering one's own nature, then we can hardly be sur-

---

[18]Erich Fromm, "Individual and Social Origins of Neurosis, " *American Sociological Review* 9 (1944): 380.
[19] Wilhelm Reich, *The Mass Psychology of Fascism* (New York: Orgone Institute Press, 1946).

prised that the conquest of external dimensions of nature — other species, the environment — is such a large occupation of political systems.

Before I move on from this discussion of the DSP and its importance to our everyday lives, I would like to pay a bit more attention to the question of consumption, the buying and selling of goods. I don't think it can have escaped anyone's attention that the pursuit of material affluence plays a large role in American life. It must be equally obvious that many of our current problems with unemployment, inflation, pollution, and energy are somehow connected to this pursuit. Let us take a look at some of the specifically economic aspects of our cultural heritage.

Becoming a Consumer

Every society has some sort of economic system, some set of arrangements for cooperating in the production and exchange of goods and services. Few societies, however, come close to our rate of consumption of goods and (underlying this) our emphasis upon consumption as a mode of social behavior, a civic duty. Possibly the best work on this subject is that of Jules Henry, an anthropologist who believed that learning to be a consumer is a major part of the task of coming of age in America:

Homo Sapien *trains his children for the roles they will fill as adults. This is as true of the Eskimo three-year-old who is encouraged to stick his little spear into a dead polar bear as it is of an American child of the same age who turns on TV to absorb commercials; the one will be a skilled hunter, the other a virtuoso consumer.*[20]

The training process, according to Henry, involves absorbing ways of thinking quite different from those of most primitive societies. He discussed this in relation to production and property accumulation. First, production:

Outstanding among the differences between simple societies and our own is the absence in the latter of what I call production-needs complementarity *and* coincidence. *In primitive culture, as a rule, one does not produce what is not needed; and objects are made in the quantity and at the time required. Thus there is a congruence or complementarity between what is produced and what is desired, and there is a coincidence with respect to timing.*

27

[20]Jules Henry, *Culture Against Man* (New York: Vintage, 1963), p. 70. Reprinted by permission of Random House, Inc., publisher.

This helps to give primitive culture remarkable stability. The primitive workman produces for a known market, and he does not try to expand it or to create new wants by advertising or other forms of salesmanship. . . . The craftsman does not try to invent new products to sell or to exchange, nor to convince his customers that they require more or better than they are accustomed to.[21]

Regarding property accumulation:

Related to our contemporary dynamics is the lack of a property ceiling. *Most, though by no means all, primitive societies are provided with intuitive limits on how much property may be accumulated by one person, and the variety of ways in which primitive society compels people to rid themselves of accumulated property is almost beyond belief. Distributing it to relatives, burning it at funerals, using it to finance ceremonies, making it impossible to collect debts in any systematic way — these and many other devices have been used by primitive cultures, in veritable terror of property accumulation, to get rid of it. Rarely does primitive society permit the permanent accumulation of vast quantities of wealth. The fact that our society places no ceiling on wealth while making it accessible to all helps account for the "feverish" quality Tocqueville sensed in American civilization.*[22]

Advertising — especially via television — is one of the main ways of socializing American children into the economic system and the property concepts that support it. The average American child has spent 15,000 hours watching television by the time he or she graduates from high school, compared to 11,000 hours spent in school. And this input is only one of many. Family, school, and peer group all do their parts in training us to be consumers.

We learn many roles as we become adult members of the system, but what role is more central to our lives — and more critical to the maintenance of the system as we now know it — than that of consumer? We measure our success by our level and quality of consumption, and we express our life style in patterns of consumption. The traditionally oriented American buys a big car and patronizes gourmet restaurants, while the seeker after a new consciousness buys a bicycle and shops for natural foods. Both are performing admirably in the consumer role. Ralph Nader, the system's most persistent gadfly, does not

28

[21]Ibid., pp. 8-9.
[22]Ibid., pp. 9-10.

"...The operator, truck driver, sales-clerk, or bookkeeper may never expect to rise much in 'the firm,' but he can direct his achievement drive into a house of his own, a car, and new furniture."

call himself a reformer or a public-spirited citizen but rather, perceiving clearly the chief activity of the American public, a consumer advocate.

Henry also noted that growing up in America calls for socialization into a work role. In order for the economic system to continue at a high rate of productivity, individuals must learn to suppress certain inner needs and direct their energies toward satisfying material needs:

This renunciation of the needs of the self — this latter-day selflessness — is, paradoxically, a product of the most successful effort in human history to meet on a mass basis an infinite variety of material needs. The man who accepts such a renunciation does indeed approach fulfillment of the wants the engines of desire-production have stirred within him, and whoever refuses to renounce his very self will get few of the material things for which he has been taught to hunger. The average American has learned to put in place of his inner self a high and rising standard of living, because technological drivenness can survive as a cultural configuration only if the drive toward a higher standard of living becomes internalized; only if it becomes a moral law, a kind of conscience. The operator, truck driver, salesclerk, or bookkeeper may never expect to rise much in "the firm," but he can direct his achievement drive into a house of his own, a car, and new furniture.[23]

30

The essence of this argument is that economic drives are internalized, that we are all socialized solidly into the linked roles of worker and consumer. And it bears repeating that when drives are internalized, they become a part of the self and are not experienced as culturally shaped characteristics.

This line of thinking about economic socialization is obviously close to the ideas I have been presenting about political socialization. That is, there is some conflict between genetic and cultural heritage, and the human being must repress some instinctive drives to function within the system.

Keep in mind that the goods we deal with are, in many ways, important for symbolic reasons. There are natural limits to how much a human being can consume or manufacture, and we now take for granted (something that would have been inconceivable in many civilizations) that people can own things they never use or even see. Lewis Mumford has written of how commerce, as it became more complex, also became more abstract:

[23]Ibid., p. 25.

In time, men were more at home with abstractions than they were with the goods they represented. The typical operations of finance were the acquisition or the exchange of magnitudes. "Even the daydreams of the pecuniary day-dreamer," as Veblen observed, "take shape as a calculus of profit and loss computed in standard units of an impersonal magnitude." Men became powerful to the extent that they neglected the real world of wheat and wool, food and clothes, and centered their attention on the purely quantitative representation of it in tokens and symbols: to think in terms of mere weight and number, to make quantity not alone an indication of value but the criterion of value — that was the contribution of capitalism to the mechanical world-picture.[24]

All this is related to scale, the size of the economic system in which we must find our places. In a small-scale tribal economy, the exchange of goods and services is an immediate and personal thing; one is in close contact with both the commodity and the other parties involved. But as our systems become larger, these operations are channeled through communications media and symbolic systems of great intricacy. As a result, the people who manipulate economic power are likely to be remote from the actual material it represents; consider absentee land ownership, for example, or the commodities exchanges where people who have never seen a field of corn perform their occult rituals of buying and selling great quantities of food. These symbolic transactions also imply that any person who does not acquire some skills in the symbolism of economics is destined to occupy a very low place in the production-consumption system.

Socialization into Nature
So far I have been stalking around the subject of how the internalization of the dominant social paradigm influences our control over the forces of nature, and I have not mentioned any specific facts or even hypotheses about the question of how we learn social values having to do with the natural environment. Oddly enough, there is no large body of wisdom to draw on in this connection. There is a large body of research and theory on the subject of political socialization and a few investigations of how people are socialized into the economic system, but scarcely any information about how we take in our culture's ideas about nature. The subject does not seem to have captured the interest of social scientists. Yet, however little we attend to

---

[24]Lewis Mumford, *Technics and Civilization* (New York: Harcourt Brace, 1934), p. 24-5.

it, this too is part of becoming an American. Our society has a definite set of values and beliefs about humanity's relationship to nature, and we must learn these in order to take our places in the system.

This learning probably begins where all socialization begins — with those first childhood experiences that teach the lesson of civilization's demand that physical and emotional energies be restrained. Gaining control over one's inner nature is the child's first task and, with variations, is one imposed by all civilizations. From that time on the growing individual proceeds into more complex relations with other aspects of nature and to patterns of behavior that are peculiar to Western industrialized society.

What one sees everywhere in such a society is nature under control, manipulated by people (usually with the help of machinery) for human purposes. If you grow up in an agricultural setting, you see crops being raised, harvested, and shipped to market, and animals being similarly processed for commercial ends. If you grow up in a city, the experience is more remote — the food comes from supermarkets and vending machines — but the basic theme of control is the same. The city is the totally managed environment, with plants only where they are planted and animals only where they are permitted to exist. All these things seem unremarkable to us because we take them for granted; we do not perceive that a child who learns to turn on a water faucet is entering into a relationship with nature and the social system that is fundamentally different from that of a child who knows of no source of water except a stream.

Socialization into our culture's patterns of interaction with nature involves perceiving the existence of control, learning the basic daily skills necessary for functioning within such a system, and learning also an ethic of control. We learn to approve of the management of nature by human technology and even to think of nature as existing for the benefit of people. Lynn White, Jr., a historian, suggests that our view of nature is part of the Judeo-Christian heritage, symbolized in the story of creation:

By gradual stages a loving and all-powerful God had created light and darkness, the heavenly bodies, the earth and all its plants, animals, birds, and fishes. Finally, God had created Adam and, as an afterthought, Eve to keep man from being lonely. Man named all the animals, thus establishing his dominance over them. God planned all of this explicitly for man's benefit and rule: no item in the physical creation had any purpose save to serve man's purposes. And, although man's body is made of clay, he is not simply a part of nature; he is made in God's image.

Especially in its Western form, Christianity is the most anthropocentric religion the world has seen. ... Man shares, in great measure, God's transcendance of nature. Christianity, in absolute contrast to ancient paganism and Asia's religions (except, perhaps, zoroastrianism), not only established a dualism of man and nature but also insisted that it is God's will that man exploit nature for his proper ends.[25]

Beyond this general world view, which we share with other Western societies, there is the specific heritage of the American historical experience with nature — all the folklore of taming the wilderness, clearing the forests, harnessing the rivers. Any study of American history puts us in touch with the image of people who came to a rough, wild land and turned it into a richly productive nation. The basic theme of our history is a struggle of humanity against nature, with humanity triumphant.

This brings us to perhaps the most important and fundamental of all our beliefs about nature, namely, the assumption that nature is one thing and civilized humanity is something else. This assumption is so basic it unites value systems that have nothing else in common. Thoreau, famed for his love of nature, said that you cannot have a deep sympathy with both man and nature. Eric Hoffer, cheering for the other side, said "the contest between man and nature has been the central drama of the universe," and that "man became what he is not with the aid, but in spite, of nature."[26]

Regardless of which side you may choose to take in this debate, you are forced by its very terms into accepting a cultural belief that is itself debatable. The assumption is built into our language and world view, institutionalized in our academic distinction between political science and biology, forced into our consciousness in a million ways. Yet this dichotomy between man and nature is no more certain than the medieval image of the Great Ladder of Being, in which all species were exactly as they had been at the time of Creation and humanity occupied a fixed place between the apes and the angels. These cultural images change, and in time we may come to see that

33

[25]Lynn White, Jr., "The Historical Roots of Our Ecologic Crisis," *Science* 155 (10 March 1967): 1203-1207. Copyright 1967 by the American Association for the Advancement of Science. Quoted in Walt Anderson (ed.), *Politics and Environment* (Pacific Palisades, Calif.: Goodyear, 1975), p. 287.
[26]Eric Hoffer, *The Temper of Our Time* (New York: Harper & Row, 1964), p. 80.

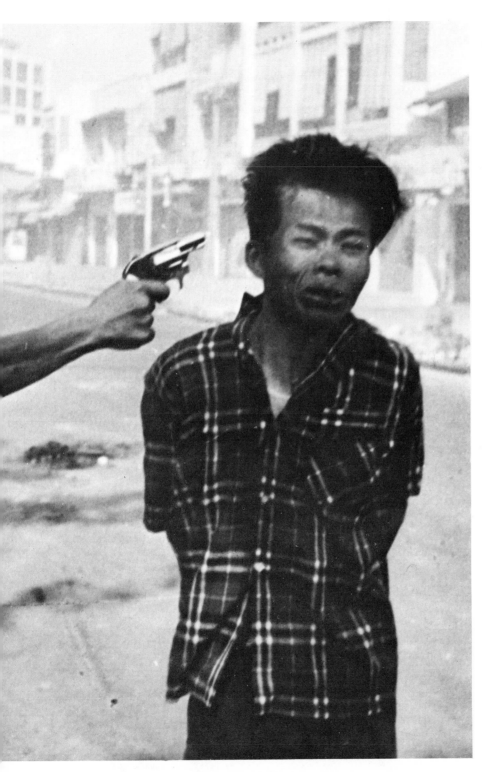

Modern mass-communications media have a powerful ability to show us where realities are inconsistent with ideals.

35

nature, endlessly experimenting, discovered a new form of evolution and adaptation, and we are it.

The Dilemma of the Ideal versus the Real

There is one final aspect of our cultural heritage that I must touch on here, even though I find it a most baffling subject to deal with: that is, the ambiguous and contradictory nature of the DSP, of the things we are taught and believe. Every feature of the American DSP has its equal and opposite number that makes its own claim to being a valid part of the culture. Americans are without doubt a materialistic people, and yet there is a deep current of mysticism in American culture. We have obviously trod heavily on our natural environment, and yet I know of no society that has a comparably organized and vociferous ecological movement. Make one generalization about the American value system and you will find somebody to contend, with evidence, that the truth is precisely the opposite. F. Scott Fitzgerald said that the test of a first-class mind is the ability to retain two diametrically opposed ideas at the same time and still retain the ability to function, and by that measure the American mind is surely first-rate.

It all has to do, I suppose, with our highly developed system of abstract symbols, which makes it possible for us to learn things at two levels. We can be taught in words and pictures that one thing is true and then learn from personal experience that something else is true. Margaret Mead says this is how we learn to deal with aggressiveness.

The American boy learns a series of lessons: aggression and fighting are wrong and are to be avoided as low, liable to arouse his mother's and often his father's disapproval; but aggression and fighting are also necessary. . . . Out of a series of conflicting traditions . . . there has emerged a special American form of aggressiveness: aggressiveness which can never be shown unless the other fellow starts it; aggressiveness which is so unsure of itself that it has to be proved.[27]

Another writer gives a similar report about education's role in preparing people to be citizens in a democracy. They are taught, says the study, that democracy works, but their actual experience within the educational system is not democratic. They are taught that tolerance is good, but their unsatisfying childhood experiences often turn them into intolerant adults.[28] Thus the

36

[27]Margaret Mead, *And Keep Your Powder Dry* (New York: William Morrow, 1965), p. 150.
[28]Elizabeth Leonie Simpson, *Democracy's Stepchildren* (San Francisco: Jossey-Bass, 1971).

institutional system that is maintained at great expense for the purpose of socializing young people into the political system ends up having, in some ways, the result of alienating them from it.

Ideals and dreams play a particularly important role in American life. "Sometimes people call me an idealist," Woodrow Wilson once said. "Well, that is the way I know I am an American. America is the only idealistic nation in the world."[29]

Gunnar Myrdal was dealing with the same point in the 1930s, when he said:

America, compared to every other country in Western civilization, large or small, has the most explicitly expressed *system of general ideals in reference to human interrelations. This body of ideals is more widely understood and appreciated than similar ideals are anywhere else. The American Creed is not merely — as in some other countries — the implicit background of the nation's political and judicial order as it functions. To be sure, the political creed of America is not very satisfactorily effectuated in actual social life. But as principles which* ought *to* rule, *the Creed has been made conscious to everyone in American society.*[30]

37

As Myrdal notes, every society has some such body of common ideals. That is, in fact, one of the things that makes a society identifiable as such, gives meaning to the world *culture*. Ideals are part of the cultural DNA passed on in a society's continuity from one generation to the next. Most societies have more genetic homogeneity than our own, and this is undoubtedly one reason why so much energy goes into making our own society's ideals visible. In other words, the presence of some readily verbalized principles — "freedom," "equality," "prosperity" — offers proof that there really is an identifiable and coherent American society.

These ideals are expressed in language and are accordingly ambiguous. Freedom means one thing to a member of the Birch Society and something else to a member of a prisoners' rights organization. The word has also changed its meaning over time, been redefined to fit new historical circumstances. In spite of this ambiguity (perhaps because of it) certain central ideals have the ability to mobilize sizable segments of the population behind major policy decisions. As Seymour Lipset, a leading political sociologist puts it, "A complex society is under

[29]Woodrow Wilson, Address at Sioux Falls, South Dakota, 8 September 1919.
[30]Gunnar Myrdal, *An American Dilemma* (New York: Harper & Row, 1944), p. 3.

constant pressure to adjust its institutions to its central value system . . . the failure to do so results in political disturbance."[31] More simply, a society with an explicit body of ideals is, so to speak, stuck with them. It must continually strive to live up to its own expectations. Ideals can, of course, be a source of smugness and self-congratulation (there are always those who are ready to assume that the society *is* already all it aspires to be and should therefore spend more energy in praise of its own greatness), but they can also be an irritant, a force for change. Again and again, some set of historical circumstances has revealed the presence of some American dilemma — a massive gap between the ideal and the reality — and the result has been pressure toward change.

In the 1960s, for example, the civil rights movement exposed the difference between our ideals of equality and the actual condition of racial minorities. Again, in the agony of the Vietnam experience, we were forced to perceive that the destruction of a country's resources, the slaughter of its populace, and the support of a military dictatorship did not square with our ideals of America's role as arsenal of democracy, defender of freedom, champion of the underdog. In the 1970s Watergate showed us a sequence of actions inconsonant with our ideals of the conduct of public officials, and the result was another period of crisis and change.

It is interesting to note the part that communications technology played in each of these: the televised broadcast of the NAACP march on Selma, photographs of napalmed villages in Vietnam, and the infamous White House tapes. Modern mass-communications media have a powerful ability to show us where realities are inconsistent with ideals.

So far this has sounded like a process whereby reality is adjusted toward the ideal, but there are many cases where the result is the opposite, where ideals are adjusted toward reality. Many of our recent shifts in cultural values seem to partake of this effect. As we learn more about the sexual behavior of human beings, for example, we let go of some of our ideals of how people *ought* to behave. This adjustment, too, may produce political decisions, such as the various moves away from laws against "victimless crimes," which are really violations of traditional cultural ideals.

We can never assume that people will voluntarily *seek* information that contradicts ideals, and as a matter of fact we

38

---

[31]Seymour Martin Lipset, *The First New Nation* (New York: Basic Books, 1963), p. 7.

can assume that people will usually work hard to *avoid* such information. Philip Slater believes that the ability to escape from whatever makes us uncomfortable is one of our chief national characteristics, an unpraiseworthy item of cultural DNA:

The avoiding tendency lies at the very root of American character. This nation was settled and continuously repopulated by people who were not personally successful in confronting the social conditions obtained in their mother country, but fled these conditions in the hope of a better life. This series of choices (reproduced in the westward movement) provided a complex selection process — populating America disproportionately with a certain kind of person. . . . we gained a critically undue proportion of persons who, when faced with a difficult situation, tended to chuck the whole thing and flee to a new environment. Escaping, evading, and avoiding are responses which lie at the base of much that is peculiarly American.[32]

Avoidance and flight are not merely physical movements but also psychological processes; the human mind is capable of blocking its own awareness of unpleasant conditions. Myrdal recognized this when he wrote: "Trying to defend their behavior to others, and primarily to themselves . . . *people will twist and mutilate their beliefs of how social reality actually is.*"[33] The tension in our society, then, is not simply a tension between an objective "American creed" and a set of conditions but between ideals as we understand them at any given time and reality as we choose, or are forced, to perceive it.

All of the things that characterize political dialogue — ideals, theories, clear statements of purpose and cloudy misrepresentations of reality — flow from our remarkable ability for abstract conceptualization and symbolic communication. It may well be that this ability is one we have not yet really mastered, that the long evolutionary span from the time human beings first acquired such a capacity is a developmental stage not yet concluded, and one that will not be passed until we develop powers of awareness and honesty commensurate with our massive technological capacity to shape the world. So here we are, the richest and most powerful society in all human history, celebrating our Bicentennial and hoping we have two centuries left.

The most appropriate symbol for America at the present stage of our history would be not Uncle Sam, that crotchety old relic of a bygone era of rugged individualism, but the Six-Million-Dollar Man. . . . He is, of course, a man of peace and friendly intentions, but he is stronger than the enemies he encounters and occasionally when they get out of line, he throws them through the wall.

39

---

[32] Philip Slater, *The Pursuit of Loneliness* (Boston: Beacon Press, 1970), pp. 13-14.
[33] Myrdal, *An American Dilemma*, p. lxxiii. Italics in original.

40

The American Predicament

It seems to me that the most appropriate symbol for America at the present stage of our history would be not Uncle Sam, that crotchety old relic of a bygone era of rugged individualism, but the Six-Million-Dollar Man, current favorite of the TV audience.

Consider this hero, who is so much like our wired and confused continent. "We can make him better than he was ... stronger ... faster," intone anonymous scientific voices, "we have the technology." So they go to work, and soon they have produced a being that is neither naked ape nor robot but some combination of the two. He has a mechanical arm and mechanical legs and a zoom eye, and he is a marvel of power. And what does he do with himself, this supercreature? Well, as it turns out, he hasn't any idea; they didn't give him a sense of purpose. He struts around in fancy clothes, mumbles vapid dialogue, and periodically is sent off by his master, a high-level bureaucrat, on missions against comic book villains who are up to no good. He is, of course, a man of peace and friendly intentions, but he is stronger than the enemies he encounters and occasionally, when they get out of line, he throws them through the wall. Unfortunately he never seems to understand the plot.

What we have done here, over the few centuries that measure the American experience, is to have created a continent that is better than it was. We had the technology. We filled it with new people and plants and animals, rechanneled its waterways, paved it, hooked it up for light and sound. We made it work in new ways — ways that require energy. We abandoned agriculture for agribusiness, meaning that we have, wherever possible, replaced the energy of human effort with the energy of farm machinery and chemical fertilizers. We have created new patterns of urban life that are, again, heavy users of energy. We have connected our resources and our urban centers and ourselves into a vast production-consumption network that keeps the great majority of us (those who can find jobs) marching through daily nine-to-five work programs for the sake of obtaining the material goods we believe we want. We have created an ecosystem, and we now find out that the system we have built is not yet a robot. It does not run of its own volition after all; it requires large inputs of fuel — oil, coal, gas, nuclear power, whatever we can find — and it requires *us*. It puts us to work, and it stridently demands that we line up for the goods it produces.

I am speaking of the system as an "it," but of course it is really ourselves, moving along within the channel of beliefs and values we have taken in with the American dominant social paradigm. Everything that we have here, good and bad, was created by human effort, and not by the effort of individuals alone but by the combined efforts of many people who shared a common vision of what they wanted America to become.

This is where the Six-Million-Dollar Man simile falters and ceases to serve as an image of the American predicament. It is true that the nation we have built is a technological contrivance, part nature and part machine. But unlike the sleepwalking hero of the TV screen, we have the ability to write the script. We can make some decisions about where we go from here, and we can and *must* also develop a greater awareness of the fact that our being in the position we are now is a logical, unfolding consequence of the social values we hold in common and a logical unfolding of our history. In fact, one of the most hopeful aspects of our present predicament is that we got ourselves into it, which suggests that we might possibly be able to get ourselves out.

In the final chapters I will return to a further consideration of where we are now. Next, however, I would like to take a look at what American history tells us about how we got where we are now. In particular I would like to pay attention to the two main elements in the development of the political/biological system we call the United States — the people who came to it and the things the people did to make the continent the way they wanted it.

42

2

The Making of an Ecosystem: Peopling the Land

The land was ours before we were the land's.
She was our land more than a hundred years
Before we were her people. She was ours
In Massachusetts, in Virginia,
But we were England's, still colonials,
Possessed by what we now no more possessed.
ROBERT FROST, "The Gift Outright"

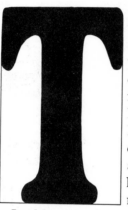he United States of America is a living system in which many lines of evolutionary activity converge. Among these are the various geological and biological processes that shaped the land's climate and its native wildlife. In this sense American history extends back millions of years. But the dimension of history we will be concerned with here is that which is usually taken to be the whole of American history — the period of its occupation by members of the human species.

In this second sense American history began with the arrival of a group of people in a new place, and its course has been marked by further new arrivals, movements within and beyond the national boundaries, and extensions of the national boundaries. The entire saga of colonization, immigration, and westward movement does not exert as strong a hold on the American imagination as it once did, but it is still true that the political order we have today was shaped by those experiences. The basic ingredient in politics is people, and the basic fact about the American people is that they came, most of them in the relatively recent past, from somewhere else.

The First Immigrants

There is not much agreement among scholars about how the American Indians came to the Western Hemisphere, but there is a general consensus that they did come: that the human species originated somewhere in Asia or Africa and gradually spread westward to Europe and eastward across the Asian continent. The most popular theory is that the Indians were of mongoloid origin and migrated across the land bridge from Asia at the point that is now the Bering Straits, gradually moving downward through North and South America.

44

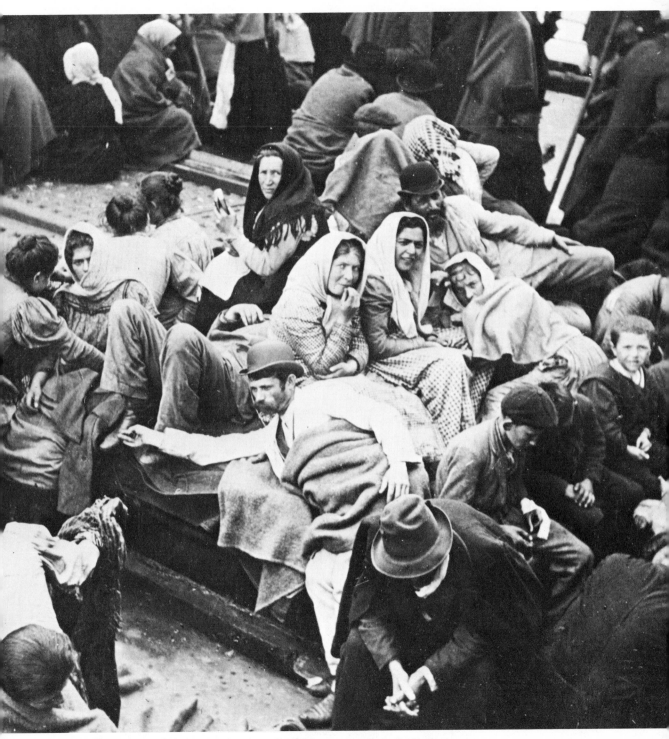

The basic ingredient in politics is people, and the basic fact about the American people is that they came, most of them in the relatively recent past, from somewhere else.

Other theories (which do not necessarily refute the first one) point toward the possibility of migrations across the water from Asia or the islands of the South Pacific. There are speculations that the American continents may have been visited in the remote past by explorers from Europe, the lost tribes of Israel, or beings from other planets. There is a record of a voyage of Buddhist priests from China to an area that may have been the west coast of North America in 458 A.D., following the same Japanese current that was later used by Spanish galleons.[1] This record and others like it suggest that the American Indian population has no single common ancestry. Edward Sapir is one of many scholars who have come to the same conclusion through linguistic analysis: "The peopling of America was not a single historical process but a series of movements of linguistically unrelated peoples, possibly from different directions and certainly at very different times."[2]

Although the Indian population was never large, Indians did occupy virtually every portion of the Western Hemisphere — the deserts, the jungles, the plains, the forests, and the barren icelands of the North. Alfred Kroeber estimated that the pre-Columbian Indian population of the areas north of Mexico was as follows:

46

AREA	POPULATION	DENSITY (per 100 km)
California	84,000	43.30
Northwest coast	129,000	28.30
Southwest	103,000	10.70
Columbia-Fraser	47,650	7.15
Eastern	426,400	6.95
Arctic coast	89,700	4.02
Great Basin	26,700	2.47
Northern	94,230	1.35
Total: 1,000,880		Average: 5.35

Source: Alfred Kroeber quoted in D'Arcy McNickle, *They Came Here First* (New York: Lippincott, 1949), p. 42.

Among these million or so people there developed an astounding variety of languages, cultures, religions, economics, and social orders. Entire civilizations, such as the Mound Builders, evolved and disappeared, leaving only relics and legends to hint at what their life was like and what became of them. There were agricultural tribes, hunting tribes, peaceful tribes, warlike tribes, large confederacies and alliances, and complex relationships of trade and commerce.

If, as most anthropologists believe, all the races of the human

[1]Jack D. Forbes, *The Indian in America's Past* (Englewood Cliffs, N.J.: Prentice-Hall, 1964), p. 6.
[2]Edward Sapir, in D'Arcy McNickle, *They Came Here First* (New York: Lippincott, 1949), pp. 37-38.

species have a common origin, then the meeting of Europeans with Indians was a momentous occurrence in human history — the merging of two long streams of movement, one westward from the place of origin across Europe and the Atlantic, the other eastward across Asia and the Pacific.

Colonials

The colonization of America, the land that was to become so identified with big business, was itself a business enterprise of great scope and daring. It coincided with the rise of capitalism in Europe and with the great new surge of world exploration and trade that resulted from new developments in the technology of navigation. Using this technology, the great nations of Europe actively transformed themselves into world empires.

It took a long time after the discovery of the New World before Europeans in any sizable numbers began to consider the possibility of living there. The first settlements were forts and trading outposts occupied by men who — although they often mated with Indian women, produced offspring, and sometimes married — had not come with the intention of making homes in America. Mostly America was thought of as a source of wealth, which would be used to make a better life back in Europe.

The idea of systematically repopulating parts of the New World grew slowly, out of the experience of the trading companies that were enriching their investors by importing various goods, such as exotic foodstuffs, from the East. The agricultural potential of the New World was reputed to be great, and some English entrepreneurs became attracted to the notion of establishing plantations that would grow into thriving communities — suppliers of goods for Europe (through the trading companies) and consumers of goods from Europe (again, through the trading companies). The word *plantation* at that time meant a plantation of people rather than of crops; the plants came later.

Although some of the colonies were founded by individual proprietors, such as Lord Baltimore, most of the early colonizing was sponsored by companies of investors. The initial investment was high (the Massachusetts Bay settlement alone cost its backers some 200,000 pounds), risks were great, and profits were slow in coming. The company that promoted the establishment of the first colony in Virginia had to resort to running lotteries to raise funds for the settlement and eventually went bankrupt.

The first colonists found it was all they could do to survive, much less produce profitable crops for export to England. The first attempt to found a permanent colony in America, led by Sir

If, as most anthropologists believe, all the races of the human species have a common origin, then the meeting of Europeans with Indians was a momentous occurrence in human history.

47

Walter Raleigh in North Carolina, failed utterly, leaving not a single living person nor even any clue to what had happened to it. Later ventures had slightly better luck, but the going was never easy and the life expectancy of those who set off for America was never high. Many did not survive the crossing, and many more died soon afterward of disease or starvation; often nearly 50 percent of a group of colonists would die before the first year was out. Those who survived the first winter and became "seasoned" to the new climate had only slightly better prospects. In spite of the companies' eagerness to see the population grow and in spite of periodic boatloads of new immigrants, the number of colonists rose slowly. For example, from 1611 to 1616 the population of colonists in Virginia actually declined from 450 to 324; two years later it rose to about 600.

The difficulty of making the colonies economically profitable was worsened by the fact that many of the colonists were ill-suited for the enterprise. By no means were all of them farmers and artisans, yet those skills were urgently needed. Many had come over with only the vaguest notions of what the new land was actually like; Europe was seething with tall tales about the ease and abundance of life in America. And many were unwilling to settle down to the hard labor of clearing and planting and cultivating; they wanted to go searching for gold or hunting for furs. In many cases colonial leaders had to become strong disciplinarians to produce enough food to keep their settlements going.

The early Virginia colonists had hoped that the Indians' corn might work out as an export crop. It did not, although it did become an important staple food locally. The crop that did prove to be exportable and that transformed the Virginia colony's history was tobacco. The English developed a taste for it, the colonists found it remarkably easy to grow, and soon the ships that came from England were returning with cargoes of Virginia-grown tobacco. Curiously this development, which offered the best chance of restoring the Virginia Company's foundering finances, was opposed by its owners. They disapproved heartily of tobacco, and in 1620 issued an order (which the colonists ignored) against any further cultivation of it. One of the company's founders, Sir Edwin Sandys, spoke of tobacco as a "deceitful weed . . . which served neither for necessity nor for ornament to the life of man."[3]

The new prosperity that came with the tobacco trade had an effect on the rate of population growth. Previously the cost of

[3]Charles M. Andrews, *The Colonial Period of American History* (New Haven, Conn.: Yale University Press, 1934), p. 153.

The Pilgrims and the Puritans wanted persons with useful skills and a willingness to settle down to a life of hard work and religious piety, and they were prepared to reject anyone who did not meet their standards.

49

recruiting new immigrants and getting them to America had been borne by the company managers in England; now, under the so-called head-right system it shifted to the colonial planters. The head-right system provided that any planter who would pay for the transportation of one new immigrant would receive a grant of 100 acres of land. In practice captains would load their boats with destitute passengers from England, Ireland, or Bermuda and bring them to the Virginia river ports where the planters would pay their fares, put the newcomers to work in the fields, and file for more land. This system was also established in Maryland; it served to populate the southern colonies and also helped shape the emerging large-plantation economy.

The colonization of New England began somewhat later and proceeded a good deal more cautiously. The Pilgrims and the Puritans came intending to establish communities of like-minded people, and they were anything but eager to open their arms to all the penniless outcasts of the Old World. They wanted persons with useful skills and a willingness to settle down to a life of hard work and religious piety, and they were prepared to reject anyone who did not meet their standards. In Massachusetts the governor was authorized to put new arrivals on a month's probation to determine whether they were "fit to sit down among us," and some of those who did not pass the probationary period were sent back to England. In New Haven a committee was authorized to judge applicants for land on the basis of their desirability, and those who failed were not only denied land but were "whipped and sent out of the plantation."[4]

This harshness in moral judgment was not confined to those who sought to join the New England communities; it seems to have extended to a desire to purify their neighbors as well. There was a man named Thomas Morton, a gentleman-lawyer who came from England with thirty servants and established a plantation at Mount Wollaston, about twenty-five miles from the nearest Pilgrim settlement. This group fell, according to a scandalized Pilgrim's account, "into great licentiousness":

And after they had got some goods into their hands, and got much by trading with the Indians, they spent it vainly, in quaffing and drinking both wine and strong waters in great excess. . . . They also set up a Maypole, drinking and dancing about it many days together, inviting the Indian women, for their consorts, dancing and frisking together. . . . Morton likewise (to show his poetry) composed sundry rhymes and verses, some tending to lascivi-

50

[4]Marcus Lee Hansen, *The Atlantic Migration 1607-1860* (Cambridge, Mass.: Harvard University Press, 1940), p. 32.

ousness and others to the detraction and scandal of some per-
sons, which he affixed to this . . . May-pole. They also changed the
name of their place, and instead of calling it Mount Wollaston,
they called it Merrymount, as if this jollity would have lasted
forever.[5]

The jollity did not last forever. A detachment of Pilgrims under
the command of Myles Standish invaded the settlement, broke
it up, captured Morton, and sent him back to England. He later
returned to Merrymount and took up his old life style, and was
again deported.

Despite the stern character of New England hospitality, the
area's population grew fairly steadily. It drew mainly from
those who were most committed to religious reform, opposed to
the rule of the Church of England, and congenial to the kind of
religious order that was being established in Massachusetts
and the adjoining colonies. After 1640, when the growing power
of the Puritans in England seemed to make their prospects
better at home, immigration to New England dropped off
sharply. The English civil war had precisely the opposite effect
on the southern colonies, which began to receive a new influx of
loyalists. By 1664 the colonial population of Virginia had risen
to 38,000.

51

Although life for the new arrivals was often precarious and
difficult, life in the Old World was even more so. Historians cite
among the various factors that encouraged emigration famines, wars (which were often accompanied by forced conscrip-
tion into the military), religious oppression, unemployment,
and scarcity of land. A token distributed in England as a kind of
advertising read: "In Virginia land free and labor scarce; in
England land scarce and labor plenty."[6] A person of any wealth
could reasonably expect to become a large landowner in
America; a person of modest means could expect to become at
least an independent farmer; and even those who came as
bonded servants had the prospect of obtaining land of their own
at the end of their period of indenture.

Although England continued for some time to be the main
source of immigration, there were colonials in considerable
numbers from other countries. Most of the Dutch settlers in the
New Netherlands stayed on there after it was seized by the
English and renamed New York. The colony founded by William
Penn welcomed Quakers from Ireland and Wales and Menno-
nites from the Rhineland. The latter group were the first of
thousands of Germans who came to Pennsylvania before the

[5]Andrews, *The Colonial Period*, p. 241.
[6]Ibid., p. 25.

Americans were developing a relationship to the land different from that of many other cultures. Now, for most people who had the good fortune to acquire title to a piece of land, it was primarily a commodity, an investment; buying and selling, moving from place to place created an important facet of the American DSP.

53

American Revolution. The Huguenots, Protestant outcasts from France, settled in various colonies and, encountering strong hostility because of the English-French conflict in the New World, quickly gave up their original language and assimilated themselves into the population.

The English colonists had generally been unenthusiastic about new arrivals from Scotland, Ireland, and Wales, but this attitude gradually changed — especially as the landowners began to realize that the best way of protecting their holdings was to encourage the settlement of the frontier. As the populations of the earlier settlement grew and land along the coast and river valleys became less available and more expensive, the newcomers from the other parts of Great Britain, in addition to freed servants from the established colonies, pressed on to the outlands.

At the beginning of the Revolution there were some 2.5 million white people in the thirteen colonies; of these about 80 percent were of English origin.

This society was already evolving along different lines from that of Europe, and different also from what a colony was supposed to be. It was turning into a social/economic/agricultural system that had no exact counterpart anywhere else in the world. Although it had social classes and a tradition of respect for rank, it had great possibilities for social mobility. This was closely connected to its high level of economic activity: every merchant, every artisan, every farmer could look about and see people no better than himself amassing great fortunes. Not all succeeded at getting rich, of course, but the possibility was always present and created a heady stimulus to economic activity — and speculation. Oscar Handlin writes:

For many artisans and shopkeepers, as for the merchants whom they emulated, speculation was an essential aspect of business. These people could not be creatures of habit or routine; the newness and instability of their situation prevented it. No accepted standards limited their visions; there was no proper income or place for the son of a carpenter or minister. Each could aim as high as he wished. Furthermore, chances were worth taking because there was in any case no security. With the cargo safely in and profitably sold, the fortunate trader always faced the question of what to do next: hold the paper and risk depreciation; accumulate idle coins that earned no interest and risk theft; double the stakes of the next voyage and risk the loss of all. The prudent merchant had to speculate and the venturesome artisan followed his lead.

54

Therefore every possessor of surplus capital was on the lookout for schemes in which to invest. They took flyers in manufacturing and shipbuilding; they sought mill rights, contracts to supply the armies, monopolies and other privileges, and they made each other loans at interest.[7]

Of all forms of speculation, buying and selling land was the most popular. Enormous fortunes were amassed in this way by those who had the requisite capital, skill, luck, or political influence. And speculation was not solely the province of large investors; many settlers on the frontiers did little more than clear the land and wait for a purchaser. Out of many such experiences Americans were developing a relationship to the land rather different from that of many other cultures — different from the Indians who had occupied the land first, and different also from the early colonists who had built their settlements in the wilderness with every hope of turning them into permanent agricultural communities. Now, for most people who had the good fortune to acquire title to a piece of land, it was primarily a commodity, an investment; buying and selling, moving from place to place created an important facet of the American dominant social paradigm.

Subsistence farming, that is, agriculture aimed primarily at meeting the needs of an independent family, was rarely practiced by choice. Most farmers aspired to produce for the market as well, and frequently specialized for the crops most in demand. The more successful commercial farms expanded their holdings and supplemented their income by other activities such as tanning and operating sawmills. Since farming was already a business, the transition to other aspects of capitalistic enterprise was scarcely noticeable. This kind of diversification was more likely to be found in the northern colonies; the South, of course, developed another kind of agricultural/economic system supported by the institution of slavery.

The Involuntary Immigrants
In a proclamation dated 23 December 1617, King James II gave royal approval to the plan of deporting "notorious and wicked offenders that will not be reformed but by severity of punishment, in order that they may no more infect the places where they abide within our realm."[8] A few years later the Virginia Company, in a petition to Parliament, said that one of its

---

[7]From *The Americans* by Oscar Handlin, by permission of Little, Brown and Co. in association with The Atlantic Monthly Press. Copyright © 1963 by Oscar Handlin.
[8]Andrews, *The Colonial Period*, p. 62n.

purposes was: "The removing of the surcharge of necessitous people, the matter or fuel of dangerous insurrections, and thereby leaving the greater plenty to sustain those remaining within the land."[9]

England in the seventeenth century was already in the early stage of the evolutionary development that became known as the Industrial Revolution. The population was growing, the acreage of cultivated farmland was decreasing (much of it was being converted to sheep grazing), food was scarce, and the cities were filling with people who had no means of supporting themselves. Crime was common, punishment was harsh (England had an astoundingly long list of offenses punishable by death), and thousands of the uprooted found their way to workhouses, prisons, or the gallows. It seemed both prudent and charitable to send these undesirables to the New World, where they could become self-supporting and contribute to the work of colonization.

Thus, with the encouragement of the Virginia Company and the king, local authorities took up the practice of transporting paupers to the New World. Among these were children. There are records of poor children sent from London in considerable numbers, and from many small towns in groups of half a dozen or so.[10] Most public charges were sent to become indentured servants, but there were occasional shipments of young women who were sent over as wives. Also, especially after the headright system was established, there were many cases of persons kidnapped and sent to Virginia involuntarily.[11]

Similarly, deportation from England became an alternative way of dealing with criminals. Persons sentenced to imprisonment or execution were offered the option of being transported to Virginia, and most of them chose the latter — although there are some reports of convicts who preferred the gallows (apparently not all the rumors about life in the colonies were favorable).[12] Some of the first English Quakers who came to America were shipped as criminals, violators of the Conventicle Act of 1664, which outlawed certain types of public gatherings. Military and political prisoners also stocked the colonies. Deportations of Scottish soldiers followed several of the battles of the civil war, and about a hundred Irish Tories were shipped to Virginia in 1653.

In many cases these deportees merged readily into the colonial populations. The number of indentured servants was high

---

[9]Ibid.
[10]Ibid.
[11]Ibid., p. 63n.
[12]Ibid., p. 65n.

(accounting for over 75 percent of the population in Virginia at one point), and there was no meaningful distinction between those who had voluntarily entered into the arrangement and those who had been given into it by authorities in England. The Scottish soldiers sent to New England were accepted there, and many of them found work and married into Puritan families.

The Quakers, who were regarded as undesirable heretics by the Puritans, found the going more difficult. Many of them were physically punished and others were shipped to Barbados or back to England. The only colony that would accept Quakers prior to the opening up of Pennsylvania was Rhode Island.[13]

Even Virginia, which had once welcomed anyone who could perform a day's work, eventually became less hospitable to deportees. In 1670 three Virginia counties officially protested against the great number of "felons and other desperate villains sent hither from the prisons of England."[14] England responded to these protests; the practice of deportation did not cease, but eventually it shifted to other colonial areas, notably the West Indies and Australia.

The colonial planters had discovered another source of labor: slavery. The slave trade began for the American colonies in 1619, when a Dutch ship came to Virginia and sold off its cargo of twenty African slaves. This is the first record of black slaves brought to Viginia, but slavery in the New World was well over a century old by that time. The Spanish had shipped slaves from Africa to the West Indies as early as 1503 and, although it has received less historical attention, Indians were enslaved in considerable numbers — by the Spanish in both North and South America, by the Dutch in the area that became New York, and by the English in all the American colonies. "With regard to enslaving the Indians," says one historian, "New England had early taken the lead and throughout the colonial period held more Indians in slavery than any of the other colonies except South Carolina, where in 1708 there were 1,400 Indian slaves against 4,100 Negroes."[15] There was nothing new or unusual about slavery, and its coming to America was gradual, almost invisible.

As the availability of free land declined, slavery replaced the head-right system. The economics of tobacco farming favored large plantations, and the large plantations provided an almost unlimited demand for unskilled labor. The planters came to recognize that, although the initial cost of buying a slave was

57

[13]Hansen, *The Atlantic Migration*, pp. 34-35.
[14]Andrews, *The Colonial Period*, p. 136.
[15]James Truslow Adams, *Provincial Society 1690-1763* (New York: Macmillan, 1927), p. 101.

Slavery in its peculiarly American form was one of the most curious developments in the unfolding of human evolution. Politically it presented a strange contradiction to the world. Here was a nation with the most democratic and egalitarian system in history offering itself as a daring model of progress at the same time that it contained within itself a flourishing remnant of a primitive and utterly dehumanizing institution.

higher than that of obtaining an indentured white laborer, the value of obtaining a worker for a lifetime — and also of obtaining the worker's descendants — made the investment worthwhile.

African slaves were less important in the economy of the northern colonies but still accounted for a significant part of the population growth. According to a recent study:

In the northern colonies, the proportion of slaves may have approached 10 percent in Rhode Island and New Jersey at one or another period in the eighteenth century. The reported proportions in the same time span in such colonies as Virginia and South Carolina ran from around 40 percent to an incredible 70 percent. The proportions in North Carolina were always relatively low and in Georgia more or less steadily rising.[16]

Although slavery was most visible in the southern colonies (and the West Indies), it had a profound effect on the economies of England and the northern colonies as well. After some initial grumbling from the throne about the immorality of the slave trade, an English company was chartered (with King James II as one of the stockholders) and embarked on an immensely profitable enterprise that soon became an important part of England's maritime economy:

The trade grew after 1731 until in 1752 Liverpool had eighty-seven vessels in the trade, Bristol one hundred and fifty-seven, and London one hundred and thirty-five. . . .

In those days the ship-chandlers of Liverpool made special displays in their windows of such things as handcuffs, leg-shackles, iron collars, short and long chains, and furnaces and copper kettles designed for slavers' use. The newspapers were full of advertisements of slaves and slaver goods.[17]

New England ports were home for the American slave traders long after the ownership of slaves in New England was outlawed. Slavery was as important to northern shipping as it was to southern agriculture. The trade that developed was also linked to the sugar plantations of the West Indies. The ships would carry molasses from there to New England, where it would be made into rum. The rum would go to Africa to pay for slaves. The third leg of the voyage was the infamous "middle

[16]Wilbert E. Moore, *American Negro Slavery and Abolition: A Sociological Study* (New York: The Third Press, 1971), p. 16.
[17]John R. Spears, *The American Slave-Trade* (Port Washington, N.Y.: Kennikat Press, 1967), pp. 17-18. First published 1900.

FIVE SHILLINGS REWARD.

RUN AWAY from the subscriber living in Fourth-street, a little above Race-street, the 25th ult. a girl named Christiana Lower, 13 years of age: Had on a blue calimancoe cap, blue and white checked handkerchief, a short red gown, blue and white striped linsey petticoat, an old pair of black stockings and new shoes. Whoever takes up said girl and brings her home, shall have the above reward and reasonable charges.

CHRISTIAN LOWER.

THREE POUNDS REWARD.

RUN AWAY from the Subscriber, living at Warwick furnace, Minehole, on the 23d ult. an Irish servant man, named DENNIS M'CALLIN, about five feet eight inches high, nineteen years of age, has a freckled face, light coloured curly hair. Had on when he went away, an old felt hat, white and yellow striped jacket, a new blue cloth coat, and buckskin breeches ; also, he took with him a bundle of shirts and stockings, and a pocket pistol ; likewise, a box containing gold rings, &c. Whoever takes up said servant and secures him in any goal, so as his master may get him again, shall have the above reward and reasonable charges paid by **JAMES TODD.**

N. B. All masters of vessels, and others, are forbid from harbouring or carrying him off, at their peril.

FORTY SHILLINGS REWARD.

RUN AWAY from Mr. Richard Dallam's on Swan Creek, in Baltimore county, on Monday the 13th ult. a servant man belonging to the Subscriber, imported the last season from Dublin, middle aged, of low stature, well set, calls himself NEAL M'LACHLAND, a native of Ireland, and speaks much in that country dialect. Had on when he went away, a dark olive coloured cloth coat, with a brown cloth jacket, sheepskin breeches, ribbed stockings, and good shoes ; he has also carried several other clothes with him. He wears his own hair, which appears very grey, and says, he lived several years in Philadelphia, with Mr. David Franks and Mr. John Reynold's, for the latter of which he drove a carriage, and professes that as his business. It is expected he will make for Philadelphia. Whoever takes up the said servant, and secures him in any goal, so that his master may have him again, shall receive the above reward; and if brought home, reasonable charges by

AMOS GARRETT.

During the year 1817, over 20,000 people came as immigrants to the United States. This was twice as many as had come in any previous year, and it was the beginning of the greatest migration of human history. We have no record of any such movement before or since, in which a comparable number of people permanently relocated over a comparable distance.

60

passage," bringing new slaves to the plantations of the West Indies or the southern tobacco-growing colonies. The following describes the way the ancestors of countless Americans came to their new home:

The space between the decks where the slaves were to be kept during the time the cargo was accumulating (three to ten months) and while crossing the Atlantic (six to ten weeks) was a room as long and as wide as the ship, but only three foot ten inches high – the space of an average Newport slaver in the days when the traffic was lawful and respected.

The men were ironed together, two and two by the ankles, but women and children were left unironed. They were then taken to the slave-deck, the males forward of a bulkhead built abaft the main hatch, and the women aft. There all were compelled to lie down with their backs on the deck and feet outboard. In this position the irons on the men were usually secured to chains or iron rods that were rove through staples in the deck, or the ceiling of the ship. The entire deck was covered with them lying so. They were squeezed so tightly together, in fact, that the average space allowed to each one was but sixteen inches wide by five and a half feet long.[18]

It took a long time for the opponents of the slave trade to mobilize enough public opinion to counter the obvious economic arguments in favor of it. Bills outlawing the trade were passed in England in 1806 and 1807, and in the United States in 1808. Even after the bills were passed, slave smuggling continued. A United States congressman estimated early in the nineteenth century that slaves were being brought in illegally at the rate of 20,000 a year. The boom in cotton farming that followed upon the invention of the cotton gin and the opening up of the new territory in Louisiana provided the market. The slave trade continued until the final abolition of slavery itself.

Slavery in its peculiarly American form was one of the most curious developments in the unfolding of human evolution. Politically it presented a strange contradiction to the world. Here was a nation with the most democratic and egalitarian system in history offering itself as a daring model of progress at the same time that it contained within itself a flourishing remnant of a primitive and utterly dehumanizing institution.

Considered in strictly biological terms, slavery was a strange coming together of life forms: people ripped from their native

[18] Ibid., p. 69.

environment, brought to a strange land and put to work growing plants — tobacco, cotton, indigo, rice — that were also forcibly thrust into new ecosystems. All this was being done by the offspring of European immigrants, while the products of their efforts were destined for shipment to European markets.

Slavery also introduced a new stream of genetic and cultural DNA into American life. We have among us today millions of people descended from the slaves and we have also the cultural heritage of their experience. This includes not only the things we customarily trace to Afro-American antecedents (jazz, for example) but also the legacy of racial bitterness and political strife that has been handed down through the generations as we strive to unravel ourselves from the consequences of that early endeavor at agribusiness.

We should understand better than we do that this historical fact has created a strain of humanity that can no longer be described as African. It is most unlikely that there is a living descendant of the slaves whose ancestry is not partly white. Furthermore, just as the input of the black experience has become part of the cultural heritage of all Americans, so have American blacks been reared in a cultural milieu far different from that of their African ancestors.

The Great Migration
There was a brief resumption of immigration after the Revolutionary War, and then from about 1806 to 1816 the conflicts among France, England, and the United States brought immigration almost to a standstill. During this period there was time to develop a national identity in America; a new generation of native-born Americans was coming of age. The conflicts with Europe and the establishment of a new governmental system helped provide a sense of a distinct American nationality. Those who arrived from this time onward came not as colonials but as immigrants who were to become citizens of a new nation.

During the year 1817, over 20,000 people came as immigrants to the United States.[19] This was twice as many as had come in any previous year, and it was the beginning of the greatest migration of human history. We have no record of any such movement, before or since, in which a comparable number of people permanently relocated over a comparable distance. This migration transformed the American continent, and it had a

[19]Hansen, *The Atlantic Migration;* William J. Bromwell, *History of Immigration to the United States, 1819-1855* (New York: Augustus M. Kelley, 1969), first published 1855; George M. Stephenson, *A History of American Immigration* (Boston: Ginn, 1926); Maldwyn Allen Jones, *American Immigration* (Chicago: University of Chicago Press, 1960).

spectacular effect on the Old World as well, permanently altering economic and social conditions in the areas left behind.

American policy toward immigration at this point was a
nonpolicy. John Quincy Adams summarized it by saying that
the republic invited no one and would not reject anyone who
had the courage and the means to make the crossing. Immigrants would receive no special privileges and could likewise
expect no special advantages. Their success would depend on
their own activity and good fortune.[20]

The European nations tended to be less laissez-faire. They
commonly believed that a decline in population meant a decline
in national economic and military strength, and many countries placed obstacles in the way of the prospective emigrant.
England was generous about giving America its paupers and
criminals but fearful of losing skilled workers. For some time
any Englishman going to the United States was required to
obtain a signed certificate that he was not a "manufacturer" or
"artificer."[21] In spite of this, many skilled workers managed to
find their way to the growing American industrial centers.

Employment prospects for both the skilled and the unskilled
varied according to the state of the American economy, which
was subject to some erratic fluctuations. For example, in 1818
when the country was getting ready for another record-
breaking year of immigration, there was a general economic
collapse that closed banks and factories and slowed down building construction. The immigrants came anyway, and thousands
of them were unable to find any means of subsistence. Many
who could raise the price of passage returned to Europe, and
others had to rely on the meager resources of charity.

In 1819 observers were shocked by the spectacle of the great
number of immigrants unloading in the harbor cities with their
sparse possessions and uncertain prospects, willing to accept
any job or endure any hardship, and more often than not hoping
to earn enough money to bring over relatives left behind. But
eventually this became a familiar part of the American scene.

Although there were skilled workers and wealthy merchants
and members of the upper classes among those who came to
America, the overwhelming majority were peasants, the poor
and landless who had managed through charity and thrift and
the sale of their last possessions (and occasionally the nonpay-
ment of rent) to scrape together the cost of a space in the
crowded hold of a ship.

The transportation of poor passengers was possible only with

[20]Hansen, *The Atlantic Migration*, p. 87.
[21]Ibid.

low fares. The business of carrying immigrants across the Atlantic was taken over by large shipping companies that circulated handbills through the cities and villages, carried the maximum number of passengers, and provided the minimum possible space and services. Death from disease and malnutrition was common; the passenger mortality rate in the early nineteenth century ran around 10 percent in the average year, and sometimes as high as 20 percent. Occasional crossings were far worse than the average: 500 of 1,100 German immigrants perished on one ship.[22]

The first American immigration laws were aimed at regulating conditions aboard these ships. Congress appointed an investigating committee and in 1819 passed a bill that put limits on the number of passengers per ship. From then on, ships that could not meet the American standards landed in Canadian ports, and the passengers who wanted to come to the United States streamed across the unguarded borders into New England.

The great migration was not simply a mass movement to America; it was also a mass movement within America. From the beginning there had been a frontier, and the new territories acquired from France, Spain, England, and Mexico opened up vast spaces for settlement. The population was not only growing, it was also in motion. This, too, was historically unprecedented. Daniel Boorstin writes:

The American transients were something new under the sun. True enough, moving peoples — bedouins, conquistadores, crusaders, explorers, barbarian invaders — are as old as man. But where before had so many people been continually in motion over a continental landscape? Where before had migrants been equipped with tools so much more advanced than those of the aborigines? Where had so many people of their own accord taken one-way passage? Where had so many men moved to unknown, remote places, not to conquer or convert or fortify nor even to trade, but to find and make communities for themselves and their children?[23]

Like the initial colonization, the westward movement was in part a business venture. Indeed the buying and selling of land was the nation's chief industry. George Washington had made a fortune in land speculation, and countless Americans aspired to

England was generous about giving America its paupers and criminals but fearful of losing skilled workers.

63

[22]Oscar Handlin, *The Uprooted* (Boston: Little, Brown, 1951), p. 51.
[23]Daniel Boorstin, *The Americans: The National Experience* (New York: Random House, 1965), p. 50.

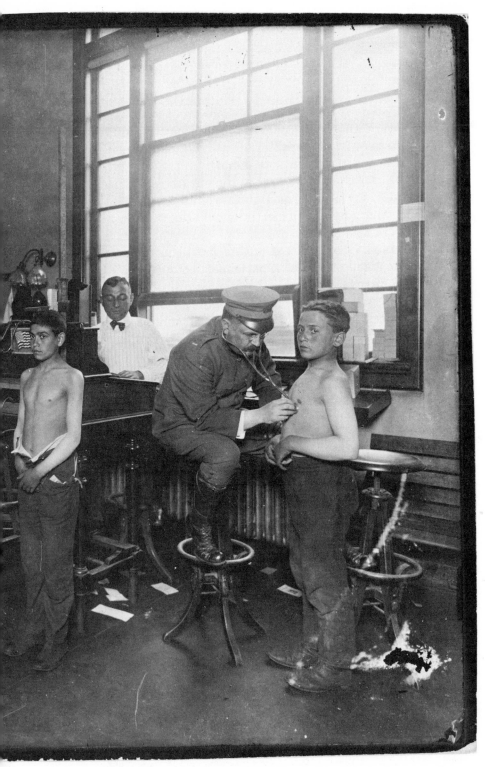

"The recent immigrants," one eugenics expert said, "as a whole, present a higher percentage of inborn socially inadequate qualities than do the older stocks."

65

follow his example. Many land companies were formed and generally proved to be far better investments than the colonization companies had been.

The national government and most of the states owned large territories; their common policy was to get money for the treasury by selling public land to such groups as the Pennsylvania Population Company and the North American Land Company. One corporation, the Ohio Company of Associates, purchased 1.5 million acres of the Ohio Territory from the Continental Congress at about eight cents an acre.[24]

Some of the land companies sent representatives to Europe to recruit settlers and founded communities in America that were transplants from communities in the Old World. But most of the new lands were taken up by Americans — people whose ancestors had arrived a few generations earlier — who were more likely to have some practical experience at pioneering.

Europeans were fascinated with the mystique of the frontier, even though it was never seen by the majority of immigrants. Samuel Gompers has written of the powerful popularity among London workers of a song called "To the West":

To the West, to the West, to the land of the free
Where mighty Missouri rolls down to the sea;
Where a man is a man if he's willing to toil,
And the humblest may gather the fruits of the soil. . . .
Away! far away, let us hope for the best
And build up a home in the land of the West.[25]

The reality was different from the image. According to Oscar Handlin:

Among the multitudes that survived the crossing, there were now and then some who survived it intact enough in body and resources to get beyond the port of landing and through the interior cities of transit. Those who were finally able to establish themselves as the independent proprietors of farms of their own made up an even smaller number.

All the others were unable to escape from the cities. Decade after decade, as the Federal government made its count, the census revealed a substantial majority of the immigrants in the urban places; and the margin of that majority grew steadily larger. Always the percentage of the foreign-born who lived in the cities was much higher than that of the total population.[26]

---

[24]Ibid., p. 53.
[25]Samuel Gompers, *Seventy Years of Life and Labor* (New York: E. P. Dutton, 1925), p. 19.
[26]Handlin, *The Uprooted*, pp. 63-64.

The immigrants came not just to the cities, but to the specific neighborhoods where they might find others who spoke their language and shared their cultural background. Biologists have noted that species that live relatively isolated existences when in their natural habitat will tend to cling together when suddenly moved to a new environment, and the development of ethnic neighborhoods in American cities would seem to demonstrate this point.

For the masses of European immigrants, the movement to America was not just a change of place. It was a total change of life situation: from rural to urban, from agricultural work to industrial work, from a monarchical (in many cases still semifeudal) political order to a democratic one. Most of the immigrants became citizens and, as property qualifications were eliminated, voters. Next to the ability to work, the vote was the most important asset the naturalized American possessed. The settling of thousands of foreign-born in the growing urban centers coincided with the rise of the political machines which organized them effectively as dependable voting blocs. Because the welfare state was still a thing of the future, and the resources of charitable organizations were limited, the one institution that was really able to deal with the needs of the newcomers — to provide jobs and loans and help in dealing with public officials — was the political machine. Thus the population patterns that resulted from immigration, the clustering of foreign-born workers in the cities, set the style for American politics for decades.

One of the greatest waves of immigration, which had a major impact on American politics, resulted from the Irish potato famine in the mid-nineteenth century. A closer look at this particular historical event shows the American system being shaped by an interplay of biological and cultural forces.

Monoculture and Politics
Ecosystems created by nonhuman natural forces are complex and relatively stable; they change, but they change slowly and usually as the result of a multitude of causes. Ecosystems created by human action are simple and unstable; they change quickly and can be totally upset by an alteration in one part of the system. Mostly human intervention creates monocultures — extensive stands (groups of plants growing in a continuous area) of a single species whose existence supports human life.

The discovery and exploration of the Western Hemisphere by Europeans led to a great forward leap in agricultural technology. Sizable portions of the New World's land were cleared of their native flora and converted to the production of European

The immigrants came not just to the cities, but to the specific neighborhoods where they might find others who spoke their language and shared their cultural background.

67

agricultural crops (an activity that we will examine at length in the next chapter), and meanwhile European life was embellished by new imports and transplants from America: coffee, tobacco, chocolate, and many fruit and vegetable species including the tomato and the potato. The potato, a humble root first cultivated by the Indians of South America, brought the first "green revolution." It quickly became a staple food in Europe and seemed to promise an end to hunger for all time.

The potato was especially important in Ireland, a country of historically low agricultural productivity. It replaced some crops and also permitted the conversion of previously unused land too poor for grain or grazing. Hillsides in Cork, Limerick, and Kerry never before cultivated now bore crops of potatoes. With the increasing food supply, the Irish population rose steadily, from an estimated 1 million in 1670 to 3 million in 1760 and over 8 million by 1845.[27] Many of these people lived by subsistence farming, and large farms were subdivided again and again into small plots of land that supported a single family. In 1845 there were some 65,000 farms of an acre or less, tilled only by the spade and producing a single crop — potatoes.[28]

The potato, like every form of life, has its natural enemies. It is particularly vulnerable to a form of fungus that destroys both the plants in the fields and the crops already harvested. There was no known method of controlling or preventing the potato blight, and those whose existence depended on the potato lived in constant fear of it. It was the greatest threat to those countries whose agricultural production was the least diversified; where other crops and economic resources were sparse, an attack of the blight became a national crisis.

That was what happened in Ireland. Other foods and foreign assistance could get the people through a failure of the potato crop one year, but a second consecutive failure exhausted those resources. So when the potato blight struck in 1845, it meant a difficult year; when it struck again in 1846, it was a national catastrophe. In 1847 fewer potatoes were planted, and the blight's impact was less severe; in 1848 farmers returned to their reliance on the potato, and there was another crop failure. It was a classic example of a monoculture's collapse.

These were years of incredible hardship in Ireland. People starved, and many who did not starve died from the diseases — typhus, scurvy, rickets, and cholera — that inevitably accom-

68

[27]Raymond F. Dasmann, *Another Kind of Country* (New York: Collier, 1970), p. 43.
[28]E. R. R. Green, "Agriculture," in R. Dudley Edwards and T. Desmond Williams (eds.), *The Great Famine* (New York: New York University Press, 1957), p. 92.

panied famines. Those who did not starve were under-nourished, scarcely capable of work. It seemed as though the country itself were dying and the only hope of survival was to leave it. America, with its great food surplus, had been one source of help, and the Irish were naturally impressed by this evidence of agricultural abundance. Many of the ships that brought food to Ireland from America returned with cargoes of immigrants.

Although the exodus from Ireland was caused by the potato famine, it continued well past the famine years. People had decided to go to America, and the general improvement in economic conditions at home did not change their minds; it simply made it possible for more people to afford the passage. Immigration from Ireland rose from 8,641 in 1845 to 162,649 in 1853. In all, approximately 2 million people left Ireland in the decade following the 1845 crop failure, the greatest single population movement of the century.

What awaited the Irish immigrants in the New World were at first new hardships and, later, a unique role in American society. The initial situation encountered by the immigrants was scarcely an improvement over the one they had left. Some of the famine's diseases also made the crossing, and many refugees died on board ship, in the ports of debarkation, or in the crowded quarantine camps. In several seaport cities arriving immigrants brought epidemics of typhus and cholera. These epidemics of course reinforced the already strong sentiments against the new population, and the antagonism was fed by anti-Catholicism, the perennial hostility of laborers to those desperate for work and willing to accept low wages, and the growing sense of native American superiority. There were anti-Catholic riots in Philadelphia, Richmond, and Charleston, and quick action in state and national legislatures to pass strict quarantine laws. "No Irish need apply" became a familiar appendage to help-wanted advertisements. The Irish were an oppressed minority at the bottom of the social structure.

But although they were a minority, they were a sizable and growing minority that soon became a significant element in the politics of the various cities, such as Boston and New York, that had large Irish communities. They were quickly recruited into the Democratic machines, which helped the Democratic party gain control over several city governments and gave the Irish access to the public jobs that were the traditional rewards for party loyalty. The Irish had certain advantages over other immigrant groups: a ready command of the English language and a familiarity with the mechanics of elections and public meetings. The new immigrants that arrived after the Civil War found the Irish solidly established in positions of political leadership.

The Irish, in spite of their political successes, were still social outcasts in the eyes of Protestant native Americans. They became, as William Allen White put it, not a ruling class but a governing class. They held appointive jobs — the Irish policeman became a familiar piece of Americana — elective offices, and positions of leadership in the party organizations. The Irish political boss was almost as common a feature of major American cities as the Irish policeman.

The Irish involvement with politics began to decline somewhat after World War I, along with the general decline in the power of most urban political machines and the increasing assimilation of the Irish into the mainstream of American society. But as a group they continue to be politically active, and politicians of Irish descent now frequently win the high-level electoral offices that were beyond the reach of their ancestors in the days when the Irish were too closely identified with urban machine politics. It had been a commonly accepted bit of political wisdom that an Irish Catholic could not be elected president of the United States; that last barrier was crossed in 1960 with the election of John F. Kennedy, a descendant of potato famine immigrants and the grandson of a Boston machine-politician.

Immigration, Status, and Power

When Alexis de Tocqueville visited the United States in the 1830s to study its social structure, he observed the absence of hereditary class distinctions and concluded that one factor — wealth — outweighed all others in determining status differences among individuals. He was probably right, but he was looking at an America that was still relatively homogeneous; its population (excluding, of course, slaves and Indians) was made up mainly of Protestants of northern European descent. There was plenty of clannishness and factionalism, but race, creed, and national origin had not yet become potent forces in society and politics. The massive immigrations that lay ahead would produce a kind of caste system, turning the descendants of the first starving colonists into aristocrats and creating a new group of untouchables out of every late-arriving minority. Along with wealth and other advantages, one of the great factors in determining one's place in the American social order has always been the simple matter of who got here first.

In early America wealth, status, and power tended to flow

together. All elective offices of any importance were held by prosperous and usually well-educated businessmen and land-owners; people without some substantial holdings in either land or money were blocked by property qualifications from voting or holding office. By the time of the Revolution the ruling groups in the various colonies were already distinct social classes. There were many local variations in the makeup of these elites — they might be shipowners of Puritan descent in Boston, financiers of Dutch descent in New York, plantation owners with a touch of Huguenot heritage in the Carolinas — but in each case they were developing into what any modern sociologist would immediately recognize as an aristocracy. There was much social mobility, but at the same time it was a firmly established part of the dominant social paradigm that stratification was a normal and necessary part of human life. Arthur Schlesinger writes:

Men in every walk of life not only accepted the concept of a layered society, but believed in its rightness. The clergy preached it; all classes practiced it. Whatever might be the shortcomings of the English aristocracy ... the American variety was no privileged group living off the unearned increment of ancestral reputations. They, by and large, had mounted the heights through shrewdness and ability and had stayed there by the continued exercise of those faculties. The ordinary citizen deemed it only proper to accord them deference.[29]

This native aristocracy produced most of the delegates to the Constitutional Convention and most of the leading statesmen in the new federal government.

The first organized challenge to the old American elites came from the coalition of frontier-state farmers, urban workers, and middle classes who supported Andrew Jackson. The Jacksonian revolution was the product of several forces that were changing the size and shape of the American system — immigration and westward movement, territorial expansion, elimination of property qualifications for voting. Industrialization was also beginning to have its effects: the rapidly expanding produc-tion-consumption economy was creating new avenues to wealth and power.

Thus began the gradual retreat of the old American elites from their exclusive position in the political order. Robert A. Dahl's study of politics in New Haven identifies 1842 as a year of

71

---

[29]Arthur Schlesinger, "The Aristocracy in Colonial America," *Proceedings of the Massachusetts Historical Society* 74 (1962): 20.

The opening-up of
the Far West pro-
duced another mar-
ket for cheap labor
and another flow of
immigration: Chinese
coolies were im-
ported by the
thousands. They built
the railroads, grew
fruits and vegeta-
bles, and worked as
cooks and servants
in San Francisco and
the mining towns.

72

transition in that city. Before that time, Dahl reports, "the typical mayor came from one of the established families of New Haven, went to Yale, was admitted to the bar, retained some connection with Yale, and spent most of his life in public affairs."[30] The mayor elected in 1842 was P. S. Galpin, a carpet manufacturer. For the rest of the century the city's mayors were mostly middle-class businessmen of English descent. After 1900 the impact of a century of immigration began to show; the mayors became first-generation Americans with names like Fitzgerald, Tully, Murphy, and, in 1945, Celentano.[31]

In the years before the Civil War immigrants came mainly from the Brisish Isles, Germany, and Scandinavia. After the war they began to come in growing numbers from southern and eastern Europe — Italy, Russia, the Balkans. Expanding American industry provided the employment. The new arrivals found work in the mines and the factories, the building trades and the public works projects. Mass production created a need for unskilled workers — men, women, and children — in the factories. The idea of organized labor was regarded as a dangerously radical notion. Rates of pay were regulated only by supply and demand, and the continual influx of new immigrants guaranteed a constant oversupply of workers.

74

The discovery of gold in California and the opening up of the Far West produced another market for cheap labor and another flow of immigration: Chinese coolies were imported by the thousands and went to work alongside the Irish building the railroads. They also grew fruits and vegetables and worked as cooks and servants in San Francisco and the mining towns.

The period between the Civil War and World War II was the time of the heaviest immigration. Over 25 million people came to America during these years, most of them from southern and eastern Europe. These "new immigrants" constituted the bulk of the urban poor, the working class. American society was a power structure shaped largely by the stages of immigration. At the top of the heap were the "Americans," mostly of English descent, who dominated business and society and the highest political offices. These "Americans" included both the upper classes who traced their descent to pre-Revolutionary elites and the aspiring new rich, politically and economically powerful and usually aspiring to intermarry with the "old American" aristocracy as the final sign of success. At a lower level, usually running the urban political machines, were the Irish. At the bottom, totally powerless at first but gradually gaining

[30]Robert A. Dahl, *Who Governs?* (New Haven, Conn.: Yale University Press, 1961), pp. 12-14.
[31]Ibid.

strength to compete with the Irish for control of the machines and then for local and state offices, were the new immigrants with Italian, Jewish, and eastern European names. Other groups — the American Indians, the freed blacks, the Orientals in the West — were out of the power structure entirely.

The heavy concentrations of immigrant groups in the cities led to a new kind of politics in which race and religion were at least as important as convictions and experience when it came to selecting candidates for office. The favorite strategy of urban power brokers was to put together some kind of a "balanced ticket" that would ally candidates from the various voting blocs — Irish, Italian, Protestant, Jewish, and so forth — to deliver a majority vote. One of the great products of this kind of politicking was Mayor Fiorello La Guardia of New York City, who was Italian, Jewish, and Episcopalian — a one-man balanced ticket.

Urban politics was exciting and profitable, but hardly respectable. The mayor's office was no longer a place for a gentleman; and the upper classes now either avoided urban politics completely or involved themselves with reform movements aimed at cleaning up city hall.

The favorite strategy of urban power brokers was to put together some kind of a "balanced ticket" that would ally candidates from the various voting blocs to deliver a majority vote. One of the great products of this kind of politicking was Mayor Fiorello La Guardia of New York City, who was Italian, Jewish, and Episcopalian — a one-man balanced ticket.

The new immigrants were slow in making their presence felt at the state and national levels. State legislative districts were usually drawn so as to give a disproportionate advantage to rural districts, and the traditional urban-rural conflict that has been so prominent in American politics took on a new dimension in areas where the state capitals were controlled by "Americans" and the cities by "new immigrant" ethnic groups. The state legislatures elected members of the United States Senate, which became known as the "world's most exclusive club," in which descendants of old colonial families mingled with multimillionaires. There was little room in this club for the sons of immigrants, and even after the change in 1913 to direct election of senators, the later-arriving ethnic groups remained underrepresented.

The fact is that the later-arriving ethnic groups have always been and still are underrepresented in political office, especially at the higher levels. Congress, for example, has far more white Anglo-Saxon Protestants than their percentage of the population. There are, of course, members of racial and religious minority groups, but as a general rule they tend to come from districts where their group is a majority or a strong plurality. The statistics show over and over again that districts containing a number of different ethnic groups resolve their differences by electing a "neutral" WASP representative.

Blacks are frequently described as a new immigrant group —

Ironically, the whites had to teach the Indians about private property in order to systematically deprive them of it.

which is accurate in a sense, even though they began arriving in America a good century and a half before the Revolution. The accuracy in the description is that blacks were effectively isolated from any sort of meaningful political participation through the long era of slavery and, except for the brief and highly overrated period of reconstruction, for a good century thereafter. The organizational actions that helped other ethnic groups establish a place for themselves in the system have commenced only recently among the black population, and usually their efforts are opposed most strongly by those groups that went through the same struggles earlier. Black representation in Congress, like that of other immigrant groups, lags well behind their percentage of the population. If it were equal, there would be forty-three black representatives and ten black senators.[32]

The point of these observations is that the era of immigration is not yet truly ended. The flow of newcomers to America has long since passed its peak, but the process of absorbing these millions into the system is far from complete. We have no adequate historical basis for predicting when it will be completed, since there has never before been a time when so many people from different racial and cultural backgrounds came together so quickly in a new environment — but it can reasonably be expected to take another century or so before our ideals of equal opportunity become social reality. Meanwhile the stages of immigration remain visible to us, like the exposed strata of a rock formation, exerting a powerful historical influence on modern politics.

Taking the Land

One of the rather less-inspiring aspects of the saga of immigration and westward movement is the fact that the country was already populated. To the European mind, it probably did not seem so. In Europe population meant farms and cities and industry. It seemed that the vast stretches of American land were not being "used," that they were empty territory, there for the taking. Europeans knew, of course, that there were people in the New World, but there were ways of getting around that obstacle. For one thing there were not really many of them by European standards; for another it was commonly accepted that since the Indians were savages, the coming of the white people would benefit them. The charters of the various colonization companies all stated their intention of converting the

---

[32]Thomas R. Dye and L. Harmon Zeigler, *The Irony of Democracy* (Belmont, Calif.: Duxbury Press, Wadsworth, 1971), p. 93.

Indians to Christianity, thereby saving their souls from eternal damnation. And throughout the years that the destinies of the Indian tribes were controlled by officials of the United States government, policies were consistently stated in terms of improving the Indians' lot by educating them and guiding them toward a civilized style of life.

But beneath that facade of benevolence lay the fact that the land was populated by people who wanted to keep it — and keep it the way it was — and that other people wanted to take it and change it, and did. The taking was sometimes peaceful, sometimes violent; sometimes by small increments, sometimes by giant swoops; sometimes through process of law, sometimes by fraud and trickery; sometimes with honest attempts at fair compensation, sometimes by outright theft. But it all moved in the same direction: more space controlled by whites, less by Indians.

Among the early colonists there was much talk of neighborliness, of Indians and whites occupying the continent together and in harmony. But that did not happen because the white population kept increasing, and because the two races represented fundamentally different patterns of adaptation that could not coexist within the same environment. It was not simply that the Indians lived by hunting and the whites by agriculture, although the conflict was often pictured that way. There were many Indian tribes that lived by farming the land, and in fact two of the chief staples of colonial agriculture, corn and tobacco, were crops that the Indians had been growing long before the colonists came. Rather it was a clash between two deeply different cultures, each of which had different ways of thinking about human existence on the land, and neither of which could quite understand the other.

The Indians had agriculture, art, government, and commerce, but they did not operate according to European concepts of consumption, private property, profit, and savings. One early missionary reported that the Indian race "takes little care for the future, but . . . enjoys the present. . . . As long as they have anything, they are always celebrating feasts, and having songs, dances, and speeches."[33] Some Spanish monks saw the same problem and proposed a solution to it: "The Indians are weak by nature and not acquisitive, and are satisfied with having enough to get along on from day to day. If there is any way to bring them out of their laziness and carelessness, it is to make them help the Spaniards in their commerce . . . and thus they

77

---

[33]McNickle, *They Came Here First*, p. 260.

will become fond of commerce and profits."[34] A couple of centuries later Henry Knox, the first official of the United States government in charge of Indian affairs, made a similar proposal: "Were it possible to introduce among the Indian tribes a love for exclusive property, it would be a happy commencement."[35] Ironically, the whites had to teach the Indians about private property in order to systematically deprive them of it.

Early colonists had found that the Indians could usually be persuaded to part with their land for small sums (the purchase of Manhattan Island for the equivalent of twenty-four dollars is the best-known example of this), and it soon became necessary for the various colonial governments to regulate such transactions. In some cases it was made unlawful for private citizens to purchase land from Indians. As early as the seventeenth century, some of the colonies had already established reservations, where land was held communally by the local tribes. It was understood, of course, that these areas were exclusively for Indian use and permanently excluded from white settlement.

Another early attempt at a permanent resolution of the land question was the British Proclamation of 1763, which established the watershed of the Appalachian mountains as a boundary, reserving all the land west of the watershed for the use of the Indians and providing that no parcels of the land could be sold except to the crown. The proclamation's intent was to create one huge reservation within which, in one historian's words, "the land was to remain untouched by the plow and where no settlement of white men should disturb the peace of the primeval forest." However, there were already white settlers west of the boundary even before the proclamation was issued. And in the general chaos of the years leading up to the Revolution, neither the crown nor the colonial governments could stop the further infiltration of the Indian territory.

Immediately after the Revolution, the Continental Congress prohibited further settlement on Indian lands and passed a law requiring congressional approval for any purchase or cession of any land "inhabited or claimed by Indians." A few years later the Northwest Ordinance proclaimed that:

The utmost good faith shall always be observed toward the Indians; their land and property shall never be taken from them without their consent; and in their property, rights and liberty, they shall never be invaded or disturbed, unless in justified and

---
[34]Ibid.
[35]Ibid., p. 261.

*lawful wars authorized by Congress; but laws founded in justice
and humanity shall from time to time be made, for preventing
wrongs being done to them, and for preserving peace and friend-
ship with them.*[36]

These were admirable sentiments, but they tended to get lost in
the confusion of conflicting opinions about how to deal with "the
Indian problem." Some of the states — most notably Georgia —
did not recognize the federal government's exclusive authority
to deal with the Indians, and members of Congress were by no
means unanimous in their assessment of what (if any) rights
the Indians possessed. There was also pressure from settlers
along the frontier who wanted the army to move in and exter-
minate the Indians.

Henry Knox, as secretary of war under President Washington, was in a position to influence the new government's
policies, since Indian affairs had been assigned to the War
Department. He investigated the situation and concluded that
a war would be both too costly and unnecessary, and that within
fifty years the Indians could be removed from all the territory
east of the Mississippi (the western boundary of the United
States) without it. In his report to the president he said:

79

*As the settlements of the whites shall approach nearer to the
Indian boundaries established by treaties, the game will be diminished, and the lands being valuable to the Indians only as
hunting grounds, they will be willing to sell further tracts for
small consideration. By the expiration, therefore, of the above
period, it is most probable that the Indians will ... be reduced to a
very small number.*[37]

Knox also believed that the Indian tribes should be dealt with
exclusively through treaties made by the federal government,
and that they should not be subject to the laws of the various
states. This policy was enacted into law by the Congress and
supported in Supreme Court decisions written by Chief Justice
John Marshall, but it remained an issue of bitter political
conflict for many years.

The conflict centered on the tribes in the South, where state
governments were most ready to defy the federal law. Many of
the tribes in the North and along the eastern seaboard had
become virtually extinct, but in the South the Indians were
numerous and increasingly sophisticated. The Cherokee nation
in Georgia was making a remarkable cultural transition. They

---

[36]Vine Deloria, Jr., *Custer Died for Your Sins* (New York: Macmillan, 1969), p. 43.
[37]McNickle, *They Came Here First*, p. 202.

80

Although Congress had passed a law reserving all of the United States west of the Mississippi (with the exception of the states of Missouri and Louisiana and the Arkansas Territory) for Indian settlement, white settlers streamed across the river anyway, effectively shifting the boundary westward to the ninety-fifth meridian. Soon the Indian country was no longer the land beyond the frontier, but rather a shrinking island within white civilization.

81

had invented a written alphabet, formed a constitutional democratic government, built schools and libraries, and were prospering in business and agriculture. Their population, unlike that of most tribes in close proximity to white settlers, was growing. They reached the point of declining to cede any further land, and when the state legislature attempted to annul their laws they took the issue to the Supreme Court, and won. Christianized and civilized, they were the model of what the whites had always said the Indians ought to become; they were also regarded as a menace by most southern leaders.

The election of Andrew Jackson brought in a new era of Indian policy. Jackson did not believe in making treaties with the Indians. "The Indians are the subjects of the United States," he wrote, "inhabiting its territory and acknowledging its sovereignty. Then is it not absurd for the sovereign to negotiate by treaty with the subject?"[38] He was also interested in the idea, which had come up frequently since the United States acquired the Louisiana Territory, of solving the problem by relocating the Indians on the other side of the Mississippi. He proposed that Congress consider "the propriety of setting apart an ample district west of the Mississippi ... to be guaranteed to the Indian tribes as long as they shall occupy it."[39]

In 1830 Congress passed the Indian Removal Act, which became the basic instrument for solving the "Indian problem" east of the Mississippi. The law authorized the president to offer land in any area not included in any state or organized territory "for the reception of such tribes or nations of Indians as may choose to exchange the lands where they now reside, and remove there."[40] In effect it permitted the government to transplant a number of tribes from the land they occupied to new reservations. The entire Cherokee nation was moved from Georgia to the Oklahoma plains in a migration known in Indian history as "the trail of tears."

While the removal process was still underway, Congress passed a law stating that all of the United States west of the Missisisippi (with the exception of the states of Missouri and Louisiana and the Arkansas Territory) would be Indian country, excluded from any settlement by whites and protected by the army. White settlers continued to stream into the lands across the river anyway, and the federal government shifted the boundary westward to the ninety-fifth meridian, running

[38]Ibid., p. 238.
[39]Ibid., p. 239.
[40]Vine Deloria, Jr., *Of Utmost Good Faith* (San Francisco: Straight Arrow, 1971), p. 41.

from the Lake of the Woods in what is now Minnesota south to Galveston Bay. But soon, as a result of the war with Mexico, new territories west of the "permanent Indian frontier" were acquired by the United States. The Indian country was no longer the land beyond the frontier, but rather a shrinking island within white civilization.

The overall effect of American immigration and westward movement was a continual increase of demands for some kind of a reduction in the Indian holdings. Every aspect of the newly developing ecosystem added to this pressure: states were being admitted to the Union, territories being organized, railroads being built, settlers and speculators seeking lands, miners discovering mineral deposits. Along the way there were countless conflicts between Indians and white civilians or between Indians and the United States Army; and there were many treaties to define the nature and boundaries of the Indian holdings. In general these treaties were made when it became obvious that some further encroachment upon the Indian lands was inevitable. Land would be ceded to the government in return for supplies and money (the latter to be held in trust by the government) and a promise of permanent protection against any further encroachment.

In 1871 Congress ended the long debate about treaty making by passing a law that made it clear that future decisions concerning Indian affairs would be determined by legislation, not negotiation. In the following decade Congress passed the General Allotment Act, which changed the fundamental legal status of Indian lands from communal holdings by tribes to individual homesteads. It was hoped that this would bring about the final conversion of all Indians to civilized farmers, making surplus land available to white settlers, and reduce the expense of maintaining reservations. One senator argued on behalf of the bill that the Indians "burn, murder and plunder with impunity; they contribute nothing, and never have contributed anything to the welfare of society. Yet they have for generations been maintained in insolent idleness or audacious hostility by the voluntary contributions of millions of money from the public revenue."[41]

The bill allotted a tract of 160 acres to each Indian, with the provision that it could not be sold for twenty-five years. It proved to be a disaster. Many of the Indians who suddenly became landowners had no knowledge of farming, and much of the land was not fertile enough — as many white homesteaders found also — to sustain a family even on 160 acres. As a result,

83

---

[41]McNickle, *They Came Here First*, p. 265.

vast amounts of land were immediately leased by Indians to white settlers, in many cases ranchers or farmers who consolidated the tracts with other holdings, and when the lease was up much of it was sold. In many cases the leases and sales were fraudulent. By 1934 Indian holdings had been reduced by another 90 million acres.[42] Hundreds of thousands of Indians were landless.

It is probably impossible for the descendants of Europeans to comprehend the traumatic effect on the Indian population of the invasion and conquest of their land. Numbers tell some of it. As late as 1920 the death rate among Indians was double the national death rate. Recent estimates place the Indian population at about half of what it was when the first colonists came. Some tribes have increased in population, while many have been totally obliterated. The Indian population in California, once the most dense of any part on the continent, virtually vanished in the years following the discovery of gold.

The most remarkable thing about the American Indians is that they and their culture have survived at all. But they have: at least one-half of the 300 or so languages spoken before the first explorers came are still in use. Art, rituals, dress, and cultural traditions from the ancient past have endured through all the movements and changes. And many of the tribes are still vigorous political institutions.

The American DSP is so attached to certain ideas of what constitutes a rational relationship between human beings and the land that there were very few people — even those who had some concern for the welfare of the Indians — who did not believe that the spread of the European agricultural/industrial adaptive system was a positive benefit to the land. There was general agreement that the Indians simply did not know how to use land and its resources. This ignorance was believed to be shared with other nationalities also. One of the justifications for the war with Mexico was that the occupants of the Southwest were not making adequate use of the land's potential, that it was going to waste. This same sense of superiority surfaced during the dispute with the British over the Oregon Territory. The dispute was not simply about who would control the territory, but about how its environment would be managed. The British were mainly interested in preserving Oregon as a resource for the fur trade; the Americans wanted to settle and develop it. The joint British-American control was strained by the influx of new American settlers, as a recent history points out:

[42]Deloria, *Custer Died for Your Sins*, p. 47.

The maintenance of an abundant supply of fur-bearing animals depended very largely on keeping the area as thinly settled as possible. It was this emphasis on small settlement that brought American demands for total control of the area. The unlimited potential of the Oregon country was not realized and never would be if the British had their way. In the final analysis, the Oregon country was acquired by the United States through a compromise that approximately halved the area in dispute. Although many Americans were disappointed that not all of it was obtained, half seemed better than nothing. This episode helped to convince many Americans that the British were no more advanced than the Indians or Mexicans, because they could not see the potential of the area for exploitation.[43]

Closing the Door

It was inevitable that such an enormous human migration as that which poured into the United States would create a variety of negative reactions. Even before the Irish potato famine Protestants were beginning to worry about the increasing number of Catholics; others were concerned that the flow of immigration from countries with no tradition of democratic government might have a damaging effect on the quality of politics in America. The rise of bossism and the political machines among the foreign-born populations of the cities gave weight to the argument that unchecked immigration would destroy democracy.

Out of this reaction emerged a political anti-immigration movement. Antiforeign secret societies and political parties sprang up — mainly in the port cities where the immigrants were the most visible and where Protestant citizens were becoming alarmed by the construction of new Catholic churches and schools. The movement coalesced into a national party, the American party, better known as the "Know-Nothings" because it was a secret society whose members took vows of loyalty and refused to divulge any information to outsiders. Although the Know-Nothings avoided the usual forms of campaigning and speech making and at first tried to conceal even the fact of the party's existence, they became a powerful force in American politics. Their most spectacular success was in Massachusetts (rapidly filling with fugitives from the Irish potato famine), where they polled two-thirds of the vote in 1854, electing the governor, most of the state legislature, and the

---

[43]Donald W. Whisenhunt, *The Environment and the American Experience* (Port Washington, N.Y.: Kennikat Press, 1974), pp. 52-53.

entire delegation to Congress. The Know-Nothing party soon died out, but the sentiment underlying it did not.

In the late 1870s unemployment in California lent force to another third-party movement, the Workingmen's party. In this case the leadership was Irish and the target was the Chinese, whose availability for low-paying jobs threatened other workers. This party, too, soon passed from the political scene, but anti-Chinese sentiment produced the first clear restriction on immigration — the Chinese Exclusion Act of 1882 — which suspended the admission to the United States of laborers from China.

During the late nineteenth and early twentieth centuries, a number of other restrictive laws were passed excluding such "undesirables" as convicts, prostitutes, paupers, people with contagious diseases, polygamists, imbeciles, and people whose passage had been paid for by others or who had been imported as contract workers. The latter exclusions were aimed at employers who recruited immigrants as strike breakers. Organized labor in the United States, a movement made up mainly of immigrants, became a major source of anti-immigration pressure. Working people were concerned about immigration's tendency to produce a surplus of available workers, and employers (members of the same social classes that most disapproved of the new immigrants) sometimes found themselves supporting free immigration for economic reasons.

In the midst of all this was still the old ideological commitment to the view of America as the land of new hope for the downtrodden. Four years after the Chinese Exclusion Act the Statue of Liberty was completed, with its famous inscription:

Give me your tired, your poor,
Your huddled masses yearning to breathe free,
The wretched refuse of your teeming shore,
Send these, the homeless, tempest-tossed, to me:
I lift my lamp beside the golden door.

The association of foreigners with radical politics was a factor in the gradual increase of anti-immigration sentiment in the United States. After President McKinley was assassinated by Leon Czolgosz (a Polish anarchist), Congress added anarchists to the list of those excluded. This was only the first of many attempts to screen out undesirable political ideas. However, the anti-immigration reaction proceeded along several fronts and resulted in public policies explicitly aimed at controlling cultural and genetic evolution.

The effort to control cultural evolution was the "Americani-

The effort to control cultural evolution was the "Americanization" movement, whose purpose was to help the immigrants "renounce allegiance to their old and prepare to live or die for the glory of the new — America."

zation" movement, whose purpose was to instill the immigrants with the cultural values that would help them to function effectively in their new economic and political roles. A post of Director of Americanization was created within the Department of Interior, and a variety of educational programs were designed to help the immigrants, in the words of a Bureau of Americanization publication, "renounce allegiance to their old and prepare to live or die for the glory of the new — America."[44] Americanization was actually an effort at large-scale adult socialization meant to excise certain elements of the cultural heritage of the immigrants and replace them with an American cultural heritage. It was a rather primitive form of the kind of cultural reprogramming that is now known as brainwashing.

Americanization rested its case on the "environment" side of the heredity versus environment debate: it assumed that the immigrants' moral deficiencies (the existence of which most native Americans were convinced of) came from their cultural heritage and could be remedied through education. But at the same time that the Americanization movement was underway, another line of thought and action was directed toward *genetic* heredity.

Genetics emerged as a separate branch of science in the late nineteenth century, largely as a result of a belated surge of interest in the laws of heredity that had been discovered by the Austrian botanist Gregor Mendel. At first the geneticists concerned themselves exclusively with simple physiological traits, but soon they were theorizing about the genetic heredity of human character traits as well. This led to the development of a special class of genetic study, eugenics. The word *eugenics* was first used in 1883 by the English scientist Francis Galton in his book *Inquiries into Human Faculty.* It comes from a Greek root which means approximately "good genes." Its subject is the relationship between human character traits and race, and the question of how the quality of the human population might be "improved" by any technological means or public policies that would, as Galton put it, give "the more suitable races or strains of blood . . . a better chance of prevailing speedily over the less suitable."[45] Galton (a cousin of Darwin's) was convinced that there was a natural hierarchy of superior and inferior races (white at the top, black at the bottom), and he worked hard to get eugenics accepted as a legitimate science. He had some limited success in England (he did manage to get a chair in

[44]F. C. Butler, *Community Americanization* (Washington, D.C.: Government Printing Office, 1920), p. 14.

[45]Francis Galton, in Frederick Ausubel, Jon Beckwith, and Kaaren Janssen, "The Politics of Genetic Engineering," *Psychology Today,* June 1974, p. 40.

eugenics established at the University of London) and much greater success in America, where eugenics became a powerful scientific and political movement.

Eugenics spoke directly to the growing American fear of immigration's effect on the quality of the society. Its alarming message was that the quality of the American population was on the decline as a result of immigration, and that this was because of inferior *genetic* characteristics — something that could not be remedied by reeducation. "The recent immigrants," one eugenics expert said in congressional testimony, "as a whole, present a higher precentage of inborn socially inadequate qualities than do the older stocks."[46]

Financial support for eugenics research was provided by grants from the Carnegie and Harriman families and cereal tycoon J. H. Kellogg. Institutes were founded: the Station for Experimental Evolution, the Eugenics Record Office, the Race Betterment Foundation. Eugenics courses were taught at the major American universities, and new concepts on eugenics were discussed at international scientific congresses and in the pages of scholarly publications such as the *Journal of Heredity*.

All of this naturally had its impact on public policy. At the state level there were legislative efforts to protect or improve the national gene pool. In the early 1900s, thirty states passed laws permitting the sterilization of people with character traits believed to be genetically inherited — drunkenness, sexual deviations, criminal violence, insanity, and feeblemindedness. Some 20,000 people were legally sterilized under these programs.[47] Most state miscegenation laws also date from this period.

At the federal level there were new efforts to restrict immigration. This was a delicate issue because any overt effort to block immigrants from a given nation could lead to repercussions both in domestic politics and international diplomacy. Nevertheless, Congress found ways. In 1917 a bill was passed — over President Wilson's veto — which excluded all European aliens "over sixteen years of age, physically capable of reading, who cannot read the English language, or some other language or dialect."[48] The bill might have seemed impartial, but it was not. It was a device for reducing immigration from southern and eastern Europe, where literacy rates were low. Earlier government actions such as the Chinese Exclusion Act and the

89

[46]Harry H. Laughlin, superintendent of the Eugenics Record Office, in Frederick Ausubel, Jon Beckwith, and Kaaren Janssen, "The Politics of Genetic Engineering," *Psychology Today*, June 1974, p. 40.
[47]Ibid.
[48]Charles A. Beard and Mary R. Beard, *New Basic History of the United States*, rev. ed. (Garden City, N.Y.: Doubleday, 1968), p. 395.

"Gentlemen's Agreement," negotiated with Japan in 1907, had cut down immigration from the Orient, another area that troubled the eugenicists.

The 1917 law, like the other restrictive acts before it, was still a "qualitative" law; it did not directly reduce the actual total amount of immigrants. That step was taken in 1921, at a time of increasing fear of an immense new postwar wave of immigration from Europe. An emergency act passed in that year established the first quota system: immigration from any nation could not exceed 3 percent of the number of persons of that nationality living in America in 1910.

A more comprehensive law, the Immigration Act of 1924, retained the quota system and also placed an annual limit on immigration of approximately 150,000 — far fewer than the hundreds of thousands who had come to America in the peak years. This marked the end of the great flood of immigration from southern and eastern Europe, which were allotted only a small part of the total quota, while 70 percent of the quota was allotted to Great Britain, Ireland, and Germany (quotas that were rarely filled).

The quota system remained in effect for about forty years and served as a fairly effective monitor of the country's racial composition. New laws in 1965 and 1968 finally eliminated the national quota system and replaced it with a ceiling of 170,000 immigrants from nations outside the Western Hemisphere, a maximum of 20,000 immigrants from any one country, and a limit of 120,000 immigrants from Western Hemisphere nations.

Immigration is no longer the heated issue it once was, but it continues to alter the American population. According to the Commission on Population Growth and the American Future appointed by President Nixon in the early 1970s, immigration is again becoming a larger factor in population growth. The commission found immigration accounting for 16 percent of growth in the 1960-1970 decade, 18 percent in 1971, and 23 percent in 1972.[49] This means, for one thing, that predictions of American population growth cannot rely solely on birthrate and death rate computations.

Immigration is having other effects on the American system. It is bringing in (as provided for by the 1965 law) a considerable number of new Americans with advanced professional and technological educations. This is consistent with the traditional belief that immigrants with job skills are preferable to immi-

---

[49]Leslie Aldridge Westoff, "Should We Pull Up the Gangplank?" *New York Times Magazine*, 24 September 1973, p. 59.

grants without them. On the other hand, the 1965 law is having unforeseen impacts on the American medical profession, for example, which is anxious about the influx of foreign doctors. Further, there is a corresponding social problem in the countries of origin that are being *deprived* of doctors. Also, and again consistent with the explicit provisions of the 1965 law, we are taking in a considerable number of refugees from Communist countries. This has had its greatest effect in Florida, which is filled with anti-Castro Cuban refugees. Its most recent manifestation was the immigration of South Vietnamese. This recent influx of immigrants from Communist countries is a curious political phenomenon, whose consequences have not been (so far as I know) studied by political scientists: in other words, what, if any, is the social impact of a selective immigration of militant anticommunists?

A third product of recent immigration, perhaps the most ironic in the light of the concerns I have discussed in this section, is the number of nonwhite immigrants. In the past twenty years there has been an increasing number of immigrants from the Asian mainland, India, and the Philippines. This Asian immigration, combined with the movements from Cuba and Puerto Rico and the nations of Latin America — all groups that have higher birthrates than the U.S. national average — means a slow but significant reduction in the Anglo-Saxon percentage of the population.

Another development that contributes to the drop in the Anglo-Saxon percentage is the continual inflow of illegal immigrants. Nobody knows how many illegal immigrants are currently living in the United States — estimates range from 1 to 5 million — but the number is undoubtedly on the rise. The Immigration and Naturalization Service, the federal agency charged with the awesome task of trying to find all these aliens and repatriate them, fears that there may be as many as 17 million illegal immigrants within the decade. About 85 percent of these illegal aliens are Mexicans — more genetic fuel for the drift away from Anglo-Saxon America.

The report of the Commission on Population Growth and the American Future called population growth "an intensifier or multiplier of many problems impairing the quality of life in the United States," and recommended new measures to tighten some areas of immigration and eliminate others.[50] The report suffered the usual fate of presidential commission findings —

---

[50]Westoff, "Should We Pull Up the Gangplank?" p. 73.

It was assumed that
immigrants would
improve their lot by
becoming Americans,
and that the land,
too, was being called
to a higher mission
by becoming part of
the United States.

92

that is, it was ignored by the president who had appointed the commission in the first place — but it is only one of many signs of growing national uneasiness about immigration. We can expect to hear more arguments in favor of a further closing of the door.

Population Patterns

Although immigration is no longer the chief cause, the American population is still changing: it is growing, and it is changing in its makeup and distribution. The American population has always been highly mobile. We can look at this in relation to three main movements: the migration from the East to the West, the migration from the country to the cities, and the migration from the South to the North.[51]

The westward movement, which we have already discussed as a major phenomenon in America's historical past, has not ended. In the decade 1950-1960 the population of the West increased by almost 40 percent, and in the state of California alone population increased by over 5 million. More recently population growth has shifted away from the coastal states, and is now more of a southwestward movement.

Urbanization has also been an important part of American history. Much immigration, as previously mentioned, was a movement from the European countryside to American cities, and there has been a similar internal movement. In 1790 the first national census revealed that only 5 percent of the people lived in towns with a population of 2,500 or more. By 1870 when the country's industrialization was already well underway, the urban population was about one-quarter of the total. By 1920 it was one-half, and today it is over 70 percent and still growing.[52] Once a nation of farmers, America has become a nation of city dwellers. Even the farms have become industrialized, dependent more on the modern technology of agribusiness and less on the labor of small landowners and their employees.

The south-to-north movement has not been as numerically large as either the movement westward or urbanization, but it has had a dramatic effect on American politics, as evidenced by the election of black mayors in a number of major northern cities. Actually it is not entirely distinguishable from the urbanization movement, since many of the people who went northward were moving from country to cities, from work on

---

[51]Everett S. Lee, "Internal Migration and Population Redistribution in the United States," in Ronald Freedman (ed.), *Population: The Vital Revolution* (New York: Anchor, 1964), p. 124.

[52]Late reports from the Census Bureau indicate that the growth of cities has begun to level off and be passed by the growth rate of some nonmetropolitan areas, especially those with large retirement communities. This means that a new form of urbanization is taking place in many areas that were recently semirural.

the farms to work in the factories. The migration of black Americans to the northern cities (accounting for not all of this movement but for an important part of it) began after the Civil War and expanded during the first and second world wars, as the demand for labor increased with the growth of defense industries. Today the black population is more heavily urbanized than the white population.

The continual growth of America's population was never entirely due to immigration. The fertility rate was at one time extremely high — about eight children per family in the colonial years — and combined with immigration to make America's population the fastest growing in the world. Robert Malthus cited this country's fantastic growth rate, which more than doubled in each generation, as support for his argument that people would inevitably multiply beyond their food resources.

The fertility rate was on the decline through the early years of this century; then during and after World War II it underwent a spectacular and unexpected change. From 1940 to 1960 the American population increased by 47.7 million, which was almost as many people as were counted in the census of 1880. This so-called baby boom produced a "bulge" in the population — an unprecedented number of young people — but as the people who represent the "bulge" grow older, we can expect to have a similarly disproportionate number of older people.

Population growth, apart from immigration, results from two things: the death rate and the birthrate. In America mortality rates have declined spectacularly: life expectancy averaged around thirty-five years in 1800, and today is about twice that. The death rate (measured as the number of deaths per year per 1,000 people) has gone down from 17.2 at the beginning of this century to about 9.0 at present.

Birthrates have been more erratic — very high over most of the early years of American history, dropping low during the Great Depression of the 1930s, rising to a new peak during the postwar baby boom, and declining fairly steadily since then. In 1950 the birthrate was 24.1 (the number of children per 1,000 people per year) and the fertility rate (the number of children the average woman could be expected to have in her lifetime) was 3.7. Today the birthrate is approximately 17.0 and the fertility rate is around 2.0. If this remains constant, the *rate* of growth can be expected to diminish, but the population will continue to increase, possibly reaching the 300 million mark by the year 2020. (Even at this reduced rate, the growing number of Americans can be expected to result in increased demands on the world's natural resources.)

Public decisions about the size and makeup of the population are among the ways that human institutions control the course of genetic and cultural evolution. Through most of American history the population policy has been simply to encourage growth, to allow immigration while striving to keep the birthrate high and the death rate low. Even when some Americans began to worry about the *quality* of population growth, there was still virtually unanimous agreement that the population should continue to grow — through immigration from the northern European nations and multiplication of the native stock — and grow it did. No census yet has reported a decline in the number of Americans.

Population growth has been equated with national progress. While the population grew, so did the nation's territorial space. It was assumed that immigrants would improve their lot by becoming Americans, and that the land, too, was being called to a higher mission by becoming part of the United States. This enthusiastic sense of progress and betterment also included economic growth. New land meant new resources, and new people meant new manpower and still more consumers. Americans became entranced with the upward march of the Gross National Product, the total output of goods and services; it became an article of the nation's faith that the economy must always grow, that more each year must be produced and consumed.

Recently the growth/progress equation has lost its prominence in the American dominant social paradigm. Some communities have reversed years of encouraging population growth and are now trying to limit it. Public and private institutions have developed a new concern for the dangers of overpopulation, and political activist groups such as ZPG (Zero Population Growth) and the more recent NPG (Negative Population Growth) have made human numbers their sole concern.

The newness of the population-control movement may give the impression that government has only begun to determine the size and makeup of the population. This is, of course, not true. There has always been an American population policy and programs to carry it out. The newness is in the sudden suspicion that growth may not be the only policy worth considering and in the awareness of the many things that governments do or don't do (through education, health programs, taxation, and welfare) to control population. This concern about population also calls for a new awareness of the relationship between people and the land. Population-control activists find their natural allies among ecologists, and land-use planners begin to speak of the "carrying capacity" of the environment. We see that population management is inseparably connected to environmental management—and again, this is nothing new. Government has always been occupied with environmental management, and the growth of the American population has been accompanied by a remaking of the American environment to accommodate it.

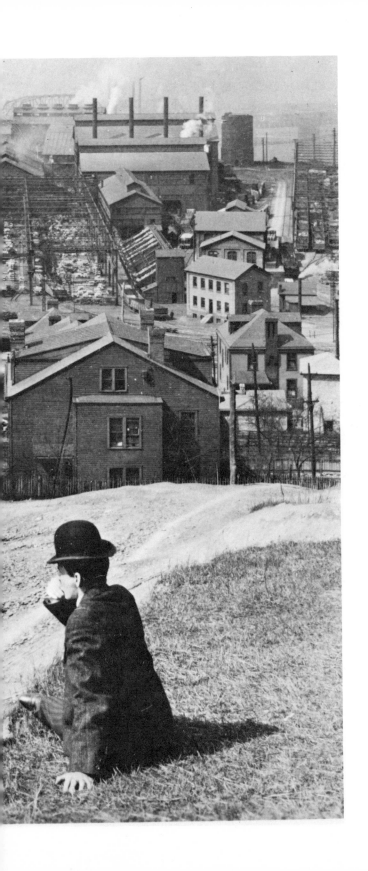

The Making of an Ecosystem: Adapting America

Mankind can be viewed as a new sort of
geological force, reshaping the landscape,
favoring some kinds of organisms and destroying others, changing the very composition of
the atmosphere with the smoke of countless
chimneys, starting new chains of radioactive decay with atomic explosions.
MARSTON BATES, *Man in Nature*

Men become fully conscious of what they
have done only some centuries after they
have done it.
JOHN STRACHEY, *The Coming Struggle for Power*

herever human beings live,
the environment changes. In
many cases where populations
are small and technology
is simple, the human species
finds a place for itself in the
balance of nature and life goes
on for centuries with only minor changes. But the changes
do take place. Naturalists
have found that even prehis-
toric tribes altered the envi-
ronments as they hunted, mined, domesticated animals, and
developed agriculture. Early civilizations created farmlands
out of deserts by the use of irrigation, and sometimes their
farming turned fertile land into deserts. Whenever people
moved, whether in tribal migrations or in expeditions of war or
trade, animals and plant species moved with them. Thus, over
the millennia the continents of Africa and Asia and Europe
were transformed. The same thing has happened in the Western Hemisphere but at a different rate. Here, with the massive
influx of new people and the spectacular development of new
technology, the change has been quick and conspicuous.
America as the first colonists knew it no longer exists; the land
we now live in is an ecosystem created by human activity. The
business of directing environmental change — slowing it down,
speeding it up, changing its course, rectifying past errors — has
become one of the chief responsibilities of modern government.

The transformation of the American continent was a deliberate and cooperative social effort. There were accidents and

100

Marston Bates, *Man in Nature* (Englewood Cliffs, N.J.: Prentice-Hall, 1964), p. 106.
John Strachey, *The Coming Struggle for Power* (New York: Covici-Friede, 1933), p. 11.

The land the pioneers found was a natural water management system that kept the streams running by steady seepage even in dry years, moderated floods, and made water available to all its plant and animal species. The first act of the farmer was to take this system apart.

Land was the great
magnet that drew
the first settlers
from the Old World,
and it was land —
more than anything
else — that kept the
white civilization ad-
vancing ever west-
ward across the con-
tinent.

unforeseen complications along the way, but the general direction of the change was not accidental; it was intended and
planned and carried out with a political consensus so strong
that there was never any need to debate the basic purpose.
People came to America with the intention of adapting to it, and
also with the intention of adapting it to them.

Plant Importation

The process of transforming the ecology got underway almost
immediately after the discovery of the New World. On his
second voyage Christopher Columbus brought with him livestock and the seeds of various Spanish crops, in addition to
samples of Canary Islands sugar cane, which became the prime
commercial crop of the West Indies. The missionaries in Mexico
and California planted citrus, figs, dates, grapes, olives, and
alfalfa — all imported from Spain.

The English explorers also brought their plants with them.
An English fisherman wrote from Newfoundland in 1578: "I
have in sundry places sown wheat, barley, rye, oats, beans,
peas, and seeds of herbs, kernels, plumstones, nuts, all of which
prospered as in England."[1] The Endicott expedition for the
Massachusetts Bay Colony in 1628 carried nearly thirty different varieties of seeds, and by 1630 the gardens of Massachusetts were growing cabbages, turnips, lettuce, spinach,
radishes, onions, peas, and beans from seeds brought from
England.[2]

Even where the native plants were grown, their cultivation
by the settlers from Europe brought ecological changes. The
Indian corn, which had grown in a few clearings in the woods,
soon filled large fields. Later, carried westward and refined by
scientific breeding, corn covered endless miles of the plains land
that had once been thought useless for farming. Tobacco, also
grown in modest amounts by the Indians, soon became the
keystone of the South's economy, the sole crop of immense
plantations carved out of the thick woodlands. But the tobacco
of the plantations was not the kind that had been grown by the
North American Indians; it was a different variety that the
Spaniards had found in Central and South America. Although
cotton is sometimes counted as a native crop, the cotton that
grows in America today is descended from strains imported
from Egypt, South America, and Mexico.

Early Americans seem to have been fascinated with the
challenge of finding out what kinds of plant species could be

[1]Nelson Klose, *America's Crop Heritage* (Ames, Iowa: Iowa State College Press, 1950),
p. 4.
[2]Ibid., p. 5.

imported and grown profitably. This was one of the many interests of Benjamin Franklin:

On excursion about the [European] countryside to seek relaxation from the formalities of court and tension of diplomatic circles, Franklin was quick to perceive new varieties of plants, along with new ideas of culture, to pass on to his American friends. On one occasion he sent John Bertram from England seeds of new varieties of turnips, cabbage and peas; again he forwarded to his wife some naked oats, recommended for oatmeal, and some Swiss barley, "six rows to an ear," with the request that she divide it among his friends. . . . then it was Penshurst peas, and again a new sort of beans that he sent home across the water.[3]

Thomas Jefferson was another Founding Father who dedicated himself actively to the cause of improving the native ecology:

The greatest service which anyone can render his country, he asserted in his autobiography, is to add a new plant to its culture, and this he himself did in ample measure. He was indefatigable in his search for different varieties of rice and obtained seed from the Piedmont, Egypt, and even Sumatra. From Italy he imported the Lombardy poplar, soon to be as familiar in America as in France and Italy. In an effort to encourage the cultivation of the olive . . . he shipped over more than five hundred olive trees — alas, in vain. He experimented with figs from France, vetch from England, grapes and strawberries from Italy, endives from France, and silk trees from China and Constantinople.[4]

103

Plant importation soon became an operation of the federal government. It had been a traditional practice of ships' captains to bring home samples of plants from their voyages; this was put on a semiofficial basis in the early nineteenth century. An 1827 Navy Department communication to a commander said: "It will probably be in your power, while protecting the commercial, to add something to the agricultural interests of the nation, by procuring information respecting valuable animals, seeds, and plants, and importing such as you can."[5] A decade later the navy dispatched its first voyage specifically for plant importation on a four-year cruise of the Pacific.

---

[3]Carl R. Woodward, "Benjamin Franklin: Adventures in Agriculture," in *Meet Dr. Franklin* (Philadelphia: The Franklin Institute, 1943), p. 206.
[4]Henry Steele Commager, "Jefferson and the Enlightenment," in Lally Weymouth (ed.), *Thomas Jefferson* (New York: Putnam's, 1973), p. 50.
[5]Klose, *America's Crop Heritage*, p. 28.

In 1839 Congress established within the Patent Office a new agricultural division to supervise the importation of seeds and plants. A few years later a tariff bill specifically exempted seeds from import duties, and the importation and distribution of seeds became a routine governmental operation. Free seeds were sent out to farmers in great numbers, by 1850 running to about 80,000 packages a year. The practice was popular among members of Congress, who could endear themselves to constituents by sending out postage-free seed packages.

In 1862 Congress created a Department of Agriculture, partly in response to the needs of farmers and partly in response to the Patent Office's desire to get out of the business of furnishing congressmen with cuttings and garden seeds to distribute among the voters. The free seed distributions continued, however, and so did the government's practice of importing and testing new plant varieties. In 1897 David A. Fairchild became head of the Office of Foreign Seed and Plant Introduction. Under his supervision expeditions traveled all over the world and imported hundreds of new plants.[6] This policy received new governmental support after the turn of the century, and experiment stations were set up across the country to test crops in varying soil and climatic conditions. In the 1920s, in some measure as a result of the work of Luther Burbank, interest and public policy shifted to breeding rather than importation as a way of improving American agriculture. But by that time, of course, the American ecology had been totally transformed by the adaptation of imported plants. In 1937 Secretary of Agriculture Henry Wallace reported that only about ten of the seventy-eight leading American crops were native to the United States (and this was probably inaccurate, since several of the "native" crops, such as tobacco, were actually imports from other parts of the New World).

The Land

Land was the great magnet that drew the first settlers from the Old World, and it was land — more than anything else — that kept the white civilization advancing ever westward across the continent. Because there seemed to be so much of it and because the Europeans who took possession of it had so scanty an understanding of its natural ecology, the American land was severely damaged.

Erosion, the washing or blowing away of topsoil which turned rich fields into barren mounds and gullies, came early to America — wherever there was excessive clearing, careless

---

[6]David Fairchild, *Exploring for Plants* (New York: Macmillan, 1930).

Railroads and land speculators touted the riches of plains land widely and wildly, and, with the help of technology, farming began. Prospective buyers were given free trips west to see the flowing wheat fields for themselves, and many of them liked what they saw and bought.

plowing, or overreliance on a single crop. A historian of the effort to adapt to the American land writes:

In the Virginia Tidewater, the first William Byrd cleared a tobacco-field and lost in one cloudburst not only the crop but "all the top of the manured land." The early British Governors tried to make the colonists plant trees and diversify their crops, but the lure of the land was irresistible and cash-cropping was necessary to pay debts in London. Long before the Revolution, American farmers discovered what it meant to raise money instead of food. Early settlers in Massachusetts had to pass a law against overgrazing in the meadows of Cambridge. In post-war years, Patrick Henry announced: "Since the achievement of our independence, he is the greatest patriot who stops the most gullies."[7]

Some of the colonies offered prizes for new techniques of reclaiming eroded land. George Washington gave up one-crop farming to halt erosion at Mount Vernon, writing that "We ruin the lands that are already cleared and either cut down more wood, if we have it, or emigrate into the western country."[8] Indeed, there is ample evidence that the westward movement was inspired not only by the promise of fertile new lands in the West but equally by the exhaustion of much of the old land in the original colonies.

Erosion resulted from clearing away the native growth on the land, draining it, and repeatedly plowing it, usually without any attempt at crop rotation or fertilization. In the crowded Europe from which the colonists had come, techniques for renewing the soil and maintaining its productivity were part of the culture and were being applied intensively, but in America they were rarely used.

The land the pioneers found was part of an ecosystem that had maintained itself in a certain way over many thousands of years. In its wild state the land had been highly efficient at holding and using water. Every part of it — grass, shrubs, trees, rocks, layers of rotting leaves and logs that covered the soil — played a part in the natural water-management system. All of this kept the streams running by steady seepage even in dry years, moderated floods, and made water available to all the plant and animal species that lived within the system.

The first act of the farmer was to take this system apart. The trees and bushes were cleared away, the rocks and stones removed, the swamps and ponds drained. What remained was

[7]Jay Franklin, *Remaking America* (Boston: Houghton Mifflin, 1942), p. 30.
[8]Ibid.

In 1934 the federal
government made a
survey of erosion
across the country
and classified 12
percent of the land,
225 million acres, as
"severely eroded."

107

the system's by-product, rich humus soil that could be plowed and cultivated immediately to produce the sustenance foods and market crops that the farmer urgently needed. Usually the farmers proceeded to take as much as possible from the land for as long as its yield was high. But, with the system that had maintained the soil's fertility dismantled, the land would begin to deteriorate from floods, erosion, and dryness. When this happened the farmer would have to turn to the hard (and not immediately profitable) work of soil preservation, or move on. Many chose to move on. There were exceptions to this pattern. In Pennsylvania, for example, the early German settlers retained some of the techniques of careful cultivation they had learned in their native land. But thousands of farms were simply used up and abandoned.

When the population moved out into the plains, a similar process took place. The ecosystems were different and some of the uses of the land were different, but the cultural values were the same. The systems that had made the land rich were disrupted and, through single-crop agriculture or overgrazing, the richness was depleted. This was accepted as an inevitable fact of life, as a Missouri farmer recorded in his memoirs: "In those old days farmers used to brag about how many farms they had worn out. Those old boys used to say 'Why son, by the time I was your age I had wore out three farms.' "[9]

In 1934 the federal government made a survey of erosion

---

[9] Leo E. Oliva, "Our Frontier Heritage and the Environment," *American West*, January 1972, p. 62.

across the country and classified 12 percent of the land, 225 million acres, as "severely eroded" — meaning that over three-fourths of the topsoil had been lost. Another 3 percent of the land, over 57 million acres, was found to have been totally destroyed.[10] The next year the Soil Conservation Service was established to take over responsibility for programs to stop erosion.

Soil conservation, which had been a part of the traditional culture in the Old World, developed as a science in America. Experiment stations were set up across the country, and agricultural scientists (mostly working for the government) began the large task of (1) turning soil conservation theories into practical farming techniques and (2) getting farmers to adopt them. Gradually, as most of the agricultural areas of the country have been organized into soil conservation districts, farming practices have changed dramatically. This does not mean that erosion has been stopped. Thousands of acres of farm and forest land are still lost, perhaps irrecoverably, every year. In addition, modern farming produces new ecological complications: flood-control projects involve construction of dams and reservoirs; irrigation places new demands on water supplies; chemical fertilizers, which raise the agricultural yield of depleted land, also create water pollution from runoff.

Patterns of land use have always been expressions of public policy. At first the governmental policy was simply to encourage westward movement by making public land available to homesteaders and land speculators, giving away seeds, forcing the Indians onto reservations, and providing for the establishment of state and local governments. In time, as some of the negative consequences of the westward movement became impossible to overlook, government (especially at the federal level) became more active in attempting to understand and manage ecosystems. Often these new programs were not implemented until well past the time when the effects of the massive conversion of land to agricultural use had become catastrophic. This was what happened in the area known as the Dust Bowl.

The Dust Bowl: A Crisis of Misuse One of the most spectacular crises in the history of American agriculture resulted from the misuse of the land on the southwestern plains. This area had once been open grassland, the home of buffalo herds and the tribes of the plains Indians who hunted them. As civilization moved westward the plains became cattle trails for moving

[10]Franklin, *Remaking America*, p. 65.

herds northward to the railroad towns from which they would be shipped to the slaughterhouses in Chicago. Then, with the advent of barbed wire, vast areas were fenced off and the grasslands became pasture for large ranches.

With the help of technology, farming began. New kinds of plows, first of cast iron and then of steel, enabled farmers to break up the hard sod. Most of the farmland was without irrigation and dependent on the rainfall, but in good years the fertile land yielded crops of feed grains, corn, and wheat. Optimistic homesteaders moved in on the available tracts of public land, while speculators bought up ranches and subdivided them into farms. The railroads and land speculators touted the riches of plains land widely and wildly. Prospective buyers were given free trips west to see the flowing wheat fields for themselves, and many of them liked what they saw and bought. New towns sprang up quickly on the plains and competed for the profitable status of state capital or county seat.

The years of the first plains-land boom were years of adequate rainfall, and the new settlers did not know that the weather tended to vary between good years and years of drought. In the 1890s the rainfall was sparse for several years running. Many of the farmers went bankrupt, businesses failed, and some of the new towns that had suddenly appeared on the plains emptied and fell apart almost as quickly as they had arisen.

The great drought ended, and after the turn of the century another land boom followed it. Nobody wanted to believe dry years would ever come again. A new generation of land promoters went to work. Between the censuses of 1900 and 1910, the population of sixty-one southern plains counties increased by almost 350 percent.

World War I gave a new impetus to plains farming: "The forces that fight for freedom," said President Woodrow Wilson, "depend upon us in an extraordinary degree for sustenance, for supply of the materials by which men are to live and fight." Conservation experts advised farmers to diversify, but the demand was for wheat, which was bringing unprecedented market prices. The scientists' advice was disregarded, and the southwestern plains moved toward a one-crop economy.

Millions of acres of grassland were brought under cultivation for the first time. The average size of farms increased, and vast amounts of land (in some areas as much as 80 percent) were farmed by the employees of absentee owners who were more sensitive to balance sheets than to ecosystems. The drive to increase crop volume was helped by new technological de-

109

velopments: tractors and trucks and combines that could harvest and thresh grain in a single operation.

Wheat prices remained high after the war's end, and the great farming boom that some conservationists called "the rape of the plains" continued. Farmers invested heavily in more machinery, and more grassland was turned into wheat fields. Between 1925 and 1930 over 5 million acres of plains land was plowed for the first time; two-thirds of it was used for wheat.

The price of wheat dropped sharply after the stock market crash of 1929, but that did not decrease the volume of wheat farming. On the contrary, most farmers increased their acreage under cultivation to bring in whatever profits they could. Agricultural scientists continued to urge diversification into feed crops and livestock, but the farms and the plains economy were geared for wheat.

Weather conditions in 1931 were ideal for wheat farming, but in 1932 there were some setbacks — a late freeze and hailstorms, followed by a cutworm invasion and a spring drought. Some farmers went bankrupt, and the rest tried to increase their farmed acreage to get out of debt. A farmer said: "One thing only mattered then — to save our investments somehow. The best way seemed to plow, and plow and plow, as long as the bank would loan us money for gasoline."

There was another dry year, and then the dust storms began. Dust storms had always been a part of life on the plains, especially wherever the land was cultivated, but by now millions of acres of the buffalo grass that had once held down the soil were gone. The topsoil blew off the fields, covered roads, and piled up in dunes.

The worst dust storms came in the spring of 1934, when it seemed as though the whole of the southwestern plains rose into the air and moved. The clouds of dust filled and darkened the skies, not just over the plains but, as the winds blew eastward, all across the country. The sun was shut out for five hours over most of the eastern seaboard; dust from the plains hung in the skies over Washington, D.C. The next day ships as far as 300 miles out in the Atlantic reported dust settling on their decks.

It was estimated that the May 1934 storm removed 350 million tons of topsoil from the plains. Other storms blew up that year, and the next. Crops failed, and people and animals fell ill from a lung ailment called "dust pneumonia."

The drought covered about half of the United States, but the area hit hardest was the southwestern plains, the land that

One of the most spectacular crises in the history of American agriculture resulted from the misuse of the land on the southwestern plains.

became known as the Dust Bowl. It was an area about 500 miles long and 250 miles wide, covering parts of Kansas, Colorado, New Mexico, Texas, and Oklahoma. Its center was the Oklahoma panhandle. Government relief programs brought some economic aid to the bankrupt farm families, but thousands of Dust Bowl residents abandoned the area. Once-prosperous farm families went west to become migratory workers in the fields of California.

Reclaiming the land became a top-priority program of the federal government, but it was a slow process. It took time to develop farming techniques that could hold down the soil, and more time to persuade farmers to use them. Meanwhile the dust storms continued. In 1937 a storm blew dust from the bowl area across the Great Lakes into Canada; government officials in Iowa estimated that soil from the southwestern plains was being dumped on that state in the amount of 200 pounds per acre.

Encouraged by free technical assistance and financial incentives provided by the government, plains farmers began to use new techniques for shaping the soil to break the wind, plowing with the land contour instead of in straight furrows, alternating crops, retaining rainfall water in the soil. The monstrous sand dunes, some of them hundreds of yards long, were cleared away from the fields and roads. Thousands of acres were returned to grassland, although the native grasses would not grow back alone in the denuded soil and so were mixed with other varieties imported from Africa. President Franklin D. Roosevelt personally conceived the idea of a "shelterbelt" of trees that would be planted as windbreaks on nearly 2 million acres of government-leased land along the edge of the Dust Bowl. That grandiose plan was discarded, but a large federal tree-planting campaign did get underway on the once-treeless plains: trees were planted beside roads, along stream beds and the edges of fields, around farmhouses. They lessened the force of the strong plains winds and also added some new visual interest to the bleak landscape. Some people believed they helped to reduce the rate of absentee ownership.[11]

The Trees
The land the first American settlers found was thickly forested, a long green wall of trees along the entire eastern seaboard, extending westward far beyond the boundaries of the original

112

---

[11]Franklin, *Remaking America;* Vance Johnson, *Heaven's Tableland* (New York: Farrar, Straus, 1947); Guy-Harold Smith (ed.), *Conservation of Natural Resources* (New York: Wiley, 1950).

The worst dust storms came in the spring of 1934, when it seemed as though the whole of the southwestern plains rose into the air and moved. The clouds of dust filled and darkened the skies, not just over the plains but, as the winds blew eastward, all across the country.

One early traveler
said that a squirrel
could travel from
Pittsburgh to Illinois
without leaving the
treetops.

thirteen colonies. The colonies were, in fact, one vast forest varying in composition from region to region: pines in the drier parts of the Southeast; cypresses and magnolias and live oaks in the wetlands; oaks, chestnuts, hickories, poplars, beech, birch, and hemlock through the central East; pines, spruce, and fir in the northern mountains.[12] Here and there were clearings made by the Indians for their farming, but most of the land was covered with trees — and wherever there were to be farms and towns, the trees had to be removed. The trees had some market value, but commercial loggers were hampered by the lack of transportation; they could operate profitably only near watercourses, where the lumber could be shipped downstream to towns or ocean ports. Most of the trees were simply obstacles, living impediments to be moved aside so that room could be made for the expansive needs of civilized life. The trees seemed to be personal enemies. They offered concealment to the Indians and sheltered the swamps that many frontiersmen, ignorant of their ecological function, saw only as dark and unhealthy places. "Letting in the daylight" was the frontiersman's preferred term for tree-cutting. One by-product of this activity was an early American technological advance — the development of a new kind of axe. The axes that the first colonists had brought over with them were little more than hatchets with straight handles, a kind that had been in use for thousands of years. The Americans soon improved on that design and produced an axe that was a marvel of balance and efficiency.[13]

Visitors from Europe were often dismayed by this war on the forests. An English traveler observed the building of the first Pennsylvania turnpike and wrote that "many thousands of trees that were cut for making the turnpike, lay rotting by the sides of it — this day only, we passed some thousands of loads of timber thus decaying. I believe I have seen more timber in this wasting state than all the growing timber I ever saw in my life in England."[14] A Frenchman who visited Cincinnati reported that "An American has no idea that anyone can admire trees or wooded ground. To him a country well cleared, that is where every stick is cut down, seems the only one that is beautiful or worthy of admiration."[15]

The logging industry grew along with the population, the construction and shipbuilding industries, and technology. The

114

[12]William R. Van Dersal, *The American Land* (New York: Oxford University Press, 1943), p. 6.
[13]George Soule and Vincent P. Carosso, *American Economic History* (New York: Dryden Press, 1957), p. 21.
[14]Van Dersal, *The American Land*, p. 25.
[15] Oliva, "Our Frontier Heritage," p. 46.

circular saw and the steam mill were invented in the early 1800s
— thereby making deforestation faster and more efficient —
and the development of the wood-pulp process for paper manufacturing created another stimulus to logging. New roads and
canals made it easier to get lumber to market. State and federal
governments helped by making public forest land available to
loggers at bargain prices. Thus a logger could economically strip
an entire forest and then simply abandon it and move his
sawmill elsewhere. The average operating life of a sawmill was
twenty years.[16]

Less than a century after the Declaration of Independence,
the federal government surveyed the effect of logging on the
eastern forests and reported:

Massachusetts — *Scarcely a vestige of the original forest is left,
even on the mountain-tops, owing to the demands of manufacturers and railroads.*
Delaware — *The best timber has long since disappeared.*
Connecticut — *Timber is being cut faster than it grows.*
Maine — *The pine timber has been shipped from the northern
half of Penobscot until there is not enough left for home consumption.*
Vermont — *It is thought that the demands of the railroads will
soon result in a scarcity of wood and timber.*
New York — *The mountains were originally covered with a
heavy growth of hemlock, which was cut for the bark, the logs
being left to decay . . . many kinds of forest-trees are dying. . . .
The forests are being exhausted very fast.*
Maryland — *Within a few years a large number of sawmills have
used up the best parts of the forests.*
Virginia — *Since the war the indiscriminate destruction of
forest . . . has been highly disadvantageous.*[17]

With the westward movement, the same thing happened in
other areas once heavily forested with oak, walnut, buckeye,
elm, ash, sycamore, hickory, and butternut. One early traveler
said that a squirrel could travel from Pittsburgh to Illinois
without leaving the treetops.[18] But this changed quickly. Some
counties in southern Indiana, first opened to settlers around
1800, were totally cleared of timber by 1875. The clearing was
hastened by the commercial value of the local black walnut
tree, whose wood was in vogue with furniture manufacturers in
the nineteenth century. Of course, as it became more scarce it

[16]Nancy Wood, *Clearcut* (San Francisco: Sierra Club, 1971), pp. 36-38.
[17]U.S. Department of Agriculture, 1875.
[18]Vernon Carstensen, "Land of Plenty," *National Observer*, 18 October 1975, p. B-2.

116

Trees offered concealment to the Indians and sheltered the swamps that many frontiersmen, ignorant of their ecological function, saw only as dark and unhealthy places.

117

became more precious. In 1875 a single shipment of logs from Indiana brought a price of $50,000. In 1965 the last privately owned black walnut tree was auctioned off for $12,600.[19]

Late in the nineteenth century (and far too late to save the eastern forests) the federal government began to withdraw some lands from the public domain to be maintained as forest preserves. By this time American boundaries had reached to the Pacific, and civilization was clearing its path through the awesome forests of the West Coast. An early settler in Oregon wrote this account of the difficulties of making room in the forest for the town of Astoria:

The place selected for the emporium of the West might challenge the whole continent to produce a spot of equal extent presenting more difficulties to the settler; studded with gigantic trees of almost incredible size, many of them measuring fifty feet in girth, and so close together and intermingled with huge rocks, as to make it a work of no ordinary labor to level and clear the ground. . . .

There is an art in felling a tree, as well as in planting one; but unfortunately none of us had learned that art, and hours together would be spent in conjectures and discussions; one calling that it would fall here; another there; in short, there were as many opinions as there were individuals about it; and at last, when all hands were assembled to witness the fall, how often we were disappointed! The tree would still stand erect, bidding defiance to our efforts, while every now and then some of the most impatient or foolhardy would venture to jump on the scaffold and give a blow or two more. Much time was often spent in this desultory manner, before the mighty tree gave way; but it seldom came to the ground. So thick was the forest, and so close the trees together, that in its fall it would often rest its ponderous top on some other friendly tree; sometimes a number of them would hang together, keeping us in awful suspense, and giving us double labor to extricate the one from the other, and when we had so far succeeded, the removal of the monster stump was the work of days. The tearing up of the roots was equally arduous, although less dangerous, and when this last operation was got through, both tree and stump had to be blown to pieces by gunpowder before either could be removed from the spot. . . . Nearly two months of this laborious and incessant toil had passed, and we had scarcely yet an acre of ground cleared.[20]

118

[19]Earl Finbar Murphy, *Governing Nature* (Chicago: Quadrangle, 1967), p. 144. At this time there were four other living black walnut trees in a public forest.
[20]Van Dersal, *The American Land*, pp. 14-15.

The redwood forest, which covered around 2 million acres of the land along the moist Coast Range, proved to be a fine source of building material. Today less than one-tenth of virgin redwood forest is left.

119

For all the difficulty of the task, western settlers managed to clear away a prodigious amount of trees. As the lumber industry developed, greater numbers of the felled trees were used rather than merely destroyed and discarded.

Before the California gold rush began, that state contained an enormous timber resource, the redwood forest, which covered around 2 million acres of the land along the moist Coast Range. This proved to be a fine source of building material, located conveniently close to the new population centers. Today less than one-tenth of virgin redwood forest is left; most of it is owned by lumber companies and is now being logged off. Some 60,000 acres of virgin redwood forest are within state and national parks, along with several thousand acres of second-growth forest. Being within a park's boundaries does not guarantee the security of the trees, because ecosystems frequently fail to observe the line of demarcation between public and private land. When a logging company clearcuts a forest on its privately held land, the process sends tons of silt moving down hillsides and along stream beds toward trees in the "protected" area; this has happened in the Redwood National Park in California, which is adjacent to privately owned redwood forests.

Because of the depletion of the redwood forests and the increasing political pressure for their protection, the lumber industry has moved farther north, into the Douglas fir forests of Oregon and Washington, thus shifting the center of the ongoing war between loggers and conservationists. Actually, this war is fought in the state capitals and in Washington, D.C., where lobbyists from the various interest groups struggle over park boundaries, logging permits, and environmental impact reports. The skirmishes sometimes seem trivial, but they are parts of a larger evolutionary truth, which is that the fate of these ancient ecosystems rests not with nature but with human political and economic institutions.

Through most of the nineteenth century the prevailing public policy regarding state and federal forest land was to get as much of it as possible into the hands of loggers at the lowest cost to them. Some of this was done under "homestead" laws that, although supposedly created for the purpose of helping establish small family farms, had the actual effect of making more land available to commercial loggers. The homestead laws had major (and not entirely unpredicted) loopholes such as the requirement that a dwelling be erected on the homesteaded land, which the loggers complied with by building houses as small as fourteen by sixteen inches.[21]

---

[21]Wood, *Clearcut*, p. 39.

Logging the American forests created still another group of millionaires, the timber barons, who used their wealth and political power to support new and generous laws such as the Homestead Act of 1862, the Timber Culture Act of 1873, and the Forest Management Act of 1897.

Opposition to such policies came from a handful of Americans, notably Emerson, Thoreau, Carl Schurz, and John Muir; finally, during the administration of William Harrison the federal government began establishing forest reserves. This practice was continued cautiously under later administrations and more aggressively by Theodore Roosevelt, who brought the total reserve land to 132 million acres. The government also bought some cutover land and placed it under the supervision of the Forest Service, which was established under the conservation-minded Gifford Pinchot in 1905.

But the creation of national forests has not meant an end to logging on them. Most national forest land is administered

As president, Theodore Roosevelt espoused the new conservation movement, making well-publicized visits to the national parks and extending the federal forest reserves.

under the "multiple use" policy, which means it may be used for logging, mining, grazing, and recreational purposes. These American public lands are carefully managed artificial ecosystems in which the type, size, and spacing of trees is determined by government officials. Even areas designated as "wilderness" are subject to human use and human management. It seems that conservation as well as destruction requires an intervention in natural processes. Richard Wagner, a botanist who has written extensively on environmental policy, argues that there is no longer an American wilderness: "A true wilderness should be viewed biocentrically; its forests must be free to burn, free to be attacked by insects, free to be blown down by storms, and free to be carried away by floods, all because these are natural events to which the forest is adapted to respond."[22]

Public foresters have developed a deeper understanding of the value of fire — how it clears underbrush, maintains a balance among types of trees — and now sometimes permit it even at the risk of traumatizing admirers of Smokey the Bear. But the kind of freedom of which Wagner speaks is hardly affordable at a time when wilderness areas have become some of our most precious and fragile national treasures; the ironic consequence is that our pockets of wilderness survive only as domesticated life systems.

Management policies also include planting new trees. In the 1930s the government began an extensive program of reforestation, carried out by the Civilian Conservation Corps (CCC). This was partly an attempt to deal with depression unemployment, but it did have a significant effect on the nation's ecology. In its first eight years the CCC was responsible for planting 8 billion trees. These were planted in overcut forest, in areas denuded by erosion, and often in places where trees had never grown before. Sometimes they were trees of the same variety that had grown there originally; often they were species brought in from other parts of the country or other parts of the world.

Many species of trees, especially fruit-bearing and nut-bearing species, have been imported. Although most came from Western Europe, they had first been found growing in lands farther to the east. Apples, native to the region between the Black and Caspian seas, came to America with settlers from Europe and spread westward quickly. Seeds were sown by the Indians, and so the apple tree was often already far beyond the advancing frontier. Apple seeds went west with missionaries and traders and wagon trains, and the apple tree soon became a

---

[22]Richard Wagner, *Environment and Man* (New York: Norton, 1974), p. 70.

familiar sight across the continent. John Chapman, known as Johnny Appleseed, became legendary for his efforts in planting apple trees throughout the Midwest. Other fruit-bearing trees such as pear, peach, plum, and cherry, which were all ancient transplants to Europe from regions farther east, flourished in America. So did nut trees such as almond and English walnut. The olive from the Mediterranean and a variety of subtropical fruits such as citrus, dates, and figs transformed the landscape in the warmer areas of the continent. The varieties of palm trees that ornament the cities of California and Florida are all imports from other parts of the world.

Effects of the importation of trees were scantily understood, but there were clearly some ecological interactions between the old species and the new. We can see such an interaction in the case of the American chestnut, a sturdy and useful tree that provided good saw lumber, wood for fences, tannic acid for leather work, nuts for food, and a location for Longfellow's celebrated village smithy. The American chestnut became nearly extinct due to the importation of Chinese chestnuts, which brought with them a fungus to which the native trees had no immunity.[23]

In many parts of the country the residents of the area have no recollection of how things once appeared, since the imported species are so familiar that they do not stand out as elements in an artificial landscape. In California, where the native flora has been so thoroughly destroyed that even botanists have only the vaguest idea of what the original ecology was like, the trees that seem most "native" are oranges and other citrus bearers, palms, and eucalyptus. The tall and fragrant eucalyptus grow so easily in the California soil that they seem to be totally at home there, natural products of the land's evolution. But they are immigrants too, and the story of their coming is one more of those small boom-and-bust sagas that turn up so frequently in American history. The first eucalyptus was planted at San Jose in 1858, and a few decades later the "eucalyptus boom" reached its height. The boom, as usual, was primarily the work of land promoters, but the promoters had as allies a number of forestry scientists who should have known better.

The eucalyptus is a hardwood: fast-growing, sturdy, and resistant to drought. In Australia eucalyptus wood was a good building material; the California promoters touted it as a sure source of wealth. Land for eucalyptus plantations sold at high prices, and soon the trees were being grown all over the state. The boom ended when it turned out that the kinds of eucalyptus

123

---

[23]Wagner, *Environment and Man*, pp. 303-4.

that grew so well in California were an inferior source of lumber: the wood tended to crack and warp in drying and was useful for nothing but firewood. The types of eucalyptus that yielded lumber in Australia did not happen to be the ones that adapted easily to California's climate. So the bottom fell out of the eucalyptus market, but the trees live on. They are commonly used as windbreaks for farmland and grow wild in many groves up and down the state.[24]

Animal Life

Animal life was also profoundly affected as the new human society spread across the American continent. Lines of evolutionary development that had been unfolding slowly for millions of years underwent sudden changes and shifts. Some species became extinct or nearly so, while other species of imported domesticated animals — selectively bred, protected from disease and predators — multiplied as quickly as the human beings who had brought them into the new environment. Civilization changed the rules of evolution; extinction and survival were now determined not by adaptability, but by economics.

The trappers and fur traders were the first to have a major influence on American wildlife. There was a time when beaver hats were in favor with men of fashion in Europe; the beaver population of America diminished accordingly. By the time the beaver hat's desirability waned, beavers were nearly extinct east of the Mississippi. So were numerous other fur-bearing species, and the trappers pressed ever farther to the north and west in search of new supplies. The fur market was, in fact, the greatest single inspiration for many of the intrepid explorations celebrated in American history.

The advance of civilization affects animal populations in many ways. Animals are hunted for food, destroyed as predators, or merely pushed aside by the destruction of their natural habitat, which inevitably accompanies farming and the construction of towns and roads.

A well-known case of a diminished American species is that of the buffalo, of which there were once about 60 million. Early travelers on the American plains sent back reports of enormous herds. One traveler wrote:

Toward evening, on rising a hill, we were suddenly greeted by a sight which seemed to astonish even the oldest among us. The

124

---

[24]Raymond F. Dasmann, *The Destruction of California* (New York: Collier Books, 1966), pp. 78-79.

The army had been trying for years to subjugate the Indian tribes of the plains, and it appeared now that the buffalo hunters might be doing the job for them. General Phil Sheridan told the Texas legislature: "Let them kill, skin and sell until the buffalo is exterminated, as it is the only way to bring about lasting peace and allow civilization to advance."

whole plain, as far as the eye could discern, was covered by one enormous mass of buffalo. Our vision, at the very least computation, would certainly extend ten miles, and in the whole of this great space, including about eight miles in width from the bluffs to the river bank, there was apparently no vista in the incalculable multitude.[25]

Although the buffalo herds were thickest on the plains, they did not live only in that area. There were as many as 5 million of them in the woods along the eastern seaboard. The herds trampled wide roads through the mountains. These roads were followed by explorers and later used for highway and rail routes.

The buffalo had been the prime food source for plains Indian tribes, and were killed for meat by many early white explorers as well. But the end of the buffalo herds resulted mainly from the growing market for hides. In 1871 a man named J. Wright Mooar sent 50 buffalo hides to his brother in New York, asking him to find out if they had any commercial value. The brother had the hides tanned, found that they were useful as machine belting in factories, and obtained an order for 2,000 more. As soon as the word was out, the buffalo hunters descended on the herds. Each hunter worked with a team of skinners who followed behind him, skinned the animals he shot (often as many as 200 a day), and left the carcasses on the plains. The herds diminished quickly. A frontiersman noted that the buffalo were thick in Kansas early in 1872, but by the following autumn "we did not meet with buffalo until we were well into the Indian Territory, and then only in scanty bands." The whole country, he said, "was whitened with bleached and bleaching bones," and along the river "the air was rendered pestilential and offensive" by the decaying carcasses.[26]

Some people were concerned about this destruction, but others saw it as a positive benefit. The army had been trying for years to subjugate the Indian tribes of the plains, and it appeared now that the buffalo hunters might be doing the job for them. General Phil Sheridan told the Texas legislature: "Let them kill, skin and sell until the buffalo is exterminated, as it is the only way to bring about lasting peace and allow civilization to advance." The same sentiments prompted President Ulysses S. Grant to veto a buffalo protection bill (the first congressional measure designed to protect a species of wildlife) in 1875.[27] Even without the appearance of the buffalo-hide market, the herds

126

[25]Van Dersal, *The American Land*, p. 19.
[26]Johnson, *Heaven's Tableland*, p. 23.
[27]Stuart Udall, *The Quiet Crisis* (New York: Holt, Rinehart and Winston, 1963), p. 58.

were probably doomed anyway by the coming of the railroads, the ranchers who fenced off the plains, and finally the farmers who plowed up the buffalo grass and sowed their crops on what had once been open grazing land.

There were also vast herds of other game animals: 40 million whitetail deer, 10 million elk, and large numbers of antelope, beaver, and bear. An early settler in Virginia noted plentiful numbers of black bear, and reported that "the beares of this countrey are good meat."[28] Today the black bear are gone from the eastern woods; the buffalo survive only in captivity; and the other game species have diminished or disappeared. Predators such as wolves (which once numbered 2 million) have been reduced in number or exterminated.

In the case of some of the species classed as predators, the effort to eliminate them from the ecosystem was deliberate. Other species were reduced or exterminated more or less accidentally, often because they were so numerous that nobody believed any human actions would ever have much of an effect on them. This inability to predict consequence is one of the persistent shortcomings of human intervention in evolution. The most spectacular example of this is the passenger pigeon; probably no species in the entire course of evolution on earth has gone from such numbers to total extinction in such a short period of time.

One day in 1813 (about a century before the passenger pigeon became extinct) John James Audubon observed a southward migration of passenger pigeons and calculated that well over a billion of the birds had crossed the Ohio River in a single day.[29] This was part of a flock that took three full days to pass. The passenger pigeon migrations would blacken the sky for miles; inevitably the ground underneath was crowded with men and boys shooting at them. Because the birds flew low, they could also be captured with nets strung between trees. This was the more effective method commercially:

The passenger pigeons were money — big money — for the man who knew his trade. A good netter with an experienced crew of helpers could capture upwards of twenty to fifty barrels of birds per day and, at three hundred birds per barrel, that was a gold mine. A single barrel of beheaded and gutted birds, iced down and shipped to Chicago, brought twenty-five dollars, and those taken alive for trapshooting could be sold right on the spot for twenty-five cents per dozen, and double that in crates aboard

127

[28]Wayne D. Rasmussen (ed.), *Readings in the History of American Agriculture* (Urbana, Ill.: University of Illinois Press, 1960).
[29]Allan W. Eckert, *The Silent Sky* (Boston: Little, Brown, 1965), p. 4.

Although native wild-life has declined enormously, there is a surviving cultural belief that hunting and fishing are among our inalienable rights.

128

boxcars in Wausau. And the best part of it all was that prices were rising every year.[30]

Using live pigeons for trapshooting probably did not contribute much to the elimination of the species, although this popular gentlemen's sport did account for the killing of many thousands of birds. For many years marksmen at the Dexter Park Trapshooting Club in Chicago strove to break the record of a Captain Adam H. Bogardus, who killed 500 pigeons in one day, loading his own guns.[31]

A more serious matter was the hunting of fledgeling birds in the nesting grounds. Squabs were a valuable gourmet delicacy, and at the stage when they had left their nests but not yet learned to fly they would be gathered up by the hundreds of thousands.

From a combination of factors — mainly hunting and the destruction of forests — the number of passenger pigeons began to decline. As the flocks became smaller, the birds ceased to mate or reproduce; apparently their very density was part of the original ecosystem. By the late 1800s there were only scattered flocks of passenger pigeons. The last wild one ever seen was killed by a boy with a BB gun in 1900. A few more survived in captivity, until the last member of the species died in the Cincinnati zoo in 1914.

At the same time that native American species of animal life were diminishing, new species, both domestic and wild, were being brought in from other parts of the world. The first shiploads of colonists who came to America carried livestock for the farms that were to be carved out of the wilderness. Today there are pigs and sheep and cattle that might, if they are so inclined, trace their ancestries back to the crossing of the *Mayflower*. And there were from the beginning accidental importations as well as deliberate ones: rats came in the holds of the wooden ships, pests of various kinds in the food and on the animals. The Pilgrims brought to America in their woolen clothing the moth, which adapted heartily to its new home.

With the exception of the turkey, virtually every species of domestic animal now known to American agriculture was originally imported. This includes cattle, chicken, pigs, sheep, goats, and horses. The first cattle in the New World were probably brought here by the Norsemen around 1000 A.D. Cattle were also brought in by the Spanish, and their offspring were the great longhorned herds of the Old West. Today most of

130

---

[30]Ibid., p. 129.
[31]Ibid., p. 181.

the breeds of cattle raised in the United States — the world's largest producer and consumer of beef and milk — are descended from strains developed in the British Isles.

Many species were imported for the purpose of furnishing new challenges to American hunters and fishermen. One example of a successfully transplanted species is the ringnecked pheasant. The pheasant was already a much-traveled species before it came to America. Native to the Orient, it was brought to Europe by the Romans, and pheasant stocks were taken to England during the time of Julius Caesar. Several attempts were made to bring pheasants from England to the east coast of America — without success. The ancestors of today's "wild" pheasants were brought to Portland, Oregon, from Shanghai in 1882. They lived and reproduced in Oregon (about 50,000 were shot during the first pheasant hunting season there in 1891) and soon spread across the country with the assistance of state fish and game commissions.

The pheasant seems almost domestic now, but other animals imported for hunters still retain their exotic quality. New Mexico imported Barbary sheep from Africa and, when that species proved its capacity to survive in its new habitat, officials felt encouraged to import other African animals — such as the greater kudi and the oryx, and also ibex from Siberia. Other states in the Southwest have proceeded along the same lines; there is an area in Texas now known to hunters as "little Africa."[32]

Although native wildlife has declined enormously, there is a surviving cultural belief that hunting and fishing are among our inalienable rights. The first governmental interventions in hunting and fishing were feeble attempts at preserving endangered species, but this has gradually developed into far more complex programs of ecological management, in which the state and federal government take the responsibility for providing fish and game. One example of increasing intervention is the U.S. Fish and Wildlife Service, which was originally charged with merely preventing or minimizing damage to fish and wildlife in federal construction project sites. In 1958, however, the law was changed to give the service explicit responsibility for *improving* these resources — in other words, stocking the reservoirs with fish.

The practice of stocking bodies of water has involved importing various types of fish, such as the brown trout from Europe, and transplanting others far from their native habitat, such as

131

---

[32]George Laycock, *The Alien Animals* (Garden City, N.Y.: Natural History Press, 1966), p. 24.

the eastern striped bass, which was planted on the West Coast and now swims in the rivers of Oregon, Washington, and California.[33]

Agriculture and hunting and fishing account for the great majority of deliberate animal importations, but some of it came about as a result of nostalgia — a desire to bring to America some familiar part of the European environment — or mere curiosity. In 1872, for example, a gentleman named Andrew Erkenbrecher, who missed the songbirds of his native Germany, invested $9,000 in a project to import them to Ohio. With the aid of a group called the Cincinnati Acclimatization Society he had several thousand birds sent from Europe, housed them for a time in the attic of a house, and then released them into the surrounding countryside.[34] Most of them died, but other imported birds, such as the common house sparrow, the starling, and the rock dove or pigeon, have adapted easily to the North American environment.

The market for zoo animals and exotic pets has also contributed something to environmental change. The United States is the world's largest importer of wildlife. Many of the species imported are kept in captivity and would be unable to reproduce if set free; but occasionally pets escape and establish a foothold in the ecology, causing what some naturalists describe as "biological pollution."

The more common pets, cats and dogs, have their own place in the American ecosystem. There are about 30 million of each in the United States today, most of them descended from breeds imported from Europe and Asia. Like other domesticated species they live in isolation from the ancient evolutionary forces of natural selection. They are safe from predators, relieved of the necessity of hunting for their food, and cared for by veterinarians; their genetic development is guided by selective breeding. But this does not mean that they are totally cut off from larger ecological systems. They still eat, and in fact the American cat and dog population takes in a quantity of protein that would go a long way toward solving the human nutritional problems of a small nation.

I have discussed a few historical examples of the human impact on American animal life and briefly indicated how this is now managed through human institutions. Evolutionary control goes by many names — game management, pest control, disease prevention — and is carried out through many organizations, both public and private. The decisions they make are

132

[33]Ibid., pp. 47-53.
[34]Ibid., p. 63.

The American cat and dog population takes in a quantity of protein that would go a long way toward solving the human nutritional problems of a small nation.

133

134

guided mainly by commercial considerations. Animal life in America is closely connected to the human society and its economic needs; it is processed by food companies, clothing manufacturers, and all the industries that use animal by-products; is part of the medical profession, which depends on animal serums for immunization and live animals for research.

Although the management of animal evolution is routinely handled by political institutions, alternative courses of management only rarely become political issues. There are occasionally controversies about the control of predators to protect agriculture or the protection of endangered species. There was a time when the United States Congress, serenely ignorant of the evolutionary dimension of its deliberations, struggled with the question of appropriating money for rat control in the urban ghettos. But these are isolated cases that become visible only when they become controversial. Most evolutionary management does not force itself into the public consciousness because there is no controversy over it. It operates out of a deep cultural consensus about the purposes and needs of life.

Building America: Roadways and Railways
While the spread of American civilization altered the forms of plant and animal life and eliminated natural habitats, it also molded the physical structure of the continent into new configurations suited to the purposes of a commercial society. With great investments of human energy, the native woods and stones were transformed into structures for the growing urban centers, and clearings were cut through the wilderness for roads to connect the cities and towns and farms.

A human social system is, among other things, a system of communication and transportation. Culture, commerce, and political institutions develop only where there are opportunities for the movement of people and goods and symbolic information. At first the separate colonies were accessible to one another only by sea, and the few roads that existed were rough paths from inland settlements to the ports. But the American population has always been highly mobile, and soon there were roads connecting the colonies. By 1673 mail was being carried along the Boston Post Road, which linked Boston to New Haven and New York; by 1717 post riders were carrying mail along the 600-mile route between Boston and the capital of Virginia. These first highways were dirt roads, often impassable in inclement weather. After the Revolutionary War the demands of commerce called for all-weather roads. The first, a sixty-two-mile stretch of turnpike (a toll road) between Philadelphia and Lancaster, was completed in 1796. The road was twenty-four feet wide and had a surface of crushed stone.

During this period there was a rapid increase in the volume of surface travel, as freight wagons and stagecoaches replaced the solitary traveler on foot or horseback and more all-weather roads were built. Major roads were usually turnpikes, that is, they were constructed by private businesses and financed by toll collections. The first federal effort in road building was a highway through the Cumberland Gap, which had once been a trail for buffalo and later a major route for settlers headed for the territories west of the Appalachians.[35]

Although the construction of turnpikes and free public roads continued more or less steadily, spreading westward with the population, it was always well behind the flow of westward movement. The Santa Fe Trail, the Oregon Trail, the California Trail, and other routes to the West can hardly be called roads. They were wagon tracks across the grass, fords across rivers, passes through the mountains — often invisible except to guides who knew the territory. These rough trails might have been transformed into roads more quickly if the job of linking East and West had not been taken over by the railroads.

The first railroad line in the United States, the Baltimore and Ohio, was completed in 1830. Throughout the remainder of the century the country went on a railroad-building spree that drew on its resources of iron, coal, lumber, and manpower; dictated the locations of new towns and cities; created vast new financial and political empires; and carried the Industrial Revolution, with a crash of noise and smoke, into the primitive heartland of the continent. For a time, before the old way of life disappeared entirely there were strange contrasts on the plains: bands of Indians trying to kill locomotives, and sporting gentlemen shooting down buffalo from the windows of passenger cars.

In 1850 the federal government began granting public land to the railroad companies, a policy which was also adopted by many of the states. Altogether the federal and state governments gave 180 million acres of public land to the railroads. The government helped the railroads in other ways as well. For example, Senator Stephen Douglas secured the organization of the Kansas and Nebraska territories partly to facilitate railroad building westward from Chicago; and the United States made the Gadsden Purchase from Mexico to provide a railroad route across the Colorado River. With this kind of encouragement, the railroad industry developed quickly: there were

135

---

[35]U.S. Department of Commerce, Bureau of Public Roads, *Highways in the United States* (Washington, D.C.: U.S. Government Printing Office, 1954), pp. 1-4.

The automobile changed America.

30,625 miles of track in operation by 1860, and six times that amount by the end of the century. The railroad companies developed larger locomotives and specialized freight machinery such as the refrigerator car, which made it possible for farmers to produce perishable foods far from the large population centers.

Toward the end of the nineteenth century, as lands farther from the railroads became settled, the demand for better surface roads grew. There were about 2 million miles of rural roads in America by 1890, but they were nearly all dirt. There had been no federal activity in road building for some time, but in 1893 — which coincidentally was the year the Duryea brothers built the first gasoline-powered automobile — Congress created an Office of Road Inquiry within the Department of Agriculture.

Seven years later there were 8,000 automobiles in the United States; by 1925 there were 20 million. The automobile, like the locomotive, changed America. It created new fortunes, altered the ways people lived and worked, made new demands on the country's mineral resources, and gave a great boost to road building. Whereas this had once been left to local governments and private businesses, it now became a matter of state and federal priority. Every state initiated a system for funding new highways, and in 1916 Congress passed the first law providing federal aid to states for road construction. Since then there has evolved a complex network of county, state, federal, and private roads that, taken together, make the United States the most paved nation in the world.

One of the salient themes of American history, as I have mentioned elsewhere, is the steady process of urbanization. This means, of course, not only a pattern of population but a complex alteration of the environment. The first colonial communities were more like forts than towns, but gradually, as the forests and the Indians retreated, as manufacturing and trade increased, buildings extended beyond the confines of the original cramped settlements. These early population centers developed slowly into towns, then into what might be called cities. Among the early colonials there were some visionaries who laid out careful plans for towns, but for the most part urban growth proceeded in a haphazard and organic way.

Later, with more rapid population growth and the increase of the land-speculation business, laying out city plans became a favorite American pastime. Scarcely a stretch of wilderness did not contain, on paper, some promised new metropolis complete with town square and public buildings. Some of these remained on paper; some came into being more or less according to plan and grew into today's urban centers; and some, like the plains farmlands and western mining areas, sprang up overnight with a boom and disappeared as quickly with a bust.

One characteristic of American urban planning still evident everywhere in our towns and streets was a fondness for neat rectangular layouts of streets and building lots. Such layouts may or may not have been suitable to the shape of the terrain or the needs of potential inhabitants (questions which most of the early planners had little time for), but they were clearly well adapted to the chief matter at hand, which was buying and selling parcels of property. According to Lewis Mumford:

If the layout of a town has no relation to human needs and activities other than business, the pattern of the city may be simplified: the ideal layout for the businessman is that which can be most swiftly reduced to standard monetary units for purchase and sale. The fundamental unit is no longer the neighborhood or the precinct, but the individual building lot, whose value can be gauged in terms of front feet: this favors an oblong with a narrow frontage and great depth, which provides a minimum amount of light and air to the buildings, particularly the dwellings, that conform to it. Such units turned out equally advantageous for the land surveyor, the real estate speculator, the commercial builder, and the lawyer who drew up the deed of sale. In turn, the lots favored the rectangular building block, which again became the standard unit for extending the city.[36]

139

And thus, even in cities such as San Francisco, whose terrain calls out most strongly for contouring and variation in planning, the straight streets and square blocks march relentlessly up and down the hills.

Each development in transportation technology also had its effect on the shape the cities took. In fact the railroads were in a position to create new towns wherever they needed them and, by their choice of route, to determine whether communities already in existence would become thriving commercial centers or out-of-the-way hamlets. Because of this power over urban fortunes, railroad companies could negotiate with a heavy upper hand for depot sites and other concessions from local governments.

The building of railroads, the growth of industry, and the shape of the new American cities were all interrelated. Often

[36]From *The City In History*, © 1961 by Lewis Mumford. Reprinted by permission of Harcourt Brace Jovanovich, Inc.

the railroad lines paralleled rivers, making it easy for factories to locate conveniently close to both water and transportation. Wherever a factory would be built there would grow up around it low-cost housing — developments that speedily became slums; "the other side of the tracks" was a meaningful social boundary in most industrial cities. In the more important towns there were often large freightyards spreading across central parts of the urban landscape. Citizens and public officials were generally pleased to have the main artery of commerce running through their community. The railroads also contributed to the development of downtown areas by creating the need for hotels and restaurants to feed and shelter the traveler.

The steady stream of immigration kept the cities growing, and in turn the growth of cities provided work for the immigrants. Oscar Handlin writes in *The Uprooted:*

The increase of urban population strained existing housing and created a persistent demand for new construction that kept the building trades prosperous. Everywhere streets pushed out into the suburbs where farms had once been; men's muscles had to grade the way, carry and fit the paving blocks. Each seaport dredged and improved its harbor, built imposing piers to accommodate the larger vessels of nineteenth-century commerce. Intricate systems of aqueducts, of gas pipes, of electric wires, of trolley tracks, supplied water and light and transportation for the new city millions.

Every one of these activities, which occupied the attention of a whole century, depended for its execution upon an ample fund of unskilled labor. The immigrants supplied that fund.[37]

While the process of railroad building and industrialization molded American cities in one way, the sudden appearance of the automobile and the resultant new spurt of highway construction began to mold them in another. At first there was growth along the rivers and railroads; now there was growth along the highways. The service station and the roadside restaurant made their appearances. Farmers began to build cabins to house traveling motorists and their families. The cabins evolved into "tourist courts," and the tourist courts into motels, which are now far more numerous in America than hotels. The development of the highway contributed to the decline of the urban core in many cities. While motels took business away

140

---

[37]Handlin, *The Uprooted*, p. 67.

Wherever a factory would be built there would grow up around it low-cost housing — developments that speedily became slums; "the other side of the tracks" was a meaningful social boundary in most industrial cities.

from the older hotels, roadside shopping centers drew trade away from downtown stores.

The move to the suburbs was already underway before the automobile came. The automobile gave the move a new impetus and gradually altered the shape of the suburbs. The first suburbs were built along the railroad lines and laid out to a pedestrian scale with identifiable downtown centers close to the railroad stations; later suburbs spread over the countryside, often with no clear urban boundaries or centers.

Suburbia has had its biggest growth in the years since the end of World War II, helped along by rising population and prosperity, a traditional American belief in the value of open space and property, and federal loan programs that encouraged veterans to buy houses. The construction industry, developing mass-production techniques comparable to those of other manufacturers, began the greatest building boom in human history. In the first twenty years after the end of the war, 6 million acres of land were covered with new houses.

Now the society is confronted with the challenge of solving some of the problems created by its earlier actions — such problems as the loss of prime agicultural land to urban use, the decay of older urban centers, the hideously wasteful dependence on the automobile as the primary mode of transportation. Some of the products of this new effort at problem solving are comprehensive planning laws, urban redevelopment and housing programs, and the construction of multimodal transportation systems. The whole effort adds up to yet another phase in the endless reshaping of the American physical environment.

Waterways

The continent's waterways have been modified to suit a number of different needs — flood control, irrigation, power generation, urban water supply, navigation, and recreation. In modern times a single engineering project is usually designed as a "multipurpose" unit to serve several such demands at once.

The first major modifications of American waterways were for navigation. The rivers were natural routes of commerce, and the technology was already available for extending their range by dredging and canal building. After the War of 1812 the state of New York authorized funds to build a canal linking the Hudson River to Lake Erie. The Erie Canal was completed in 1825, making New York City the terminus of an artery to the Great Lakes area. This stimulated much enthusiasm for canal building, not all of which was realistic. For instance, there was some discussion at one point of the possibility of building a series of canals to connect Philadelphia to the Pacific Ocean.[38] The state of Pennsylvania did, however, build a canal linking Philadelphia to Pittsburgh; and the Chesapeake and Ohio canal, an interstate project, was completed a few years later. In 1855 the first of the canals at Sault Ste. Marie was opened, enabling the iron and copper ores of Michigan's upper peninsula to reach the industrial centers of the lower Great Lakes. Several other canals were built, mostly in the area between the Great Lakes, the Ohio River, and the Atlantic seaboard.

The canals were soon forced into competition with the railroads. The Baltimore and Ohio line, for example, competed directly with the Chesapeake and Ohio canal. By 1850 the amount of railroad mileage passed the amount of canal mileage, and some of the canals ceased operation. The Pennsylvania canal was no longer used after the early 1860s, and after the 1870s some 4,000 miles of canals were abandoned.[39] But canal building still goes on, and there are thousands of miles of canals still in use.

It is no longer easy to make a clear distinction between a canal and a river as a result of the engineering that has been done on the natural riverways. Some levee building was done along the Mississippi as early as 1717. In 1879 Congress created a new federal agency, the Mississippi River Commission, for the purpose of improving the river's navigational capacity and coordinating flood-control projects. Throughout this century the federal government has built scores of dams and locks along the Mississippi, and its riverbottom dredging operations have amounted to building a 650-mile canal.[40]

The Constitution gave the federal government responsibility for interstate waterways, an authorization that formed the basis for the growth of a huge bureaucracy and a massive complex of construction projects. In 1824 Congress allocated to the Army Corps of Engineers a budget of $75,000 and directed them to remove snags and other impediments from the Ohio and Mississippi rivers. That modest project launched the corps on its way. Today it is the world's largest construction organization and developer of waterways. By 1967 the corps reported that it was custodian of 3,828 public works projects and had modified 19,000 miles of rivers and other waterways by various kinds of construction.[41]

American efforts in altering water systems have produced some impressive successes, as well as a monumental amount of waste, corruption, bureaucratic squabbling, and ecological bungles.

143

[38]Edwin J. Foscue, "Our Waterways and Their Utilization," in G. Smith (ed.), *Conservation of Natural Resources*, p. 287.
[39]Foscue, "Our Waterways," p. 311.
[40]Franklin, *Remaking America*, p. 125.
[41]George Laycock, *The Diligent Destroyers* (Garden City, N.Y.: Doubleday, 1970), p. 6.

One of the corps' perennial occupations is attempting to prevent flooding in flood plains. The flat lands along river courses, which have the natural function of taking the overflow in years of heavy rainfall, are also attractive to human purposes. They are frequently rich agricultural land and also convenient for the construction of factories and houses and the laying out of railroad lines. Thus farms and cities crowd in along the rivers, and when the rivers flood there is costly destruction of property and a renewed clamor for public action to "tame the rivers."

For several decades the government has been attempting to do just that. The principle of full federal responsibility for flood control was firmly established by the Flood Control Acts of 1928 and 1936. These laws have the effect of supporting the commercial value of land in flood plains at considerable public expense. Expenditures for this purpose have been running well over $1 billion annually in the eastern United States alone, and the corps predicts this will reach $2.5 billion by 1980.[42] So far this activity has not put an end to flooding, but by encouraging the development of flood plains it does guarantee that the losses will be more costly when floods do occur.

One of the simplest flood-control measures is levee building. Another is what is known as "channel improvement," which means increasing the river's carrying capacity by dredging its bed and straightening out its course. The earlier straightening operations were generally done by opening shortcuts across bends in the river; more recent and more ambitious river-straightening projects often abandon a river bed entirely and run the waters through canals.

Dam building became an important — and a controversial — part of the government's flood-control activities. Conservationists often oppose dams because they destroy natural waterways and turn valleys and canyons into reservoirs. In order that certain areas may not be flooded occasionally, other areas are flooded permanently. There has also been an ongoing controversy over the size and location of dams. Some agricultural scientists favor soil-conservation and flood-control projects that rely on small dams and holding ponds, rather than on big dams. Frequently there is a difference of opinion about where dams should be built. Senator Frank Moss, a specialist in waterways legislation, writes:

Reservoirs upstream offer protection to their immediate areas, but the protection grows less with distance downstream from the

144

---

[42]Murphy, *Governing Nature*, p. 53.

There are no American water systems — river basins or watersheds — that have not been modified.

dam. Like lakes, reservoirs eventually die because of vegetable growth and sedimentation. In most cases, dredging sludge out of the bottom is too expensive. Usually, a more economic solution lies in adding to the height of the dam or in building another dam in a new location.[43]

Politics, as well as economics, also favors the construction of more and bigger dams. Although such projects are usually funded and administered by public agencies, they are built by private contractors. A dam contract means money and jobs; many congressmen measure their legislative success by the number of dams that have been built in their districts.

The development of hydroelectric power was another impetus to dam building. The first hydroelectric power plants operated off of small dams or natural waterfalls, but with the improvement of electrical transmission technology it became possible to locate generation sites at massive dams, such as the Hoover and the Grand Coulee, which were far distant from the consuming market.

Agricultural needs — irrigation and soil conservation — have also figured in the modification of American waterways. The Bureau of Reclamation, created by the Reclamation Act of 1902, is the major federal agency involved in irrigation projects. Its vast empire of construction works rivals that of the Army Corps of Engineers. In fact there is a long history of competition between the two agencies, which were frequently at odds with each other. Some of these conflicts were resolved by cooperation, and others by dividing the territory.

The Bureau of Reclamation was created originally for the purpose of "reclaiming" for agricultural use land that had previously been unsuitable for farming — in other words, converting the land into an artificial ecosystem. One of the bureau's first undertakings, begun in 1904, was to irrigate the valley of the lower Yellowstone River in Montana. Using the technology of the times — manual labor and workhorses — the bureau dug 75 miles of canals and 250 miles of irrigation ditches, built a dam across the river, and created 60,000 acres of new farmland for crops such as sugar beets.

Later the bureau and its projects became more ambitious. In the Northwest it undertook the development of the main stem of the Columbia River with the Bonneville and Grand Coulee dams. The latter, when completed in 1942, qualified as the world's largest dam and the world's largest single producer of

146

[43]Frank Moss, *The Water Crisis* (New York: Praeger, 1967), p. 107.

hydroelectric energy. Ten years later the project began delivering water to lands previously covered by sagebrush and other desert vegetation, the first of a million acres projected for irrigation. In California the bureau took over the Central Valley project, which became another world's largest: this time the world's largest artificial water system, with a complex of dams, pipelines, pumping stations, and canals transferring water from the Sacramento and Trinity river basins to fertile but arid parts of the San Joaquin Valley.

The Soil Conservation Service (SCS) is another federal agency that plays a part in the managing the American waterways. It has traditionally opposed the "big dam" philosophy of the Army Corps of Engineers and the Bureau of Reclamation, but in its own way it has done a considerable amount of ecological rebuilding. SCS projects have constructed dams in the headwaters, straightened streams, and built small reservoirs and holding ponds for flood control.

American efforts in altering water systems have produced some impressive successes, as well as a monumental amount of waste, corruption, bureaucratic squabbling, and ecological bungles. The root cause of the difficulty has been the failure to think holistically, to understand that water management is ecosystem management. The political process strives to fence off separate functions to be assigned to separate agencies and to approve projects on a one-thing-at-a-time basis. This is consistent with our political traditions, but it is unrealistic because it fails to comprehend the complexity of what is being undertaken when rivers and lakes are engineered into artificial systems. The basic problem is roughly the same as the one that results from the creation of monocultures; these artificial systems, as a naturalist explains well in the following passage, are unstable.

Balances in nature are never eternal, but they have a permanency that comes close to being interminable. The wildest river in a state of nature has its patterns of conduct and limits of performance, at least until upset by some catastrophe like an earthquake or a basic climate change. But in its normal reach, the limits have been set in nature for this river.

When human economics, therefore, decides to tame such a river by dams, concrete banks, water withdrawals, effluent discharges, flumes, and canalization, something like a natural catastrophe external to the functioning of the stream has occurred. A new order for that stream has been created; and if any part of that new order is to operate for long, every aspect of the stream must

147

be brought into a reciprocal relationship similar to the kind of interlocking functionings that had existed in the natural wild river. The refusal of authorities to recognize this duty has brought America's rivers to their rather sad plight.[44]

Although the plight of the rivers may be unfortunate from an ecologist's point of view, there are worse things that could happen to a bureaucrat than to have projects turn out to be more complicated than they had at first appeared. What ordinarily happens when things begin to go wrong with artificial water systems is that the new funds are appropriated and new work projects are begun, usually under the supervision of the same people who created the problem in the first place. This sort of difficulty might be partly avoided by relying less on single-purpose agencies and creating instead institutional structures with general responsibility for environmental management in a region. The Tennessee Valley Authority is a cautious step in this direction. Created by the federal government in 1933, the TVA has undertaken one of the most ambitious programs of ecological management in human history. Its field of operation is a river basin of some 40,000 square miles, covering parts of seven states — much of it poor land that had been cleared and overfarmed. TVA build nine major dams and several hundred miles of inland waterway. It generated and sold electrical power, created recreational facilities, planted trees, and carried out research in chemical fertilizer manufacture.

It also contributed significantly to the development of atomic power by providing electricity for the uranium plant at Oak Ridge, Tennessee. For all its size, TVA is still far less than a comprehensive environmental management agency, and its existence has been complicated by struggles with state and local governments, other federal agencies (notably the Corps of Engineers and the Soil Conservation Service), private corporations, and legislators who saw it as a serious case of creeping socialism.

Although there has been much conflict and controversy associated with the creation of American water-management policy, there has also been an overriding general consensus that the waterways *should* be reengineered to help produce consumer goods. Senator George Norris, the father of the TVA bill, spoke for this consensus when he praised the TVA as a step toward "the dawning of that day when every rippling stream that flows down the mountain side and winds its way through the meadows to the sea shall be harnessed and made to work for

148

---

[44]Murphy, *Governing Nature*, p. 15.

the welfare and comfort of man."[45] The conservationist crusade for the maintenance of wild rivers is a distinct minority voice struggling to win a debate that pivots on the use of the term *wild river* to describe what used to be called simply a river. There are very few American rivers that have not yet been dammed or channelized, and there are no water systems — river basins or watersheds — that have not been modified. Most of the political conflict is about how the system should be modified, who does the construction and administration of it, and who gets the water.

These issues are big politics and big business. America's water resources are immense, and so is its consumption. The United States is the world's largest consumer of water, by 1980 reaching the amount of about 600 billion gallons a day. The consumption can be accounted for partly by household use, but the needs of industry and agriculture are also prodigious. A single modern paper mill uses more water in a day than a city of 50,000 inhabitants. To grow a ton of corn takes 350,000 gallons of water.[46]

Simply stated, water is a fundamental support of the nation's industrial and agricultural productivity. It is also a fundamental support of urban growth. Most American cities and towns have long since grown beyond their own local water resources, their continued existence depends on the construction of dams, reservoirs, and pipelines far beyond their own boundaries. A classic example of this is the case of Los Angeles.

149

Water for Los Angeles: A Case Study   Like many cities, both ancient and modern, Los Angeles has a population far beyond its local water supply. To provide the amount of water it needs for drinking and bathing, for industrial use, for filling its swimming pools, and for watering its lawns, the city has had to reach ever farther beyond its own boundaries.

Curiously, the very thing that attracts people to Los Angeles — its climate — is directly connected to its inability to provide water to keep up with its population growth. The area has an average annual rainfall of fifteen inches, with periodic dry spells. One such drought occurred around the turn of the century and seriously threatened the real estate boom that was turning many local businessmen into millionaires.

Public officials began to search for some way of increasing the water supply and concluded that the most likely source was the

[45]Frank E. Smith, *The Politics of Conservation* (New York: Pantheon, 1966), p. 206.
[46]Robert Rienow and Leona Train Rienow, *Moment in the Sun* (New York: Ballantine, 1969), pp. 71-72.

Owens Valley, approximately 200 miles to the north. The valley is much higher than the Los Angeles basin and is located just east of the Sierra Nevada peaks, which receive rain and snow even in the driest years. With the blessing of the federal government, the city bought up the necessary land and, in a remarkable engineering project, constructed an aqueduct that carried water down from the high valley and across the Mojave Desert to Los Angeles.

One immediate consequence of the project was a sharp rise in agricultural value of the San Fernando Valley, which adjoins Los Angeles. (Insiders had prudently bought up land in the San Fernando Valley in anticipation of the new supply of water for irrigation.) Another consequence was a sudden decline in the prospects of the Owens Valley, where local farmers had been developing irrigation and anticipating a land boom of their own. So began a series of skirmishes known as the Owens Valley War. In one episode a group of armed citizens of the town of Big Pine occupied an irrigation canal that was about to be closed off for the Los Angeles system and threw the city's grading equipment into the water. An Owens Valley branch of the Ku Klux Klan was organized for the purpose of uniting opposition to the Los Angeles project and terrorizing those whose loyalty to the valley seemed in doubt. In 1924 a group of about forty men blew up a portion of the Los Angeles aqueduct with dynamite. Peace was finally made, but not until Los Angeles passed a $12 million bond issue to buy up more Owens Valley land at prices that brought prosperity after all to many of the local ranchers.

Even before the conflict was fully resolved and the final construction work on the aqueduct completed, the city's growth had already outreached it, and the search for still another water source was underway. The next choice was the Colorado River, fed by streams as far away as Wyoming and the Rocky Mountains. This started another controversy, far more complex and drawn out (although somewhat less violent) than the Owens Valley War. There were also some engineering disasters involved, most notably one resulting from the first attempt of a group of developers to divert Colorado River water into the Imperial Valley to turn that Southern California desert into farmland. The developers accidentally diverted the entire Colorado River, which for a time flowed down into the Imperial Valley and turned a dry saltbed into the lake that is now known as the Salton Sea.

The political conflict had to do with the fact that various other states also had plans for the Colorado River water and were most unwilling to see it taken away by California, which was no

In America water has been used as if there were no limit on its capacities, as if there were no quantities of waste that could not be diluted and carried away.

151

part of the river's source. At one point the governor of Arizona called out the state's militia to prevent the completion of the dam that was to become part of the Los Angeles water system. Water from the Colorado was flowing to Los Angeles by 1941; the question of the proper allocation of the river's waters was finally settled by a Supreme Court decision in 1963.

But the combined inflow from the Owens Valley and the Colorado River was also insufficient, and the planners turned next to the far reaches of Northern California. California had begun the Central Valley Project in the 1930s to shift water southward from the often-flooded Sacramento Valley to the fertile but relatively dry San Joaquin Valley. This massive engineering project, as completed in its original form in 1951, did not reach into Southern California. But a few years later the state legislature approved a much more elaborate project, the California Water Plan, which was designed to carry water all the way from the Upper Feather River — 500 miles north of Los Angeles — to the water districts of Southern California.

As a result, water now flows to Los Angeles from the Colorado River and from both sides of the Sierra Nevada Range. Future growth of the city and adjoining metropolitan areas may require further extensions into the northernmost regions of California. There have also been serious proposals to connect the California Water Plan with the rivers of Oregon and Washington.[47]

Water Pollution   Whenever water is channeled through an ecosystem, natural or artificial, always among its functions is to carry away wastes or sediments. Up to a certain point in the growth of human population and technology a stream can fulfill this function and many others as well: it can pass through a primitive irrigation system or a mill and still provide drinking water for human and animal populations, and it can still accommodate all the species of plant and animal life that inhabit it. But when the effluents from human civilization become too great, the stream tends to become a single-purpose system; it is no longer drinkable and it begins to destroy life. It is solely a receptacle, a moving garbage disposal unit carrying its poisons into the lakes and oceans. When this happens — and it is happening to every American waterway — the society is forced to recognize the problem of water pollution and to deal with it as a matter of public policy. As a consequence, management of the rivers and lakes and oceans, the fundamental support

152

[47]Sources for this section include: Dasmann, *The Destruction of California;* Remi Nadeau, *The Water Seekers* (Garden City, N.Y.: Doubleday, 1950); Vincent Ostrom, *Water and Politics* (Los Angeles: The Haynes Foundation, 1953); Albert Williams, *The Water and The Power* (New York: Duell, Sloan and Pearce, 1951).

systems of all life, becomes an operation of human government.

In America water has been used as if there were no limit on its capacities, as if there were no quantities of waste that could not be diluted and carried away. And it is easy to understand, given the vastness of the natural system of lakes and rivers, how such an attitude could come into existence in a society and continue to survive — even when it no longer has any foundation in reality.

Urban sewage, industry, and agriculture are the three main sources of water pollution, which is another way of saying that virtually every functioning part of our social system is connected to some use of water as a receptacle for waste.

Early in the nineteenth century Americans began to install in their houses ingenious new inventions called water closets. At first, authorities insisted that water closets had to be connected to cesspools, but soon they were being connected to public storm-drainage sewers. Sewage emptied into the streams and frequently found its way back into the water supply. Sewage-contaminated water caused the typhoid epidemics in New York in 1843 and in Pennsylvania in 1885; fear of typhoid and cholera spurred the first attempts to study and control water pollution.

By 1900 some American cities had installed sewage-treatment facilities, "primary-treatment" plants that screened and settled out the largest chunks of solid sewage and sent the rest — still laden with bacteria and chemicals — into the water. In 1914 the United States Public Health service established national standards for drinking water; and in the 1930s millions of dollars were spent on waste-treatment projects under New Deal public works programs. Now about two-thirds of sewage plants also have "secondary-treatment" processes, in which bacteria are used to break down the settled solids into inorganic wastes, which are then filtered and chlorinated and released into the water systems. This treated sewage still includes phosphates, nitrates, and other chemicals.

Most cities now have separate storm-drainage systems, but many, including New York City, Chicago, and Boston, still have combined sewer systems. In both cases there are serious pollution problems. In the cities with separate systems the storm sewage, containing a variety of organic and inorganic wastes, goes straight into the water without treatment. In the cities where the systems are combined, a storm can overload the capacity of the treatment plant, and then both the domestic sewage and street runoff flow into the water untreated.[48]

153

---

[48]David Zwick and Marcy Benstock, *Water Wasteland* (New York: Grossman, 1971), p. 39.

Water pollution control tends to become a federal concern. The federal government is currently spending billions of dollars to monitor water quality and construct treatment plants. The Federal Water Pollution Control Act of 1970 is the largest single source of environmental protection employment: it brings the total number of people working in water-cleanup operations to over 200,000.[49]

The effort to improve water quality can boast of considerable progress as seen in laws passed, dollars spent, people employed, and plants constructed. However, the amount of pollution from urban sewage systems has not declined. Most sewage-treatment facilities are inadequate for the cities they serve, and construction of new plants is not keeping up with population growth. In fact it is falling behind; at the present time the amount of pollutants from urban sewage entering the water systems is about three times what it was in 1900.[50]

Industry, although we may think of it as a totally artificial activity, has a surprisingly high dependence on nature: natural fuels, mineral resources, and water. Especially water. Water systems as receptacles for waste are integral parts of major industries such as steel, paper, and chemical manufacturing, oil refining, electrical power generating, and food processing. The normal daily operation of these and other industries pours into the water millions of tons of chemicals, nutrients, and organic wastes. Some of the industrial wastes go into city water systems which are not equipped to handle them, and the great majority of these wastes go from factories located along rivers or lakeshores directly into the water. The total volume of industrial waste is far greater than the volume of waste from domestic sources, and it is increasing at a faster rate.

A further problem is that the technology for dealing with industrial wastes, especially chemicals and radioactive materials, is less sophisticated and more expensive. There are also economic and politcal complications in the way of any rapid and easy cleanup. Industries have used the water systems without cost for years and complain that the cost of treating pollutants would be impossibly high. Meanwhile they invest heavily in lawyers and lobbyists to delay governmental pressure to solve the problem, and in public relations campaigns to proclaim that the problem has already been solved.

Agriculture is the third major cause of water pollution. Irrigation systems provide water to crops and also carry away

154

---

[49]Patrick Heffernan, "Jobs and the Environment," *Sierra Club Bulletin*, April 1975, p. 26.
[50]Zwick and Benstock, *Water Wasteland*, p. 38.

fertilizers and pesticides. The irrigation runoffs proceed directly into streams and lakes without treatment, and in some areas they also percolate downward to contaminate underground water tables. This has caused serious well contamination in California's San Joaquin Valley, when the completion of a new canal raised the water table and began to dissolve nitrate concentrations that had been building up in the ground over decades of irrigation from local water sources.[51] Pollution from agriculture is steadily increasing, partly because more land is being brought under irrigation as a result of the Bureau of Reclamations's efforts and partly because agriculture is becoming more dependent on chemical fertilizers and pesticides. The trend in agriculture is toward a more intensive crop production relying heavily on technology — farm machinery, irrigation, artificial fertilization, pesticides. As agriculture becomes more of an industry, like other industries it produces wastes beyond the capacities of the natural water systems.

A greater reliance on chemical fertilizers to enrich the soil, for which purpose animal wastes were once used, has curiously resulted in natural wastes becoming as much of a pollution problem as chemicals. All across the country are feedlots and farms where meat-producing domestic animals — millions of descendants of the cattle and hogs and sheep and chickens imported to America — are crowded together and fed rich diets in preparation for slaughter and marketing. Their wastes accumulate and then wash away with the rains into the nearest stream. In the basin of the Missouri River, an area with more than its share of commercial feeder operations, the organic wastes that go into the river system equal the untreated sewage from a human population of 37.5 million.[52]

The cumulative effect of the vast outpouring of wastes from homes, factories, refineries, mines, farms, and feedlots is, not surprisingly, an alteration; like the land and the life systems on it, the waters have been transformed by the effects of an industrial civilization.

Every American river is polluted to some extent and several of them — the Calumet, the Colorado, and the Missouri, for example — are rated by the Federal Water Quality Administration as seriously polluted along more than fifty miles of their length. All of our larger lakes are polluted, the worst being those closest to heavy concentrations of population and industry. Lake Erie, receiving a daily inflow of 17 million tons of

155

[51]Wagner, *Environment and Man*, p. 53.
[52]Zwick and Benstock, *Water Wasteland*, p. 97.

pollutants, is probably the world's most contaminated body of water.

The contamination is not only in the water but in the living inhabitants of aquatic ecosystems. Agricultural or industrial chemicals may end up poisoning human beings not as a result of their drinking the water but as a result of their eating the fish that live in the water—that is, as a result of the food chain. This becomes more critical as the species lower on the food chain develop more resistance to the chemicals, a common form of genetic evolution influenced by human activity. A zoologist reported some time ago that some species of fish in the Mississippi Delta now survive with concentrations of pesticides in their bodies 120 times greater than what would once have been fatal to them.[53]

The ecological changes in the water from overabundant nutrients are as profound as the changes caused by poisons. Agricultural runoffs and household wastes, especially detergents, fill the water systems with nitrates and phosphates that stimulate rapid growth of algae. The algae reproduce at incredible rates, exhausting oxygen supplies and making the water unsuitable for other life forms. This process is called "eutrophication"; it is the natural aging process by which lakes turn into swamps, and it is being accelerated thousands of times over by the chemical changes in the water systems.

156

What will happen to the American water systems will be determined by human institutions — by the cities and the states, by the corporations and, increasingly, the federal government. There is little likelihood that the water systems are about to be "cleaned up," that is, returned to a condition similar to that of 200 years ago. No such undertaking has been started, nor is one contemplated. The direction of public policy is to determine the "acceptable" levels of pollution — how much arsenic, mercury, lead, nitrates, herbicides, pesticides, and so forth we can have in the water and still survive — and to keep the concentrations from exceeding those levels.

Mining

In the sixteenth century all Europe was stunned by the news of the precious metals Spanish explorers were bringing back from Mexico and South America, wealth that for a time appeared to guarantee Spain a new position of world power. Gold, in addition to land and religious freedom, was part of the colonizing agenda. The charter given by James I to the London and

---

[53]Roy Reed, "Pesticides Make Cotton Prosper But Endanger Life," *New York Times*, 16 December 1969, p. 12.

In the nineteenth
century coal became
the most important
energy source.

Plymouth companies specified that the crown would get a share of any precious metals.

Some of the early English colonists did some prospecting (Captain John Smith reportedly looked for gold and copper in Virginia) but no discoveries of note were made along the eastern seaboard, and most colonials settled for the profits to be found in America's fertile land, forests, fish, and game. Minerals did not seem to be an important part of the country's wealth. In 1790 Benjamin Franklin, arguing for a paper currency, said: "Gold and silver are not the produce of North America, which has no mines."[54]

Although no gold or silver had yet been found in 1790, copper had been discovered in Massachusetts and New Jersey, and iron was being mined in several states. By 1810 the secretary of the treasury estimated the national iron production at $13 million a year. Coal mines were operating in Virginia and Pennsylvania, forerunners of the great mines that would fuel the railroads and mills and factories as the country industrialized. Then gold, too, was discovered: first in Virginia and the Carolinas, then in Georgia and Alabama. In 1833 and 1834 the gold mined out of these southern states amounted to about $1 million a year.[55] But all of this was eclipsed by the discovery in California.

Gold was discovered in California just nine days before the signing of the treaty of Guadalupe Hidalgo, which ended the Mexican War and ceded California to the United States; neither government knew of the discovery. The United States paid $15 million for the ceded land, which included the present states of California, New Mexico, Arizona, Nevada, and Utah, and parts of Colorado and Wyoming — territories that subsequently turned out to have some of the richest mineral deposits in the world. Within a year California alone yielded gold valued at three times the amount of the payment made to Mexico.

The discovery of gold changed the face of California in many ways. As soon as the word was out, the gold country swarmed with men who had come to dig up the hillsides and pan the waters. The techniques used by the first prospectors were relatively harmless compared to the hydraulic mining operation that evolved a few years later. Stuart Udall has described this:

158

[54]Jared Sparks (ed.), *The Works of Benjamin Franklin*, Vol. 2 (Boston: Hilliard, Gray & Co., 1840), p. 347.
[55]T. A. Rickard, *A History of American Mining* (New York: McGraw-Hill, 1932), p. 18.

In 1852, Anthony Chabot, a California gold miner, ingeniously devised a canvas hose and nozzle that would wash banks of gold-bearing gravel into the placer pits for processing. Chabot's labor-saving short cut caught on in the Mother Lode country above Sacramento, and by 1870 his crude hose had evolved into the "Little Giant," a huge nozzle that could tear up whole hillsides.

The result of the hydraulic mining was the massive movement of soil into the rivers that drained the Sierra Nevada. For every ounce of gold collected, tons of topsoil and gravel were washed into the river courses below. With the spring floods, clear streams became a chaos of debris, rocks, and silt; communities downstream were inundated with muck, and fertile bottomlands were blanketed with mud and gravel.[56]

Hydraulic mining was the subject of a long conflict between the miners and the residents of the flatlands below the Mother Lode; it was finally outlawed in 1884, but its effects are still visible.

The mining itself had the most immediate impact on the land, but other indirect processes set in motion by the gold discovery were no less important: the rapid growth in California's population, the construction of cities and towns and roads, the need for a local food supply, the stimulus to railroad building. This process was repeated with variations wherever gold was found — in Nevada, Colorado, and Alaska. There would be a sudden boom in the population of the mining area itself, an urgent demand for food, and a sudden market for transportation systems to bring out the minerals and bring in new miners and the necessary tools, machinery, and supplies. A new discovery could transform an area overnight. Consider this account of what happened at Nome, Alaska:

In 1899 some of the gold-seekers that congregated on the seashore at Nome were disgusted to find that all the creeks were plastered with location notices; fortunately for them, the gold was not only in the creek-beds, but also in the detritus under the moss at the edge of the plain where it was broken by the wash of the waves. . . . Early in June a soldier found that the beach contained gold in paying quantity; it was a mine! Soon scores of men went to work feverishly with pan, shovel, and rocker. . . . The next year, of

Gold was discovered in California just nine days before the signing of the treaty of Guadalupe Hidalgo, which ended the Mexican War and ceded California to the United States; neither government knew of the discovery.

159

[56]From *The Quiet Crisis* by Stewart L. Udall. Copyright © 1963 by Stewart L. Udall. Reprinted by permission of Holt, Rinehart and Winston, Publishers.

course, there was a rush thither, and a white-tented city, like a snow-drift five miles long, fringed the shore of Bering Sea. In the summer of 1900 there were 30,000 people at Nome. . . . The beach itself has yielded altogether about $5,000,000. . . . Every kind of gold-saving device was brought to Nome, from patent cradles to cumbrous dredges; the shore became littered with fearsome machines.[57]

The acquisition of Alaska was another one of those curious pieces of luck that added to America's mineral wealth. Alaska was purchased in 1867 for $7.2 million — only a fraction of what was taken out of it in gold and, at a later stage of its exploitation, oil.

The gold and silver discoveries increased America's population, created great new private fortunes, and stimulated the growth of industry. But the growth of industry in the post-Civil War years relied heavily on the development of other mineral resources. In the nineteenth century coal became the most important energy source. In 1899 at its peak demand, coal accounted for 89.1 percent of the energy produced in the United States. The country's rapid development as an industrial and military power can be partially accounted for by the fact that it possessed this resource in abundance. The Appalachian region and the Pittsburgh coal seam stretching through Pennsylvania, Ohio, and West Virginia were found to contain some of the world's largest deposits of soft coal. The location of coal influenced the location of industry. The Pittsburgh seam, for example, supplied the ore for the furnaces of nearby Connelsville, producing the coke that made possible the development of Pittsburgh's iron and steel industry.[58] Another factor in industrial development was the abundant water supply provided by the rivers and the Great Lakes. In an amazingly short time this region was transformed from a sparsely populated frontier into one of the world's great industrial centers.

Coal went through a period of declining importance until the 1970s energy crisis stimulated a new respect for its usefulness as a power source. Using coal for energy has two significant ecological drawbacks: (1) coal is a heavy air polluter, and (2) it is now obtained mainly by strip mining. Once nearly all coal was mined from underground tunnels, but since the early 1930s there has been a steady increase in strip mining, which means using large power shovels to remove the surface soil above the coal. Strip mining requires a heavy initial investment in

160

[57]Rickard, *A History of American Mining*, pp. 50-51.
[58]E. Willard Miller, "The Mineral Fuels," in G. Smith (ed.), *Conservation of Natural Resources*, p. 354.

"... The gushers
went uncontrolled
because early oilmen
did not understand
geology."

161

machinery, but over the long haul it is the more commercially attractive method from the mine owner's point of view. It is also easily the most ecologically traumatic form of mining ever devised.

The United States Geological Survey estimated in 1970 that 2,450 square miles of land had been strip mined; it is projected that by 1980 the area stripped will total 4,287 square miles.[59] These figures do not convey the total ecological trauma of stripping, since adjoining areas are also affected by erosion and changes in the water table. Some states have passed laws requiring the reclamation of land mined by stripping, and about half the acreage stripped so far has been planted with trees or returned to agricultural use. To date most of the reclamation projects have been inadequate for both economic and technological reasons. The cost of reclaiming land is high and reduces the profit margins that made strip mining desirable to begin with. Replacing the removed soil often leaves it so tightly packed that seedlings cannot take root; and there has usually been heavy erosion before any restoration projects begin. In Appalachia, erosion losses from stripped lands run as high as 27,000 tons per square mile annually — up to 1,000 times greater than erosion of similar lands before stripping.[60]

Strip mining is now moving west. Ranchers in the Southwest, in Montana and Wyoming and the Dakotas, are suddenly discovering that they "own" only the surface of the land, that the mining rights are retained by the federal government. And the federal government's clearly stated policy is that development of power is more important than preservation of grazing lands. As a result some of the open spaces that went through an ecological transformation scarcely a century ago, as Indians and buffalo gave way to cowboys and cattle, are now going through a second and even greater change. The new heirs of the West are power plants and strip mines.

There has been an intensive effort in the Congress to place new restrictions on strip mining. The attempt has pitted environmentalists against power companies, but so far the power side of the battle has been the victor. The political consensus is that developing new energy sources is an overriding national priority.

Oil is another major support of American industrial development. When oil was first discovered they called it "black gold" and took it from the ground in the way gold had been taken —

---

[59]Peter Borelli, "The Biggest Ripoff," *Sierra Club Bulletin*, September 1972, p. 13.
[60]Ibid., p. 14.

with a rush for the wealth, accompanied by waste and destruction:

When oil came, it was usually in gushers that spewed the black liquid across the landscape with volcanic force. In the first big oil boom in Pennsylvania, just after the Civil War, gushers wasted oil at the rate of 3,000 barrels a day. But that record was soon broken and, in 1901, Spindletop in Texas flowed wild for nine days at the rate of 110,000 barrels a day before it was brought under control. The gushers went uncontrolled because early oilmen did not understand geology. Gushers caught fire, oil was allowed to evaporate in earthen dams, or to escape down creeks and gullies in an orgy of waste.[61]

The waste of the oil was nothing compared to the waste of natural gas, which accompanies oil deposits but was not considered worth saving by most early oil producers. It was allowed to escape freely into the atmosphere, a tremendous loss of a potentially valuable energy source. It has been estimated that the natural gas lost in the Texas Panhandle alone could have powered an electric generating plant equal in output to four times that of the Grand Coulee dam.[62] In 1934 one single field blew into the air every day a billion cubic feet of gas — enough to supply the daily demands of all the houses in the country.[63]

Conservation technology for oil and natural gas has improved, but oil production continues to affect the environment. In recent years the most conspicuous evidence of this was the oil spill off the coast of Southern California. The impact of the pipeline across the frozen tundra of Alaska is yet to be seen, and there will also be some major ecological/economic changes in California as the Alaskan oil is received and processed there.

Coal, iron, oil, and precious metals are some of the more spectacular parts of America's mineral wealth, but by no means all of it. There is, for example, copper, first mined along the eastern seaboard, then around the Great Lakes, now mainly in the West. There are several other metal deposits that have found their way into American industrial development. Also, as agriculture becomes more dependent on inorganic fertilizers, sources of fertilizer minerals are becoming valuable new additions to the mining industry.

In spite of its enormous mineral deposits, the United States is no longer a "surplus nation," although at the beginning of this

163

---

[61]From *The Quiet Crisis* by Stewart L. Udall. Copyright © 1963 by Stewart L. Udall. Reprinted by permission of Holt, Rinehart and Winston, Publishers.
[62]Miller, "The Mineral Fuels," p. 381.
[63]Franklin, *Remaking America*, p. 28.

century it was — producing about 15 percent more raw materials (except for food) than it consumed. By 1950 it was consuming about 10 percent more than it produced.[64] As the consumption of energy and manufactured goods becomes greater, the country becomes increasingly dependent on other parts of the world, and the per capita consumption rate becomes more disproportionate to that of other people. A former resource administrator in California estimated that "If present trends continue, the United States within fifteen years will have about 9½ percent of the world's population. At this time this 9½ percent will be consuming some 83 percent of all the raw materials and resources produced by the entire world."[65] As this consumption depletes the wealth of other nations, it augments domestic ecological problems, such as solid waste and pollution.

Solid Waste

The United States is the world's leading consumer nation, but few goods are consumed entirely. Food and manufactured goods produce solid waste, as do the containers they come in. And so the world's richest country also happens to be the world's greatest producer of garbage. Each of us produces well over a ton of garbage a year, and the total volume is increasing much more rapidly than can be accounted for by population growth alone. One factor in this growing mountain of waste is the packaging industry, which emphasizes individual wrappings and disposable containers. The department of Health, Education, and Welfare estimated that in the decade 1966-1976 the annual amount of packaging waste alone increased by 136 pounds per person.

In addition to the ordinary household wastes, which are processed through garbage collection and disposal systems, there are many solid substances that require some kind of separate handling. Among them are industrial scrap, wastes from the demoliton of buildings, agricultural wastes, residues from power plants, discarded furniture, and discarded automobiles. Each of these generates enormous volumes of material. In Los Angeles County alone, demolition produces 5,000 tons of solid waste per day. About 7 million automobiles and 100 million tires are discarded annually, and every American city has its sprawling graveyards for old automobiles. Mining processes often pile up billions of tons of waste material near mine sites.

The oldest method known for disposing of solid waste mater-

[64]Rienow and Rienow, *Moment in the Sun*, p. 19.
[65]Ibid., p. 20

About 7 million automobiles and 100 million tires are discarded annually, and every American city has its sprawling graveyards for old automobiles.

Underground in South Carolina is one of our more curious imports — 5,000 drums of topsoil from the fields near Palomares, Spain, where an American bomber crashed in 1966 and scattered radioactive plutonium fuel.

ial is the open dump. Garbage is simply hauled to an open area, usually on the outskirts of the urban area, and left there without any special form of treatment. This is the cheapest method, and it accounts for about 75 percent of solid waste disposal in the United States.

A more complex technology for garbage disposal is the "sanitary landfill" method. Compacted layers of waste are covered with layers of soil; the resulting "filled" area can be used for other purposes. Canyons or abandoned quarries, for example, are sometimes developed into parks and golf courses. In some areas where the terrain is flat, the landfill creates a hill, which is then landscaped. There is one of these near Evanston, Illinois, known locally as "Mount Trashmore." Coastal communities often use the nearby body of water for landfill, thereby creating new land for buildings or other development. Several towns and cities around San Francisco Bay have used water for landfill; as a result, the bay is now reduced to about two-thirds of its original size.

Both open dumps and sanitary landfill eventually run into the same problem: lack of space. The volume of waste increases while available land decreases. With the expansion of suburbia, convenient spaces just outside the urban area are harder to find. Engineers consider sites such as swamps desirable disposal areas, but conservationists oppose the idea. Several American communities have already begun to use trains to carry solid wastes to distant disposal sites.

Other methods of solid waste disposal account for a small percentage of the total volume of waste. Incineration could, in theory, dispose of about 90 percent of the volume of ordinary household garbage — and produce some electrical energy as well — but its effectiveness is reduced by technological limitations and by the fact that it produces air pollution. Recycling of glass, metal, paper, and other substances may also have great possibilities, but at the present less than 1 percent of American solid wastes are recycled.

Also, a sizable amount of solid waste is created when materials such as coal are burned to create electrical energy. The recent development of atomic power as a source of electrical energy offers one way out of the dependence on coal but produces a new problem of its own: radioactive wastes. These substances will remain lethal for thousands of years, and they present a remarkably ticklish challenge to waste disposal technology. Radioactive wastes are normally encased in concrete and steel drums, which are then deposited somewhere. Some are dumped into the ocean, some are buried. There are over 70 million gallons of radioactive materials buried underground in Washington and South Carolina. Also underground in South Carolina is one of our more curious imports — 5,000 drums of topsoil from the fields near Palomares, Spain, where an American bomber crashed in 1966 and scattered radioactive plutonium fuel.[66]

Solid waste disposal has traditionally been a concern of city governments, but as the garbage piles up and the open space for it diminishes, regional arrangements become necessary. Most of the states have now passed laws to create regional agencies for working with the cities on solid waste disposal. There has been some federal support for research on new technology to deal with solid waste, but unfortunately more progress is being made in figuring out new kinds of individualized packaging to increase the volume of waste and in using new materials to make the garbage more durable. The old-fashioned tinned steel can, for example, would rust away in a few decades, but modern steel cans with chrome or resin coatings last much longer, and aluminum cans last indefinitely. Meanwhile the technology for removing garbage has changed little in the past thousand years or so. It used to be hauled away in wagons; now it is hauled away in trucks.

Solid wastes have definitely contributed to the transformation of the American landscape. Billions and billions of tons of material buried or piled up on the land or dumped into the water are enough to make a difference. At present the pile is continuing to grow at the rate of about 150 million tons a year. The prospects for a change in this pattern boil down to two things: reuse and recycling.

Reuse of containers is a rather hit-or-miss operation determined by the personal habits of individuals, but it can be encouraged by governmental policies. The first major effort in this direction was Oregon's "bottle bill," requiring all beer and soft-drink containers to have a refund value, which is actually a return to the arrangement that was in effect until the 1950s, when the trend toward nonreturnable containers began. Further laws of this sort would reduce the volume of solid waste and also cut down on the energy expended in container manufacture. According to the Environmental Protection Agency, a return to 1958 levels of packaging (per person) would conserve the equivalent of 550,000 barrels of oil per day by 1980.[67]

Recycling now accounts for only about 7 percent of solid wastes, but some cities with active recycling programs have

167

[66]Henry Still, *The Dirty Animal* (New York: Hawthorn Books, 1967), pp. 43-44.
[67]Harold Gilliam, "The 'Secret' Storehouse of Energy," *San Francisco Chronicle*, 31 August 1975, p. 18.

already managed to reverse the trend toward ever-expanding volumes of garbage. The materials most often recycled are tin, aluminum, glass, and paper. Another form of recycling is composting organic kitchen wastes. This, too, is practiced only on a very limited scale at present, but in a nation that throws out 22 million tons of food annually — and has water pollution problems from chemical fertilizers — systematic, large-scale composting programs could make a real difference.

Actually, there is a third approach — in addition to reuse and recycling — to the solid waste problem. That is energy conversion. Various processes for converting municipal garbage into fuel are already fairly well developed and in use in American cities. These offer the promise of solving, at least partially, the solid waste problem and the energy problem as well.

I have been speaking mostly of the solid wastes from residential and commercial sources, and have not mentioned the enormous volume of waste from industry. "The true magnitude of the industrial waste situation," reports an EPA official, "is now beginning to come into focus, and the picture we see is alarming. Not many people appreciate the fact that industry produces about 260 million dry tons of waste per year which is almost *twice* as much waste each year as is generated by residential and commercial sources. Further, industry generates about *thirty-five times* more waste than do the sewage treatment plants; yet one hears a lot more talk about the sewage sludge problem than the industrial sludge problem."[68]

Ironically, governmental pollution-control regulations are, so far, making this problem *worse*. As new pollution-control devices are installed in factories to reduce smokestack emissions and reduce the amount of wastes dumped into the rivers and lakes, there is a corresponding buildup of sludges, liquids, and solids — many of them extremely hazardous — that have to be dumped somewhere else. They are mainly dumped onto the land. They go into landfills along with the other garbage, or to special industrial-waste disposal sites. Some of the most dangerous materials are liquids, which are either buried in drums or poured into open evaporation ponds. The material in the ponds evaporates (causing new air pollution) and in some cases seeps into surface or underground water (causing water pollution). The best that can happen is that these liquids evapo-

168

[68]John P. Lehman, Director of the Hazardous Waste Management Division, Office of Solid Waste Management Programs, U.S. Environmental Protection Agency, in *Industrial Waste Management: Seven Conference Papers* (Washington, D.C.: U.S. Environmental Protection Agency, 1975), p. 16. Italics in original.

rate safely, and leave their chemical residues forever in the ground.

This situation is bleak, but not hopeless. The glimmer of hope is the possibility that industry can learn to recover and reuse many of the wastes that are now dumped. This is technologically possible, although at the moment most industries generally find it easier and cheaper to combine wastes and haul them away than to keep them separate and find new uses for them. But it can be done. Several European countries now have "clearinghouses" for this purpose, and there is one American company (Zero Waste Systems of California) that performs the service of accepting waste and surplus chemicals from industries and finding purchasers for them.

The Air

The atmosphere is an essential, limited, and fragile part of our system. Air is consumed in great quantities by every living being (the average person's daily intake is about 3,500 gallons). And, like the water and the land, air serves as a receptacle for waste. Motor vehicles, power plants, factories, and other sources exhale millions of tons of chemicals and suspended solid particles into the air every day. Like other parts of the American environment, the air is not the same as it once was, and like other basic resources of life, its management has been taken over by human institutions.

Air pollution, another by-product of civilization, has been with us for a long time. In the last century the widespread use of coal for heating, the expansion of industry, and the practice of burning household wastes and lumber left over from construction and demolition work all contributed to the heavy clouds of smoke that gathered over some cities, especially in winter, and sometimes brought darkness in the middle of the day. By the turn of the century most major cities had passed (but were not enforcing) smoke abatement laws.

In 1948 one of the worst air pollution disasters in American history occurred when a heavy blanket of smoke settled in around the industrial community of Donora, Pennsylvania, and remained there for five days. After it cleared, twenty people were dead from damage to the respiratory system and 14,000 were ill, some of them with permanent health impairments. At about the same time people began to talk about something called smog — mostly in relation to Los Angeles, where the interaction of sunlight, temperature inversion, and automobile exhaust produced eye irritation and damage to artificial sub-

170

A Bureau of the Budget official reported that "unlike water pollution, air pollution . . . is essentially a local problem." The winds, unaware of any of this, continued to blow across state lines while local governments struggled ineffectually to enforce their pollution control policies.

171

stances such as nylon. According to a recent study, an automobile with smog control equipment emits the following quantities of substances into the air for each 1,000 gallons of gasoline consumed:

EMISSION	QUANTITY (in pounds per 1,000 gallons)
Carbon monoxide	3,200
Organic vapors	200-400
Oxides of nitrogen	20-75
Aldehydes	18
Sulphur compounds	17
Organic acids	2
Ammonia	2
Solids (zinc,	.3
Metallic oxides,	
Carbon)	

Source: John T. Middleton and Diana Clarkson, "Motor Vehicle Pollution Control," *Traffic Quarterly*, April 1961, pp. 306-17.

Automobiles now account for about 60 percent of air pollution in the United States. Other major sources are coal-burning power plants and various industries — petroleum refineries, iron and steel mills, paper mills, phosphate fertilizer plants, and smelters. Each of these pours vast quantities of various pollutants into the air. Oil refining, for example, produces 8.4 billion pounds yearly of particulates, sulfur oxides, hydrocarbons, and carbon monoxide.[69]

The short-term consequences of air pollution, such as its effects on animal and plant life and damage to paint and exterior surfaces, are fairly well known. Long-term consequences, such as the possibility of permanent atmospheric change and contribution to lung ailments, are still being studied and debated. Some climatologists now believe that the cumulative effects of various human activities — farming, industry, driving automobiles — may be causing permanent changes in the air and the weather.[70] There is also a developing technology of deliberate weather control through seeding clouds with silver iodide crystals to produce rainfall, reduce hail and lightning, and lower the wind velocity of hurricanes. The Vietnam War produced the first successful efforts at meteorological warfare, when American planes seeded clouds for rain to interfere with enemy troop movements. In 1975 the United States and Russia negotiated an agreement to refrain from meteorological warfare, another mark of humanity's growing capacity to control nature.

172

[69]John C. Esposito, *Vanishing Air* (New York: Grossman, 1970), p. 70.
[70]See statements by Dr. Reid A. Bryson of the University of Wisconsin Center for Climatic Research, *New York Times*, 15 March 1966, p. 19; and "This World," *San Francisco Chronicle*, 31 March 1974, p. 25.

The effort to deal with the air pollution problem in America closely resembles the situation surrounding water pollution: it is fairly recent; it shows a trend toward increasing involvement of the federal government; and it has not yet produced any net improvement.

Federal interest in air pollution began stirring to life in the 1950s with the Donora disaster and the obvious buildups of smog in several major cities. In 1955 the Air Pollution Control Act was passed, a modest piece of legislation that appropriated money for research and reaffirmed that the primary responsibility for air pollution control lay with the state and local governments. This was consistent with the prevailing view that air pollution was not really an interstate, hence a federal, problem. Health, Education, and Welfare took the position that "instances of troublesome interstate air pollution are few in number," and a Bureau of the Budget official also reported that "unlike water pollution, air pollution . . . is essentially a local problem."[71]

The winds, unaware of any of this, continued to blow across state lines while local governments struggled ineffectually to enforce their pollution control policies against large and politically powerful industrial corporations. Some legislators and officials began to believe that pollution control was a national issue that would have to be resolved through federal enforcement; during the 1960s several new laws gradually extended federal involvement. By the end of that decade the number of air pollution control agencies and the size of federal appropriations had increased, but so had air pollution. In the 1970s a new federal body, the Environmental Protection Agency, took over responsibility for the nationwide programs in air quality control, with mixed results: some kinds of pollution have decreased, and some kinds have increased.

The decreases can be accounted for by enforcement of laws to control burning of wastes, new technology to reduce emissions from factories and power plants, and air pollution control devices on cars. The increases come with more factories and cars, abandonment of restrictions against using coal for generating power in some areas, construction of power plants in previously unpolluted remote areas, and (ironically) from some of the pollution control efforts. Early control devices on automobiles, for example, reduced the release of hydrocarbons and carbon monoxide into the air but produced a rise in nitrogen oxides.

The air, like the water, stands in no danger of being cleaned

173

---

[71]J. Clarence Davies III, *The Politics of Pollution* (New York: Pegasus, 1970), p. 51.

up. The federal government now sets uniform air quality standards for major polllutants — sulfur dioxide, nitrogen dioxide, particulates, carbon monoxide, nonmethane hydrocarbons, photochemical oxidants — and requires state governments to work toward keeping the air within these standards. This suggests that certain levels of pollution are accepted as normal. Whether these levels may be dangerous to life over a long term is not really known. The whole pollution control effort continues to use the air as a waste receptacle — known as "optimum use of air resources" in official jargon — which means maintaining an atmosphere that is quite different from the atmosphere of preindustrial America.

The American System
And so, in many ways, the ecosystem changed. The ultimate effect of England's colonization of America was not only the transplantation of a new human population but also the disappearance or drastic reduction of many plant and animal species, the introduction of new ones, and the alteration of the continent's land and water and air. These changes were not brought about merely to sustain the lives of the new human inhabitants; other human beings had lived on the same land for many thousands of years without altering it to a comparable extent. Instead these changes were necessary parts of a new kind of life system that was emerging on the continent, a pattern of interaction among human beings — and between human beings and the environment — that was marked by such activities as commercial agriculture, manufacturing, trade, and finance. To serve such purposes as these the forests were cleared, the seeds sown, the domestic animals bred and tended, the canals dug, the harbors dredged, the highways built. This economy became something different from what had existed in the Old World (Europeans had never traded land the way Americans did, and land trading was a central part of the new system). Nevertheless this new economy was essentially derived from the European society that had generated the commercial systmm over long centuries of historical change. The transformation of the American continent was a major evolutionary upheaval that decreed the fate of many living things. Although it had genetic consequences, it was first of all the product of cultural DNA. The passenger pigeon became extinct not because it was ill-adapted to its environment but because human beings had come to its environment and changed it; they changed it because their values held such change to be

desirable and their technological achievements — another part of the cultural heritage — made them capable of bringing it about. We see, then, that cultural evolution affected not only the development of the human species but that of other life forms as well.

Another aspect of this cultural heritage to which I will now turn is the legacy of institutional forms that were available to the American settlers. These were an essential part of the new life system that was taking form.

4

Arrangements
of Power

Man evolved physically as a result of genetic-somatic changes, with the survival of those which best fitted the prevailing circumstances. Man's fitness for survival has been amply tested under circumstances heretofore dictated by nature. Now, however, man creates the circumstances in which he finds himself.

JONAS SALK. *Man Unfolding*

The enormous task of transplanting millions of people to the American continent, organizing them into new patterns of life, and meanwhile transforming the continent into an artificial ecosystem was possible only through large-scale cooperation within the framework of institutions. Political institutions are strategies of adaptation whereby a people organize to use their environment and distribute its resources among themselves. Political institutions are also arrangements of power, with the ability to mold the shape of human lives and decree the evolutionary fate of countless other living things.

The forms of human institutions are part of the content of cultural heredity; we build on the accumulated experience of the past and on our culture's ideas of the goals and purposes of life. The American people made generous use of the storehouse of human experience. Forms and concepts distilled over thousands of years of human struggle — the nation-state, parliamentary procedure, separation of powers — were adopted and applied. We revere the Founding Fathers as inventors, but they deserve equal credit as discriminating borrowers; there is scarcely a line in the United States Constitution that does not echo back through colonial charters, English politics and jurisprudence, and the writings of political philosophers.

Although our institutional structures owe much to this cultural heritage, there has also been a prodigious amount of innovating along the way. There had to be. The American nation came into being at a time of accelerating cultural and technological change. It was, in fact, a product of such changes, and history did not stand still for a leisurely consolidation of the basic arrangement that had emerged from the Constitutional Convention of 1787. Additions of people and land required admitting new states and creating new counties and urban gov-

178

Jonas Salk, *Man Unfolding* (New York: Harper & Row, 1972), p. 124.

ernments. Advances in transportation and communication changed the rules that had affected the basic day-to-day operations of government for centuries. Other technological developments brought forth new industries, new concentrations of power and wealth that called for new laws and administrative agencies. The nation became bigger, more crowded, richer, more industrialized, and more complicated; its institutional arrangements did the best they could to keep pace with this headlong current of change.

The U.S. Constitution: An Economic and Ecological Document
The human species, in adapting to different environments, has developed many different kinds of social systems, and by no means all of these have been organized on the basis of what we call commerce, or the production of goods in surplus quantities for the purpose of trade. A subsistence agricultural society or a hunting society may engage in some exchanges of goods and services without making trade a central and indispensable part of its existence, or without embarking on the quest for new markets and increased productivity. When a society does embrace commerce it begins to interact with its environment in different ways, moving resources across greater distances. This alters the environment and also the society itself, as people are organized into new relationships for production. New institutional arrangements become necessary. In Europe the institution of feudalism crumbled with the increase of trade and gave way to nation-states; the nation-states, vigorously extending their commercial activities, became world empires.

The value system that evolved in Western Europe during the colonial era was marked by a great emphasis on commerce as a fundamental human activity. Commercialism was the driving force of England's colonization project in the New World, and it took its place in the value system of the new American population. This value system, which Max Weber called "the Protestant ethic," was a unique blending of materialism with piety that made profit seeking — not simple greed but organized commercial activity — a virtue. Out of the religious upheavals of the seventeenth century, Weber said, had emerged a new set of morals permitting people to go about the business of acquiring money with a clear conscience:

A specifically bourgeois economic ethic had grown up. With the consciousness of standing in the fullness of God's grace and being fully blessed by Him, the bourgeois businessman, as long as he remained within the bounds of formal correctness, as long

179

as his moral conduct was spotless and the use to which he put his wealth was not objectionable, could follow his pecuniary interests as he would and feel that he was fulfilling a duty in doing so. The power of religious asceticism provided him in addition with sober, conscientious, and unusually industrious workmen, who clung to their work as to a life purpose willed by God.[1]

We are told by Charles Beard and more recent historians that the U.S. Constitution was an economic document: the men who wrote it were prosperous entrepreneurs, and the new federal government was specifically intended to serve as the institutional framework for orderly commerce.[2] This intent is clearly expressed in Article I, Section 8 of the Constitution, in which Congress is granted powers to levy taxes, borrow money, regulate foreign and interstate commerce, establish bankruptcy laws, coin money, fix standards of weights and measure, secure patents and copyrights, establish post offices and post roads, and punish pirates — all measures calculated to protect economic stability.

The Constitution was also an ecological document: it expressed a certain set of cultural values and, in creating the framework for a national economy, it also created the framework for exploiting the continent's resources through a cooperative effort to channel its latent natural energies into human systems of industry and agriculture. The Founding Fathers did not yet appreciate the full potential of the territory they possessed, but they knew it was a rich resource (that knowledge, after all, was what had spurred the whole colonization enterprise to begin with) and they had some specific ideas about how to use it. The uses they envisioned were the uses of commerce and industry and farming for profit. This meant that goods would be produced in quantity, merchants would travel between the states, and American ships would carry American surpluses abroad and return with cargoes of consumer goods and industrial supplies. It meant also that the government would consolidate its boundaries and make it safe for Americans to seek out the mineral and agricultural wealth of the land without interference. All these activities required an institutional arrangement to protect them; the federal government was precisely that. The Constitution laid down the ground rules whereby the Americans could continue, with greater efficiency and less interference, the process of transforming the continent

[1]Max Weber, *The Protestant Ethic and the Spirit of Capitalism*, trans. Talcott Parsons (New York: Scribner's, 1958), pp. 176-77.
[2]Charles Beard, *An Economic Interpretation of the Constitution of the United States* (New York: Macmillan, 1913).

180

We are told by Charles Beard and more recent historians that the U.S. Constitution was an economic document: the men who wrote it were prosperous entrepreneurs, and the new federal government was specifically intended to serve as the institutional framework for orderly commerce.

from a forest wilderness into a densely populated industrial society, whose wealth would accrue to a new elite of bourgeois businessmen.

With the adoption of the Constitution the Americans effectively took possession of the land they inhabited and created the basis for future expansion and growth. It is hard to believe that the weak association of states under the Articles of Confederation could have survived its own internal factionalism, withstood the threats of the various European powers that were still interested in exploiting the resources of the North American continent, and handled the acquisition of new territories and the influx of new population. To bring all this about it was necessary for the thirteen states to become a nation.

The concept of the nation-state was an important part of the cultural heritage of the American population. The nation-states of Europe were fairly recent inventions, consolidations of land and people under monarchs who could successfully maintain control over the nobility and resist the political aspirations of the Roman Catholic church. The main theoretical support of the nation-state was sovereignty, meaning that no external authority could exert any power whatever within the boundaries of the political unit. The idea of sovereignty was well understood among the authors of the Constitution and presented a ticklish political issue. In response to the fears of some, sovereignty was nominally retained by the states, but the fact of the matter (as later historical developments have made clear) was that the new union was a nation-state. The diligent merchandising of the continent's resources, which Americans were engaged in, could not be expected to proceed safely without the protection of national power. This was brought out by John Jay in one of the *Federalist* papers:

With France and with Britain we are rivals in the fisheries, and can supply their markets cheaper than they can themselves, notwithstanding any efforts to prevent it by bounties on their own or duties on foreign fish.

With them and with most other European nations we are rivals in navigation and the carrying trade; and we shall deceive ourselves if we suppose that any of them will rejoice to see it flourish. . . .

In the trade to China and India, we interfere with more than one nation. . . .

The extension of our own commerce in our own vessels cannot give pleasure to any nations who possess territories on or near this continent, because the cheapness and excellence of our pro-

ductions, added to the circumstances of vicinity, and the enter-
prise and address of our merchants and navigators, will give us a
greater share in the advantages which those territories afford,
than consists with the wishes or policy of their respective
sovereigns.[3]

These commercial activities, Jay argued, could lead at any time
to military action (such being the practice of nations), and the
Americans stood a far better chance of going their profitable
way without interference if they were united under a national
government of their own.

The nation-state model was one of several forms of social
organization available to the Americans. Others were colonial
status, which they had forcibly rejected; loose confederacy,
which they had tried and found wanting; and separate sovereign independence of the states, which appealed strongly to
some. The choice that they made was the kind of choice that can
be made only by a society at a fairly high level of cultural
evolution, which has at its disposal a repository of knowledge
about the experience of different societies with different governmental forms. In their choosing, however, the Founding
Fathers did not range too far from the mainstream of their
cultural heritage. They adopted the principles of their leading
political philosophers, many of the structures and procedures of
the parent government, and the nation-state form that had
already been adopted by the three powers whose presence was
most visible in the New World — England, France, and Spain.
There was some reluctance to adopt the nation-state model;
this flowed from another readily available item of historical
data, namely, the knowledge that the other nation-states were
monarchies with a built-in predisposition toward tyrannical
interference with the rights and property of individuals.

One of the most important cultural values built into the
American system was private property. Anthropological research has revealed an enormous variety of ways that different
peoples relate to the land and its products, conceptualize the
rights and obligations of ownership. Many societies have existed without monetary systems, others without private ownership of land, still others with scarcely any idea of private
property. Such value systems — and we cannot describe them
all as simply primitive — would never have produced the kind of
economic and political arrangements that we have.

Our concepts of property had evolved over centuries of ex-

183

[3]James Madison, Alexander Hamilton, and John Jay, *The Federalist* (New York: Modern Library, 1937), pp. 18-19.

184

perience in Western Europe, particularly in England, where conflicts with the monarchy had generated some strong convictions that were expressed in English law and political theory. The English philosopher John Locke, whose works were especially influential in America, had consistently spoken of human rights in terms of human *property* rights, and of freedom in terms of freedom from capricious abuse of private property by government. In his *Second Treatise of Government*, which was the theoretical basis for the Declaration of Independence,[4] Locke advanced such propositions as these:

Man being born, as has been proved, with a title to perfect freedom and an uncontrolled enjoyment of all the rights and privileges of the law of nature, equally with any other man, or number of men in the world, hath by nature a power ... to preserve his property, that is, his life, liberty and estate. ... Men unite into societies that they may have the united strength of the whole society to secure and defend their properties.

A major cause of the rebellion against the English crown was its interference with free trade and property rights in the colonies; consequently, a main concern of the framers of the Constitution was to make sure that the new government would not similarly interfere. The framers did not do their job to the satisfaction of all the states. The Bill of Rights, which deals explicitly with property in Articles III, IV, V, VII, and VIII, was created to remedy the defect.[5]

The *Federalist* papers reveal the importance of property to the political thought underlying the Constitution. Resources were being exploited in many different ways, and this was creating divergent economic interests that would have to be reconciled within some orderly institutional framework if the whole enterprise of developing the land for the American population's benefit were to continue. James Madison made the classic statement of this in *Federalist* No. 10:

The most common and durable source of factions has been the various and unequal distribution of property. Those who hold and those who are without property have ever formed distinct interests in society. Those who are creditors, and those who are

> A strand running through all the various factional and sectional differences was the fundamental division between those who favored a strong central government and those who wanted either a very limited one or none at all. The centralists tended to be urban, northern, oriented to business and industry; their opponents tended to be rural, southern, oriented to agriculture.

[4]See Joe Allman and Walt Anderson, *Evaluating Democracy* (Santa Monica, Calif.: Goodyear, 1974), p. 70.
[5]Of particular importance is the provision of Article V: "No person shall be ... deprived of life, liberty, or property without due process of law; nor shall private property be taken for public use, without just compensation." This provision has been applied in many court cases involving zoning and other restrictions on land use. See Fred Bosselman et al., *The Taking Issue: An Analysis of the Constitutional Limits of Land Use Control* (Washington, D.C.: U.S. Government Printing Office, 1973).

debtors, fall under a like discrimination. A landed interest, a manufacturing interest, a mercantile interest, a moneyed interest, with many lesser interests, grow up of necessity in civilized nations, and divide them into different classes, actuated by different sentiments and views. The regulation of these various and interfering interests forms the principal task of modern legislation, and involves the spirit of party and faction in the necessary and ordinary operations of government.[6]

In practice the Founding Fathers were much more concerned about mediating between the various kinds of property interests than between those having property and those having none at all. There were extensive debates in the Constitutional Convention about property qualifications for voting, which missed becoming a part of the Constitution only because the delegates could not agree on what *kind* of qualifications (land, shares, money, and so forth) ought to be imposed. They agreed to leave it up to the states, all of which had property qualifications of one sort or another. In general the delegates were not at all reluctant to disenfranchise the propertyless, who were, of course, the major part of the population. One delegate spoke of property qualifications as a "necessary defense against the dangerous influence of those multitudes without property and without principle, with which our country like all others will in time abound," while another with a good deal of foresight warned: "Give the votes to the people who have no property and they will sell them to the rich who will be able to buy them."[7]

185

The Constitution gave form and institutional support to the basic ideas about property that had developed in Europe's commercial society, and it established the ground rules for political competition among the various propertied classes that were emerging in America. In so doing it provided an orderly framework for dealing with America itself — its land, its minerals, its plant life, its wild and domestic animals — as property. The ancient religious tradition of stewardship held that the land belonged to human beings, who would use it in human ways. To the writers of the Constitution, the obvious unwillingness of the Indians to use the land in a "civilized" manner established that they were not the sort of people God had in mind when He entrusted the world to human care. The successful revolution against England and the legal tradition of national sovereignty guaranteed that no other nation could inter-

[6]Madison, Hamilton, and Jay, *The Federalist*, p. 56.
[7]Thomas R. Dye and L. Harmon Zeigler, *The Irony of Democracy* (Belmont, Calif.: Duxbury Press, Wadsworth, 1971), pp. 39-41.

fere in domestic policy. Thus fortified by the Constitution, the Americans consolidated their claim to the territory and began anew the cooperative project of shaping it to fit their needs.

Federalism and Internal Improvements

The various modes of exploitation of America's resources by its new resident population produced several distinct forms of private property and thus several distinct economic interest groups, what the *Federalist* writers called "factions." There was much discord and competition among these factions, but there was also a prevailing recognition of the need for an institutional arrangement to facilitate interstate commerce and provide united military protection. They had chosen to create a nation-state, but they knew well that a nation-state is a formidable concentration of power, and there was a widespread fear that one faction might gain full control of this power and use it to the disadvantage of other factions. The best available safeguard against this was to diffuse power, separate it among different branches of the government.

To achieve this the delegates to the Constitutional Convention drew heavily upon the past political experience of Western civilization. Several separation-of-powers arrangements had been tried in ancient Greece and Rome, and their successes and failures had been extensively documented by historians and philosophers. In the era of the Roman republic, Polybius had written of the interaction among the consuls, the people, and the senate, in which "each part of the state has the power of hampering the others or cooperating with them."[8] By the time of the Enlightenment this concept had evolved into an abstract principle used by Montesquieu in his attempt to build a general science of politics. Failure to separate powers, warned Montesquieu, led inevitably to tyranny: "There would be an end to everything if the same men or body — whether of the nobles or of the people — should exercise these three powers: that of enacting laws, that of carrying them out; and that of trying the cases of individuals."[9]

The United States Constitution instituted not only the legislative-executive-judiciary separation but also a further division of powers between the federal government and the state governments. The federal system was an ingenious innovation and a necessary one, if there were to be a nation-state at all. Institutions have rarely been eager to legislate themselves

[8]Polybius, *The Histories*, Vol. 3, trans. W. R. Paton (Cambridge, Mass.: Harvard University Press, 1923).
[9]Montesquieu, *The Spirit of the Laws*, Vol. 1, trans. Thomas Nugent (New York: Colonial Press, 1899), pp. 151-52.

out of existence; the thirteen independent states were no exception. They delegated to the new national government such powers as they considered minimal, and wrote into the Bill of Rights a guarantee that all other powers were reserved to the states.

A strand running through all the various factional and sectional differences was the fundamental division between those who favored a strong central government and those who wanted either a very limited one or none at all. The centralists tended to be urban, northern, oriented to business and industry; their opponents tended to be rural, southern, oriented to agriculture. These two groups expressed different visions of what the new nation was to become. The centralist ideal was expressed in Alexander Hamilton's image of a prosperous and activist government, closely allied with the nation's financial elites and able to hold its own in world affairs; the alternative was manifested in Thomas Jefferson's vision of a nation of small farmers, self-sufficient and remote from the corrupting influences of finance and politics. These views represented two different patterns of adaptation to the American land. The course of events has favored the Hamiltonian vision.

Hamilton's policies as first secretary of the treasury were directly aimed toward the goal of strengthening the federal government — notably through establishing the Bank of the United States, an action not explicitly authorized in the Constitution. The landmark Supreme Court case of *McCulloch* v. *Maryland* upheld the legality of Hamilton's action under a broad interpretation of the Constitution, which allowed the federal government to adopt measures not explicitly within its delegated realm of responsibilities as long as they were "necessary and proper" to the execution of its constitutional powers. The same decision also established the principle of judicial review, meaning that a state law that conflicts with a national activity can be declared unconstitutional — another consolidation of authority in the central government.

Ironically, Jefferson also contributed greatly to the development of a strong central government. His major accomplishment in this respect was the purchase of the Louisiana Territory. Purchasing land was another act that was not within the federal government's explicit powers, and the event helped in many ways to transform American loyalties and institutions. The new states were in a sense the creations of the federal government. Their populations did not develop the sense of allegiance to state-before-nation that had often existed in the older states. There was another, much more tangible, result of the massive land acquisition: the lands were owned by the federal government, and they were thus a source of power. Long before the federal government began making grants of money, it was in the business of making grants of land. Then as now federal grants served federal policies.

In spite of the ideological differences between the advocates of strong central government and the defenders of state sovereignty, there was an overriding commitment to the development of American resources, which resulted in cooperation between the federal government and the states. Daniel Elazar's research into the actual workings of federalism in the nineteenth century has revealed that, while all the ideological bickering went on, the federal and state governments in fact worked together rather well at the common task of adapting America. This was carried out through a multitude of "internal improvement" projects in which governmental agencies participated:

The term "internal improvement" covered a multitude of specific problems, all basically concerned with facilitating the geographic and material expansion of the American people, while at the same time binding the various sections of the country more closely together as one political and economic system. Roads, canals, railroads, harbors, public buildings and institutions, river improvements, land reclamation, mineral production and extraction, agricultural development, and the creation of a banking system to finance all these projects, constituted the internal improvement programs of the day. All demanded a share of the interest, energy, and money, both public and private, of the expanding nation. Internal improvements provided a major portion of the intergovernmental programs that emerged during the century, simply because they provided a major portion of all governmental activity.[10]

Elazar identifies three different periods in this huge cooperative effort. In each period different institutional arrangements were used toward the basic purpose of converting the American environment to serve as a more effective vehicle for commercial activity. In the earliest period, the joint-stock company was the most commonly used device. For a project of this nature—for example, the Chesapeake and Ohio canal—a company would be created and its shares purchased by the federal government, a number of states and cities, and private investors. The federal

188

[10]Daniel Elazar, *The American Partnership* (Chicago: University of Chicago Press, 1962), p. 298.

government would provide various kinds of technical assistance such as surveying routes and assigning specialists from the Army Corps of Engineers, and would continue to oversee the project's operation as a major stockholder.

As the focus of development turned to the new "public land" states created out of the Louisiana Territory and other acquisitions, land-grant programs became the predominant form of intergovernmental cooperation. One marker of this transition was the demise of the greatest of all the joint-stock companies, the United States Bank, during the Andrew Jackson administration. As American energies shifted to developing the frontier, and as the federal government found itself in possession of incredible amounts of land, the practice of granting public land was used as a way of facilitating internal improvements. Typically in the construction of a transportation facility such as a highway, canal, or railroad, the federal government would grant the right-of-way and also additional sections of land that could then be sold to finance the project. Initially the federal land grants were made almost exclusively to the states; after 1862, as the idea of a transcontinental railroad took hold on the American imagination, the federal government began the practice of making land grants directly to private entrepreneurs. In so doing the government not only got the railroads built but also contributed to the rise of several gigantic corporations, a number of multimillionaires, and a powerful new interest group. As often happens, environmental alteration and resource distribution resulted from a public policy not explicitly concerned with either.

Elazar marks the beginning of the third period of federalism at about 1913, as the federal government shifted from the grant of land to the grant of cash. This was really only the beginning of a gradual transition that became more pronounced in the era of the New Deal.

The term "New Deal" was coined by Franklin D. Roosevelt at the beginning of his 1932 campaign for the presidency, when he promised "a new deal for the American people." Coming at a time when the American commercial system was on the verge of a total collapse, the Roosevelt administration launched itself immediately into the most intensive period of institutional innovation in American history. Scholars are still arguing about whether the New Deal had any significant influence on the great economic depression it was designed to combat, but there is general agreement on one point: the New Deal transformed American federalism by greatly extending the federal government's activist role in guiding the workings of the

Although land was
the magnet that
drew immigrants to
America, city life
was the reality that
awaited most of
them.

191

economy. Also, although this effect has been less clearly understood, the New Deal carried the government a giant step farther in the direction of taking over active management of the environment.

During the celebrated Hundred Days of the first Roosevelt administration, the Congress approved fifteen major pieces of legislation aimed at reviving the economy. Among these were the Emergency Farm Mortgage Act, a stimulus to agricultural production; the Tennessee Valley Authority Act, launching the greatest single ecological management project in human history; and the establishment of the Civilian Conservation Corps, which resulted in the employment of several thousand young men and the planting of several billion trees.

The New Deal also created a new Public Works Administration (PWA), whose mission was to stimulate employment and the economy through an energetic program of internal improvements. Arthur Schlesinger, Jr., summarized the PWA's accomplishments in his history of the New Deal:

It built roads and highways, sewage systems and water systems, gas plants and electric power plants; schools and courthouses, hospitals and jails; dams and canals, reclamation and irrigation projects, levees and flood control projects, bridges and viaducts, docks and tunnels. . . . PWA made it possible . . . to put up the Triborough bridge in New York. PWA gave Chicago (on the loan-grant arrangement) a new sewage system, Kansas City a great municipal auditorium, Denver a water supply system, the University of Washington a set of buildings, the Muskingum Valley of Ohio a flood control project. It rebuilt the schools of Los Angeles after the earthquake of 1933, and it built roads and bridges connecting Key West with the mainland of Florida. It helped build the Tennessee Valley Authority, the Grand Coulee and Bonneville Dams on the Columbia, Fort Peck Dam on the Upper Missouri, and Boulder Dam on the Colorado.[11]

The PWA spent $6 billion during the 1930s. This money went into the economy in the form of salaries for workers and profits for stockholders in construction companies and production industries. The legacy of those years, says Schlesinger, was "a splendidly improved national estate."[12] Contemporary critics of big-dam building question whether all of the PWA's projects were in fact improvements of the environment, but there is no

192

[11]Arthur Schlesinger, Jr., *The Coming of the New Deal* (Boston: Houghton Mifflin, 1959), p. 288.
[12]Ibid.

question about its importance as an example of a new direction in federal policy. "Big spending" by the federal government was denounced as unsound economic and political policy by opponents of the Roosevelt administration, but big spending has continued to be a solid fixture of American government through subsequent administrations, both Democratic and Republican.

The practice of annually appropriating large sums of federal money for projects to rebuild the environment has generated a powerful and apparently unstoppable momentum. Large bureaucratic institutions such as the Army Corps of Engineers and the Bureau of Reclamation depend for their continued existence on new projects and are adept at getting multibillion-dollar appropriations from the Congress. For the individual congressman, a federal public works project in the home district is a plum that can bring in several million dollars and perhaps make the difference at election time — hence the phenomenon of "pork barrel" appropriations bills with something for very nearly everybody.

One of the products of this bureaucratic and political momentum is continual environmental alteration; another is a concentration of power at the federal level. The states and local governments have extensive powers over environmental management in areas such as zoning and administration of public utilities; still the federal involvement tends to grow. The power of the central government has been increasing at the expense of the "sovereignty" of the states for two centuries. State and local authorities frequently resent this trend at the same time that they perpetuate it by seeking the federal grants that inevitably come with policy-making conditions attached.

Many people disapprove of the central government's power, but hardly anyone doubts that it has been growing and will probably continue to do so. This is true of all areas of governmental activity, not just those I have described as environmental management. Less clearly understood is that environmental management activities are also a *cause* of this growth. The first round of internal improvement programs were, as Elazar said, basically concerned with facilitating the geographic and material expansion of the American people, while at the same time binding the various sections of the country more closely together as one political and economic system. That goal has been rather successfully reached. A result of the achievement is one system — not fifty different systems, but one system.

If the American people had chosen an adaptive system along the lines of the Jeffersonian vision of independent farmers,

Urban areas have
flowed together into
supercities, called
"conurbations" or
"megalopolises," that
spread across city
limits, county lines,
even state bound-
aries.

there would have been far fewer pressures tending to erode the power of the separate states. But the choice was to build an energetic commercial society that carried on intensive trade between the states; that was what the road building and canal digging were all about. The growth of interstate commerce naturally fed the institution that had been given the power to regulate it — the federal government. And at a later stage of commercial development, as industrialization and urbanization increased the strain on the common systems of air and water the federal government was turned to as the logical level at which to attack what had become a national problem.

Deliberate environmental alteration becomes big business and big government and gives birth to powerful federal bureaucracies such as the Army Corps of Engineers. Accidental environmental alteration like pollution creates new bureaucracies such as the Environmental Protection Agency. In either case the course of development of a commercial society does not seem to favor the autonomy of smaller units of government.

Regionalism and the Urban Problem

America was occupied during a major part of its history with an unprecedented amount of activity in drawing boundary lines and setting up new governmental structures. The spread of the American population across the continent required the creation of a multitude of regional arrangements for the purpose of administering public works projects, education, law enforcement, and tax collection. Thus the vast American wilderness was divided into territories, states, counties, and cities. Rough frontier towns would evolve, often with remarkable speed, into centers of government: recently arrived citizens would organize themselves into electorates and select administrators, magistrates, and legislators.

The structure used to organize the American wilderness borrowed basic units of government that had grown up in Europe over the centuries. The county, an administrative demarcation that had been in use in England since the time of the Norman invasion (and before that in similar form as the shire), seemed equally suitable to American needs. Several colonies were divided into counties well before they were settled; in some cases the initial work of mapping county lines was done in England by people who had never seen the areas they were dividing up.

One peculiarity of the division of American space into administrative units is the fact that, although the institutions have a general similarity to those in Europe on which they were modeled, they developed in a reversed sequence of events. In Europe the populations were there first and the institutional forms developed later. In America political boundaries were generally laid out in territories populated mainly by Indians, in the planners' expectation that the area would eventually be filled with Americans.

The laying out of American political units depended heavily on the abstract symbolic system of lines of latitude and longitude, and less on traditional natural boundaries such as rivers or mountain ranges. State and county lines run across the American map in straight lines that clearly reveal the method of creation; states and counties have a tendency to come in rectangular forms. The people who drew the boundaries of American political units were interested in creating demarcations that could be reasonably administered by state and county governments; they were also concerned with providing for the orderly transfer of land ownership. The granting of land by the federal government to the states and private corporations, and the sale of land by speculators and mobile frontiersmen were, as I have mentioned elsewhere, main activities of American life. Dividing land into sections and drawing neat rectangular political boundary lines were parts of the same process and the same way of thinking about the proper human relationship to geographic space.

The size of administrative units was determined by the life needs and technological capabilities of nineteenth-century rural America. A county was normally laid out so that the county seat would be within a day's travel by horse-drawn wagon and thus provide an accessible center where farmers could come to transact business. Normally county seats became centers of commerce as well, since the same trip could conveniently include banking and purchasing supplies. This potential for commerce was not lost on local businessmen and promoters in towns that might aspire to the designation of county seat; sometimes conflicting claims to that status were bitterly disputed, with two or more towns making the claim at the same time. A nineteenth-century plains newspaper editor wrote that "If the people of Southwest Kansas have a passion for anything that cannot be satiated short of possession, it is their hungry desire for county seats. Most of the counties have three, and the residents anxiously, madly long for more."[13]

The counties are normally entrusted with responsibility for providing law enforcement, firefighting, and similar services

[13]Vance Johnson, *Heaven's Tableland* (New York: Farrar, Straus, 1947), p. 146.

for areas outside the city limits, and also for certain local improvement projects such as public roads to permit automobile access into farm areas. In areas that have remained predominantly rural, the original functions of counties are still carried out approximately as they were in the last century. However, most counties contain areas of urban growth, and some counties are now overwhelmingly urban. County government has changed markedly in these areas in response to population growth; still further changes can be expected to come about. Even in rural areas, technological change has rendered the size of counties obsolete: most farmers can now reach their state capital as easily as their ancestors could reach the county seat a century ago.

In America, despite the early commitment to agriculture, cities appeared soon and developed rapidly. By 1700 there were already five distinctly urban centers: Boston, Charles Town, Newport, New York, and Philadelphia; by 1860, before the Civil War brought a temporary pause to immigration, there were nine cities with populations of over 100,000.[14] From 1820 onward the rate of urban growth has mushroomed while the rate of rural growth has declined.

The early American cities served certain purposes that were necessary supports to the advance on the wilderness; they were harbors, storehouses, fortresses, and communications centers. As they grew they became centers of commerce, creating tension between urban and rural populations. Farmers and trappers resented the power of urban businessmen; city dwellers resented the dominance of country representatives in the provincial assemblies and the high taxes levied on urban property. The urban-rural split was a basic factional division in the emerging nation and has been a familiar feature of American politics down to the present time.

Each wave of immigration increased the population of the major seaboard cities and brought new consumers of basic goods and new workers for manufacturing and construction. I mentioned earlier that, although land was the magnet that drew immigrants to America, city life was the reality that awaited most of them. The cities were the ports of entry, the cities contained neighborhoods of countrymen and relatives, and the cities offered opportunities for employment. Many industrial skills in occupations such as mining or textile work were readily transferable to the New World, whereas agricultural skills were not; peasants from Europe frequently lacked

196

---

[14]Constance McLaughlin Green, *The Rise of Urban America* (New York: Harper & Row, 1965), p. 74.

either the money to buy land or the techniques for farming under new conditions, especially on the frontier. Many immigrants did become farmers in America, but many more remained in the cities; some of them arrived in America and lived out their lives without ever traveling outside the port city.

For these new city dwellers survival meant dependence on different sources for basic human necessities. Food, shelter, and water were now obtained not from the earth and the nearby environment but from political and commercial institutions. These immigrants had moved, whether they knew it or not, into new and much more complex life systems, making the leap in a few weeks' time over centuries of cultural evolution. And while the new city dwellers were adjusting themselves to this vast social organism, the cities themselves were growing and reaching out ever farther for building materials, energy sources, water and food supplies. The rapid growth of American cities recapitulated the long history of urban growth since the beginning of civilization.

The first primitive cities probably appeared in agricultural societies rather than hunting and gathering societies, and they had to exist in close symbiosis with the lands around them. The first cities were usually located close to agricultural spaces and were constructed of whatever materials the local terrain afforded. They took in the materials their populations needed for survival from the immediately surrounding life system, and the city's wastes were collected and returned to the soil as fertilizer. At a later stage of cultural evolution cities became larger, their technological capacities more advanced, and their ecological impact more wide ranging and complex. Lewis Mumford's description of the development of Rome tells us something about the problems of modern American cities.

Rome of the Seven Hills is an acropolis type of city, formed by a cluster of villages united for defense; and the plain of the Tiber was the original seat of their agriculture. The surplus population of this region conquered first the neighboring territories of the Etruscans and then those of more distant lands. By systematic expropriation, Rome brought wheat, olive oil, dried fish, and pottery back to the original site to sustain its growing population. To facilitate the movement of its legions and speed up the process of administration, it carved roads through the landscape with triumphant disregard of the nature of the terrain. These roads and viaducts went hand in hand with similar works of engineering, the aqueducts and reservoirs necessary to bring water to Rome. By short-circuiting the flow of water from moun-

tainside to sea, the city monopolized for its special uses a consid-erable amount of the runoff; and, to offset some of the effects of metropolitan overcrowding, it created a cult of the public bath that in turn imposed a heavy drain upon the fuel supplied by the near-by forest areas. The advance of technology, with central hot-air heating, characteristically hastened the process of de-forestation. ... Meanwhile, the sewers of Rome, connected to public toilets, polluted the Tiber without returning the precious mineral contents to the soil, though even in Imperial Rome dung farmers still collected most of the night soil from the great tenements of the proletariat. At this stage the symbiotic relation turns into a parasitic one; the cycle of imbalance begins, and the mere massing of the demand in a single center results in denuda-tions and desiccations elsewhere. The more complete the urbani-zation, the more definite is the release from natural limitations; the more highly the city seems developed as an independent entity, the more fatal are the consequences for the territory it dominates.[15]

Rome's extension of its ecological support system was paral-leled by, and inseparable from, an extension of its institutional structures: the city became an empire, and along the way the democracy became a monarchy. The development of American urban centers has some analogies to that of Rome (every American city is in some ways an empire), but their growth has taken place at a higher stage of human evolution, under differ-ent cultural and environmental conditions, and at greater rates of speed. The daily biological existence of the modern city dweller is sustained by an incredibly complex and far-reaching support system, and the institutional technology of modern urban government has reached a level of complexity and power that would boggle the mind of any Caesar.

Although city governments are creations of the states, most cities have enjoyed a considerable amount of home-rule au-tonomy, actually becoming formidable concentrations of power to modify the environment and distribute resources. The cities had their own internal improvement projects in the form of public works and utilities which were generally carried out by private operators. Awarding contracts for public works proj-ects are the urban machine's standard source of wealth. All the technological marvels of the growing American city — street lights and sewers, pavements and transportation systems — were built by private operators with public money. To win a

[15]Lewis Mumford, *The City in History* (New York: Harcourt, Brace & World, 1961), p. 388.

The modern city is probably the closest we have yet come to the mechanistic image of a society: it is the great automat whose technology produces water, heat, and light as if by magic, and whose stores stock all the resources needed to sustain the physical body as well as a great number of things not needed at all.

199

contract for such a project meant profitable business for the private operator, and kickbacks to the officials who controlled the contracts were an accepted part of business life.

At another level, the machines doled out small business loans, jobs, and gifts of food to the masses in return for votes. The system helped the immigrants survive in the cities, it created new elites of wealth and power, and it guided the transformation of American cities into the massive, artificial life systems they have become.

The machines were a natural expression of industrializing America (the choice of the word *machine* to describe such institutions is itself significant) and were also part of the change in the ethnic composition of the American population, which was taking place as a result of immigration. The old political elites were displaced by leaders from the new ethnic groups and either withdrew from city politics entirely or occupied themselves in support of "reform" or "good government" movements.

Reform movements and welfare programs gradually whittled away at the machines and although some traces of old-style machine politics persist, the governing of American cities is now done through institutional arrangements that do their best to look like technocracy — rule by experts. Public agencies are staffed by career bureaucrats and high-level decisions in many cities are made by city managers who profess a "nonpolitical" expertise in urban administration.

The depoliticizing of city government was possible mainly because business elites have so totally dominated politics in American cities that they could reasonably appear to represent a consensus about what cities needed and how they should be governed. In city after city across America, administrative decisions are made by bureaucrats on the basis of policy guidelines formulated by elective bodies composed of local businessmen, realtors, developers, and others who share their basic values. The new-style technocratic city government is still a way of carrying out the basic imperatives of a commercial and industrial society. We are now somewhere in the process of evolving still newer styles of urban government, brought about by new patterns of ethnic distribution in the cities and by patterns of urban growth that make it increasingly difficult to say where the city ends and the country begins.

The basic units of government — states, counties, and cities — grew out of the cultural heritage, out of the nineteenth century's communications and transportation technology, and out of some basic assumptions about country and city as two distinct forms of human settlement. But urban growth has taken place in such a way that it is no longer possible to identify the American city as a distinct entity except by reference to its arbitrary political boundaries. Urban areas have flowed together into supercities, called "conurbations" or "megalopolises," that spread across city limits, county lines, even state boundaries.

Megalopolises began with the coming of the railroads and the first suburbs, which made it possible for segments of the urban middle classes to take up a new life style that combined some of the best features of city and country living. Suburban growth was accelerated by the next technological advance, streetcars, and still more by the mass manufacture of private automobiles. The early suburbs were fairly recognizable as distinct communities and formed their own city governments. Other urban developments, especially after World War II, crept across the countryside in meaningless patterns that placed severe burdens on traditional governmental forms. Some of these urban areas were incorporated as new cities, some remained under the jurisdiction of the county governments, others were annexed by the cities.

In some cases, then, older American cities became encircled fragments of the greater urban area, usually with concentrations of black and other minority group residents coexisting uneasily within the city limits alongside the remnants of the "new immigrant" comunities from Eastern Europe; white middle and upper classes resided in the suburbs beyond. In other cases county governments have had to travel a long distance from the original rural purpose and take on new responsibilities of urban administration. One innovation of this sort was the Lakewood Plan devised by Los Angeles County, wherein the county not only provides fire and police protection in unincorporated areas but also acts as a contractor to supply these services at a cost to new cities, which are thus spared one of the burdens of civic administration. Another innovation was the county federation plan adopted in Dade County, Florida — an echo of the creation of the federal government by the thirteen states. In Dade County the cities created a countywide metropolitan government, to which they assigned functions such as fire and police protection, water and sewage, transportation, comprehensive growth planning, and slum clearance. In other cases cities have extended their limits, annexing suburbs and unincorporated areas and creating in the process some exceedingly strange urban shapes.

State governments have responded to the new problems of

The oil crisis of 1973, when the intricate interactions of multinational corporations and Near Eastern potentates closed down American service stations, gave urban America the first uncomfortable hint that the urban machinery, indeed the national machinery, literally does not run on its own fuel.

Hills that the city dweller never sees are carved open to produce coal for power plants, forests are cleared to produce paper and paneled walls, cattle fatten in feedlots to produce steaks and hamburgers, chickens sit in their metal cellblocks and produce eggs for the city dweller, whose sleep will never be disturbed by a rooster's call.

increasing population and spreading urbanization by creating a multitude of one-purpose special districts authorized to deal with sewers, solid waste disposal, air quality, water, and various other needs over a region that may encompass a number of cities and counties.

Although city governments are still technically subordinate to state government, there has been an increasing amount of direct federal involvement in urban programs. The availability of federal funds makes a life-or-death difference to countless programs in every city in the country.

These various developments add up to the fact that there is no longer any necessary congruence between the city as a geogaphic entity and the city as an institution. A conurbation, which might logically be regarded as a single system connected by networks of commerce and transportation, can cover several counties or states. Even a fairly distinct urban entity with recognizable outlines is actually governed by a complex of local, regional, state, and federal agencies and also by private or quasi-governmental bodies such as chambers of commerce. There are, in fact, very few people in any American city who know how many official institutions they are governed by, a condition that is hardly congenial to democratic politics.

The modern city is probably the closest we have yet come to the mechanistic image of a society: it is the great automat whose technology produces water, heat, and light as if by magic, and whose stores stock all the resources needed to sustain the physical body as well as a great number of things not needed at all. Water and power flow into it from distant sources, goods arrive from all over the world, and its effluents of solids and liquids flow effortlessly away somewhere (although its gaseous wastes sometimes refuse to disperse so conveniently). There are signs now and then that the machinery is not running well — crises of energy or financing or public order — but most urbanites accept the city as the source of life and assume that somebody somewhere is running it.

Meanwhile the cities grow, and everything that is not urban is converted to the role of resource for urban life. Hills that the city dweller never sees are carved open to produce coal for power plants, forests are cleared to produce paper and paneled walls, cattle fatten in feedlots to produce steaks and hamburgers, chickens sit in their metal cellblocks and produce eggs for the city dweller, whose sleep will never be disturbed by a rooster's call. Mumford speculates that there is inherent in city life "a tendency to loosen the bonds that connect its inhabitants with nature and to transform, eliminate, or replace its earth-bound aspects, covering the natural site with an artificial environment that enhances the dominance of man and encourages an illusion of complete independence from nature."[16]

This tendency, Mumford says, is nothing new. It has manifested itself time and again in earlier proud urban societies — and has had a good deal to do with their eventual demise:

Unfortunately, as the disintegration of one civilization after another reminds us, the displacement of nature in the city rested in part upon an illusion — or, indeed, a series of illusions — as to the nature of man and his institutions; the illusions of self-sufficiency and independence and of the possibility of physical continuity without conscious renewal. Under the protective mantle of the city, seemingly so permanent, these illusions encouraged habits of predation or parasitism that eventually undermined the whole social and economic structure, after having worked ruin in the surrounding landscape and even in far-distant regions.[17]

The undermining of the social and economic structure, rather than the impact on environmental support systems near or remote, is the part of this process most likely to be recognized as an "urban problem." There are certain policy areas that are recognized as urban — welfare, housing, law enforcement, transportation — and a host of other problems that are not, even though they may have immediate consequences for the maintenance of the urban machine. The oil crisis of 1973, when the intricate interactions of multinational corporations and Near Eastern potentates closed down American service stations, gave urban America the first uncomfortable hint that the urban machinery, indeed the national machinery, literally does not run on its own fuel, that our cities' lifelines now extend around the world. In a very real sense all our problems are urban problems: problems of how to create possibilities for enriching human life in vast urban areas that draw heavily on the environment for resources, that fill the air and water and land with wastes, that grow by spreading across the very agricultural land that sustains them, and that give rise to problems that seem to be solvable only with further bureaucratization and regimentation of individual citizens.

Urbanization in America has created such a host of institutional innovations that it is hard to discern a pattern in the

205

---

[16]Lewis Mumford, "The Natural History of Urbanization," in William L. Thomas, Jr. (ed.) *Man's Role in Changing the Face of the Earth* (Chicago: University of Chicago Press, 1956), p. 386.
[17]Ibid., p. 387.

multileveled jumble of agencies currently struggling to impose some sort of human order on it. One trend appears to be in the direction of areawide government: the Dade County model, the councils of governments that bring city and county officials together to look at programs from a wider perspective, the creation by the states of area-planning agencies, and the experimentation with statewide zoning and land-use planning. Some recent laws, recognizing at last that local political boundaries are arbitrary and artificial, call for special-purpose regional agencies with a more logical relationship to ecological systems. One example of this is the attempt to enforce air pollution control on the basis of natural "air basins" rather than city or county lines. Such efforts generally run into resistance from the local bureaucracies, which are unwilling to relinquish their power to new regional agencies.

While these governmental innovations edge toward the unified management of larger spaces, other political trends strain inward in search of a sense of community, a workable human scale. This is visible in "no-growth" political movements across the country, in the organizational schemes of poverty agencies and unofficial self-help groups, in the rise of the urban commune.

Both of these trends have promise and, although they may appear to be marching in opposite directions, I suspect they will turn out to be complementary. But we will have to realize, as we grope for new urban institutional forms, that they can only cope in part with the larger urban problem — how to sustain the massive clusters of population that have grown up all over America (and much of the rest of the world) without destroying the ecological systems that give them life.

Technocracy

At the same time that power in the American system has tended to concentrate in the federal government it has also tended to differentiate and specialize. Most policy making and administration is *not* done by generalists who concern themselves with the "big picture" of the total system; instead, power is fragmented. Government is separated into discrete subject areas that are then entrusted to the care of experts, bureaucrats, and interest-group representatives.

Government has evolved in this direction because the society has changed into something far different from what it was when the original institutional structures were created. The system is larger and more complicated, and it has developed within it a number of specialized power concentrations — interest groups.

Groups have been amply studied by observers of American political life, from the *Federalist* authors down through Arthur Bentley and David Truman and the pluralist school of political scientists. Some of these writers have come to the conclusion that the individual is both powerless and meaningless as a unit of political analysis and that our system of representation can only be understood in terms of representation of groups: "In a great part of our political life," one study asserts, "the average citizen is an innocent bystander and also a bewildered one. He feels that his vote is futile, but he seldom grasps the fact that the Congress, like the state legislatures, never has functioned as a truly representative body, but only as a means of registering organized pressures."[18]

Most of the attention has been paid to *organized* groups. Some believe that unorganized groups may be equally important, but we know that organized groups do exert a formidable amount of power in our system. The way they go about it explains a great deal of why our system has produced the kinds of policies it has.

Interest groups come in a variety of shapes and sizes, but mainly they represent specialized segments of the economy. We recognize them by names such as American Farm Bureau Federation, AFL-CIO, American Medical Association, National Association of Real Estate Boards, U.S. Savings and Loan League, National Coal Association. The function of each is to look after the group's "interests" — defined in a very limited and special sense — and to bring about whatever legislation, executive or administrative policies, or judicial decisions that might further such interest. Interest in most cases means income or profit. There are exceptions, such as when a labor union seeks laws protecting the safety of workers on the job, but overwhelmingly the objective is an economic benefit: workers want higher wages, farmers want higher prices, businesses and industries want to maximize profits. The function of interest groups, it is commonly held, is to get a bigger cut of the pie.

The kinds of interest groups we have reflect the nature of our system — the way we manage the environment and distribute its resources, our level of technological achievement, and our cultural assumptions about the purposes of life. They also depend for their existence on a certain amount of standardization of society so that, for example, chemical manufacturers in different parts of the country can organize themselves into a national group with certain shared values.

The sense perceptions of interest groups are attuned to a narrow waveband of reality defined by economic roles: each interest group focuses on a special segment of public policy.

The daily biological existence of the modern city dweller is sustained by a complex and far-reaching support system.

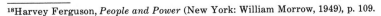

[18]Harvey Ferguson, *People and Power* (New York: William Morrow, 1949), p. 109.

Because this is so, and because an increasingly technological political system is cut up into separate compartments of interest and expertise, government sorts itself out into subject areas. This is evident in the committee structure of Congress, the cabinet departments, and, much more sharply, the independent regulatory commissions.

These commissions were created in response to public fear of the enormous concentrations of power that arose out of the rapid industrialization of the United States. One such concentration of power was the railroad industry, which had become a government unto itself, able to decree the success or failure of farmers and businesses, dictating the policies of city and state governments. Thus the first independent regulatory agency, the Interstate Commerce Commission, was to "regulate" the railway industry. A few years after the ICC was created, President Cleveland's attorney general wrote a reassuring letter to a railroad tycoon and unwittingly summed up much of the criticism that has been made about the independent regulatory commissions ever since:

The Commission is, or can be made, of great use to the railroads. It satisfies the popular clamour for government supervision of the railroads at the same time that supervision is almost entirely nominal. Further, the older such a commission gets to be, the more inclined it will be found to take the business and railroad view of things. It thus becomes a sort of barrier between the railroads and the people and a sort of protection against hasty and crude legislation hostile to railroad interests. [19]

The development of independent regulatory commissions was not only a response to public pressure, it was also a way of dealing with the increasing complexity of the system. It began to seem as though technological changes were making it impossible for the rather slow-moving processes of representative government to regulate the economy. The regulatory commissions were an institutional innovation designed to govern with greater flexibility, expertise, and rationality. They were created by a delegation of power in which the Congress, realizing that some aspects of interstate commerce had become too complex for the traditional legislative processes, granted to the new agencies the authority to issue rules and regulations that would have the force of law. This was a giant step toward technocracy.

[19]Jack Newfield and Jeff Greenfield, *A Populist Manifesto* (New York: Praeger Publishers, Inc., 1972), p. 110.

Each regulatory agency developed a special relationship with the interest areas it was meant to regulate. This was no accident of power politics; from the beginning it was intended that regulation should be a new form of authority somewhere between law and private self-regulation. Many of the interest-group organizations came into existence only with active encouragement of the government. Lowi notes:

The Department of Commerce fostered the trade associations where they already existed and helped organize them where they did not yet exist. Thus the Department took the initiative in founding the U.S. Chamber of Commerce. Without official endorsement in 1912, the fusion of local chambers into one national business association would more than likely never have taken place. Most of the negotiating sessions among local leaders, the National Association of Manufacturers, and others were arranged by, and took place in, the office of the Secretary of Commerce and Labor. The final organizational charter was written there.

The practice of official recognition and representation of trade associations in the inner processes of policy formulation was established . . . during the war years of the Wilson Administration. This was fostered and given doctrinal support in the 1920s, primarily by Secretary of Commerce Herbert Hoover.[20]

Hoover correctly believed that he was taking part in a new stage of American institutional evolution, in which vast areas of policy making would be removed from politics, as it was then understood. "Legislative action," he said, "is always clumsy — it is incapable of adjustment to shifting needs. . . . Three years of study and intimate contact with associations of economic groups convince me that there lies within them a great moving impulse toward betterment."[21]

At about the same time that the U.S. Chamber of Commerce was being nourished into being by the government, another of our "watchdog" agencies, the Federal Trade Commission, was created and given authority to regulate unfair business practices. In order to determine officially what such practices might be, the FTC went to work immediately to draft codes — in consultation with representatives of the industries involved.[22] The more government seeks to govern with expertise, the more authority devolves on those who are to be governed. In the case

It fits neatly into the technocratic value system that decisions are most likely to be made rationally and wisely by people who know something about the subject matter and are not merely amateurs; then what better source for experts in a given industry than the industry itself? And, accordingly, regulators and regulatees nimbly switch places to an extent that raises serious questions about which is which.

209

---

[20]Theodore Lowi, *The End of Liberalism* (New York: W. W. Norton, 1969), p. 117.
[21]Ibid., p. 118.
[22]Ibid., p. 151.

just cited, government delegated to interest groups responsibility for regulating their own actions. The legislative committees, the executive departments, and the regulatory agencies all depend on interest groups for information.

Government also depends on interest groups for personnel. It fits neatly into the technocratic value system that decisions are most likely to be made rationally and wisely by people who know something about the subject matter and are not merely amateurs; then what better source for experts in a given industry than the industry itself? And, accordingly, regulators and regulatees nimbly switch places to an extent that raises serious questions about which is which. Newfield and Greenfield give some samples of this:

Of the last eleven ICC commissioners, four became railroad executives, one became a lobbyist for a group of bus companies, one became a rail freight executive, and three became ICC lawyers, representing private interests before the very agency they had helped to run. This pattern runs through all the agencies.

One of the most pro-industry of all FDA officials, Dr. Joseph Saudek, Jr., became a vice-president of Parke, Davis shortly after leaving his federal job. In the fall of 1971, a high FDA official and one of the biggest pharmaceutical lobbyists simply swapped jobs. The defender of the public against dangerous drugs was now going to fight against "excessive" federal regulation, while the industry's mouthpiece was now going to protect the public.[23]

Such special relationships inevitably develop between the interest group and the regulatory agency; the result is self-government by segments of the economy that has the same legitimacy as legal regulation. This has been justified by the philosophy of technocracy, which characterizes much regulatory policy making as "administrative" and thus free of the corrupting influences of politics, and by the philosophy of pluralism, which pictures the system as an intricate machinery of "countervailing power," in which one interest balances another.

David Truman, one of the most eminent spokesmen for the pluralist philosophy, has stressed not only the competition of organized groups but also the existence of unorganized "potential groups" representing minority elements as well as the power of general adherence to the "rules of the game." These

---

[23]Newfield and Greenfield, *A Populist Manifesto*, pp. 113-14.

rules, says Truman, "are interests the serious disturbance of which will result in organized interaction and the assertion of fairly explicit claims for conformity."[24]

The rules-of-the-game hypothesis may be valid in relation to the rules Truman has in mind, which are the basic democratic values of fairness, democratic process, and equal rights — and it may not. Political scientists get a good deal of exercise debating whether or not democratic values are well served in the pluralist system. At this point I would like to expand our scope of vision and consider how interest groups function in relation to ecological management. In this respect I fear that very few people really know what the rules of the game are, and most don't even know what the game is. The game is evolution, the survival of species, and nature's "assertion of fairly explicit claims for conformity" (quoting Truman) may not always be perceived in time.

Policies regulating ecological management, which result from interest-group influence in government, are rarely debated in depth or checked by the "countervailing power" of opposing organizations, government, or the general public. Sizable areas of policy making are staked out by interest groups and their attendant cadres of experts, and their programs are carried out, frequently over a long period of time, with very little interference from "outside." This is the case with agriculture, which Lowi describes as "that field of American government where the distinction between public and private has come closest to being completely eliminated," which has been accomplished "not by public expropriation of private domain — as would be true of the nationalization that Americans fear — but by private expropriation of public authority."[25]

The management of most of the American land surface (in effect what agricultural policy is) is carried out by an alliance of institutions whose nature confounds not only the traditional concepts of private-public separateness but also the old ideology of federalism. This alliance constitutes the "agricultural community"; among its membership are farmer-elected associations at local, state, and national levels, agencies of county government, agencies of state government (including agriculture departments at the state colleges created by federal land grants), and various federal agencies. The American Farm Bureau Federation is customarily described as an organized private interest group, but it is a federation of local associations that are protected and *required* by law, and which have reg-

211

---

[24]David Truman, *The Governmental Process* (New York: Knopf, 1951), p. 511.
[25]Lowi, *The End of Liberalism*, p. 102.

ulatory powers of their own. Like the U.S. Chamber of Commerce, the American Farm Bureau Federation is a creation of government.

The agricultural community also includes various businesses and industries that are not directly involved in farming the land but participate in determining how it is done. Among these are financing institutions, agricultural equipment manufacturers, and manufacturers of pesticides and chemical fertilizers. Each of these has its own connections with legislators, administrative agencies, and the university departments whose research furthers agricultural technology. A good example of what the agricultural community looks like when incarnated in a single individual is Earl C. Butz, secretary of agriculture under the Nixon and Ford administrations. Dr. Butz has been a member of the board of directors of the Standard Life Insurance Company of Indiana, Stokely-Van Camp Company, Ralston-Purina Company, and the International Minerals and Chemical Corporation; director of the Farm Foundation; research economist for the Federal Land Bank; trustee of the Nutrition Foundation and the American Society of Farm Managers and Rural Appraisers; and chairman of the Agricultural Economics Department at Purdue University.

The Department of Agriculture is the apex of the structure of public and private groups. It is one of the cabinet departments described by political scientists as a "client" department, with a special relationship to the people it regulates. The agricultural community does not include consumer or conservationist organizations. Such organizations might well have political power, but their power is ad hoc, mobilized on occasion around specific issues, and is usually spent in attempting to halt policies already underway. Consumer groups may protest against food prices and may even succeed here and there in lowering prices, but they do not influence the long-run policy making that *causes* high food prices. Conservationists, similarly, may succeed in halting the construction of a dam or getting a ban on DDT, but they do not penetrate or change the network of cultural values and managerial practices that culminate in dams and pesticides.

Even more significant are the many other interest groups that simply take no "interest" whatever in agricultural policy. Technocracy compartmentalizes areas of policy and isolates one from another. Zeigler and Peak observe that "while the American Farm Bureau Federation is very influential in the affairs of the Department of Agriculture, and while the American Legion has come close to total domination of the Veterans

213

Consumer groups may protest against food prices and may even succeed here and there in lowering prices, but they do not influence the long-run policy making that *causes* high food prices.

In the American
two-party system the
parties are coalitions
to begin with and
contain groups that
have precious little
in common beyond
their party
identification.

Administration, neither of these organizations can muster much influence with the Department of State"; each group has "considerable influence in its own unique area of activities, but virtually no influence when ventures into other policy areas are undertaken."[26]

The political science literature on this subject (much of which is insightful) neglects the obvious fact that these interest-group-government communities have evolved into subcultures. The Zeigler-Peak study comes within range of recognizing this when it states: "The weight of evidence would seem to indicate, as we and others have suggested, that agencies and their clients tend to develop coincident values and perceptions to the point that neither needs to manipulate the other overtly. The confident relationships that develop uniquely favor the interest groups involved."[27] Although the interest-group-agency clusters are specialized and parochial, they nevertheless make policy for the whole system. The "policy outputs" of the agricultural community affect every American, and for that matter a sizable part of the world's population, even though the decisions are made by a relatively small number of specialists.

Sometimes other governmental bodies attempt to intervene in an area of agricultural policy, and the result is usually an intragovernmental jurisdictional dispute. This happened when the Environmental Protection Agency banned the use of various pesticides (aldrin, dieldrin, and DDT) against the wishes of farmers and pesticide manufacturers. The Department of Agriculture powerfully expressed its resentment of the "outside" usurpation of agricultural policy making, and in 1974 the House Agricultural Committee (another part of the community) voted to require EPA to get the views of the department before banning any more pesticides. At about the same time the Department of Agriculture was involved in a skirmish with the Department of State over its attempts to restrict grain sales to communist countries; Secretary Butz protested the invasion of agricultural policy by "striped pants" diplomats. These disputes are not, as they may seem on the surface, merely arguments about which governmental agency has the power to regulate agriculture. They arise from infringements of the agricultural community's power to regulate itself.

Compartmentalization of government into separate, and in large part self-regulating, segments is characteristic of our system at its present stage of evolutionary development; there

---

[26]L. Harmon Zeigler and G. Wayne Peak, *Interest Groups in American Society*, 2nd ed. (Englewood Cliffs, N.J.: Prentice-Hall, 1972), pp. 166-67.
[27]Ibid., p. 180.

are many similar clusters that resemble the agricultural community.

The practice of this kind of technocratic government is to take as much policy making as possible out of the noisy arena of politics. It steers away from the kind of policy making that we learn in school to think of as "democratic": the discussion of issues in political campaigns and public hearings, the choice among alternatives on the basis of informed public opinion. Technocrats and interest groups generally prefer to avoid this kind of political process; it is inefficient and costly. Insofar as possible, each community will conduct its business quietly, make changes only in small increments, and avoid confrontations with other communities. There is much to be said in favor of this kind of governmental process. Its major weakness is that government by specialists may lack any apparatus for thinking about the system as a whole and considering where it is going. The closest thing we have to an institutional structure for that purpose is the party system.

Parties, Echoes, and Choices

Political scientists have struggled long and hard (and without success) to arrive at a universally acceptable statement of what political parties are or what they do. This confusion is understandable, since one of the functions of political parties is to confuse. And beyond that there is something elusive about an American political party; the "same" party turns out to be a different thing at different places, at different times, at different levels of the system.

The matter is further complicated by the fact that an American political party combines a miscellany of economic interests, sectional interests, social classes, ethnic groups, and ideological viewpoints. In the multiparty political systems of some countries, leaders of different parties form a coalition after an election; in the American two-party system the parties are coalitions to begin with and contain groups that have precious little in common beyond their party identification. The classic example of this is the fragile alliance of southern rural conservatives with northern urban liberals in the Democratic party.

Parties have always suffered from a certain lack of respectability in America. The Founding Fathers hoped to get by without them, and even Hamilton and Jefferson — who did as much as any two men in history to bring the two major parties into existence — were theoretically opposed to them. Richard Hofstadter notes in his history of the American party systems:

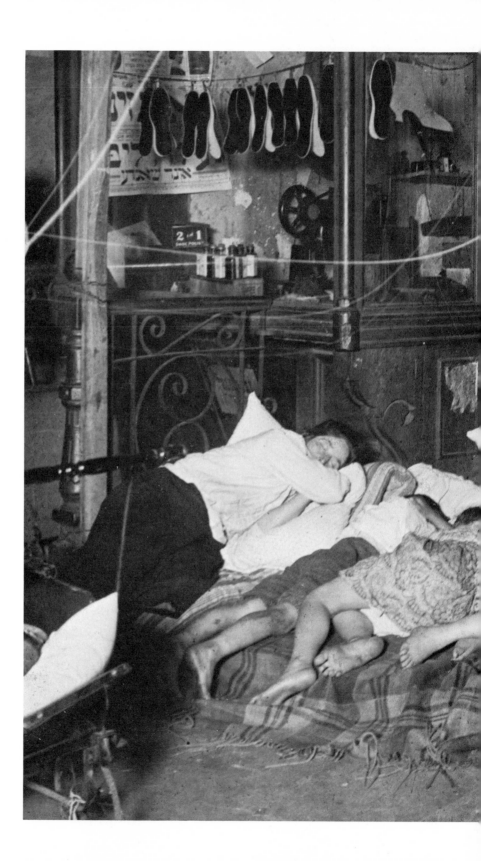

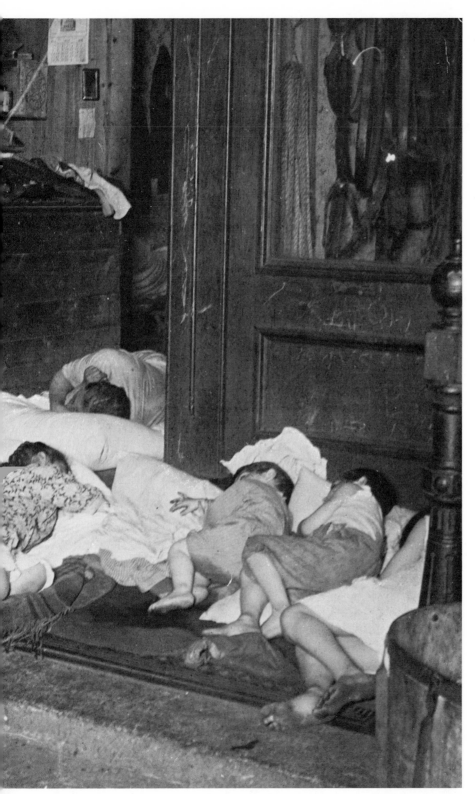

Thirteen million immigrants had been added to the American population; they and their children were a majority in most of the urbanized North, and a discontented one. They lived in a society that extolled consumerism, but their access to its wealth was limited.

217

The whole tradition of anti-party writing is full of the works of men who were strong partisans; this tradition is, in very large part, the work of partisan writers and political leaders who are actually appealing to a general distrust of the idea of party in order to subvert some particular party or to advance the interest of another party whose greatest claim to glory is that it will surmount and eliminate the party battle itself.[28]

But in spite of the general distrust of them, parties did form, and although individual parties come and go the party system itself appears to have become a permanent fixture of the American political system. Most students of American political history believe that the parties are an indispensable part of the system, that they perform necessary functions in making the formal institutions of government work. Frank Sorauf, in a representative analysis of the role of parties, describes them as having three "manifest functions" — electing, propagandizing, and governing — and six "latent functions": "They reduce effectively the number of political options to manageable numbers, bring order and focus to the political struggle, simplify issues and frame alternatives, compromise conflicting interests, recruit political leadership, personalize and dramatize politics, stabilize political debate and allegiance, and enhance the political power of the 'insignificant' individual."[29]

One thing parties have done is organize various elements of the society into coalitions. Party leaders generally aspire to assemble a coalition large enough to elect a president and gain a majority in the Congress. Thus the parties shape the structure of political conflict. The multitude of groups and individuals competing for access to the decision-making centers of the system resolve themselves into two large and rather amorphous assemblies. The fragmented strivings of various regions, interests, and ideologies are abosrbed into a national pattern.

Major transitions in American history have been marked by the emergence of new coalitions. Andrew Jackson came to power with the support of voters in the new frontier states and newly enfranchised propertyless voters in the eastern states. The Jackson coalition combined the farmers of the frontier with the workers, shopkeepers, and middle class of the older states. That period of Democratic ascendancy brought basic changes

---

[28]Richard Hofstadter, *The Idea of a Party System* (Berkeley: University of California Press, 1969), pp. 17-18.
[29]Frank Sorauf, *Political Parties in the American System* (Boston: Little, Brown, 1964), pp. 165-66.

in institutional structures (the spoils system), a new chapter in internal improvement policy, and a vigorously aggressive expansion of American territory.

The Republican era in American history began with Lincoln's election and was consolidated during Reconstruction as another coalition supported by votes from the increasingly populous northern states. This era launched America into a long period of intensive industrialization supported by high tariffs, laissez-faire ideology, opposition to the labor-union movement, and construction—with generous public support — of a nationwide railway transportation system.

By the 1930s the time was ripe for the formation of a new coalition. Thirteen million immigrants had been added to the American population; they and their children were a majority, and a discontented one, in most of the urbanized North. They lived in a society that extolled consumerism, but their access to its wealth was limited. They worked for an industrial system that depended on their human energies for its prosperity, but they were not among the prosperous. Still another large segment of the body politic — the "solid South," which had been a one-party political system since the end of Reconstruction — was assimilated into the coalition that, under the leadership of Franklin D. Roosevelt, provided the electoral support for the New Deal and its venture into new programs of environmental management and distribution of wealth.

The Roosevelt coalition appears to have run its course, but the concept of the coalition still beguiles American politicians. Seekers of all persuasions look for a new combination that can form a clear majority and make decisions for the decades to come. Kevin Phillips endeared himself to the Nixon administration with his game plan for the creation of a new Republican coalition made up of Wallace voters, white southerners, voters in the southwestern "sun belt" cities, working-class Catholics, and residents of the "heartlands" and "ordinary suburbs."[30] More recently another conservative spokesman, William Rusher, talked of a coaliton of "producers" from business, labor, and agriculture that would rise up in rebellion against "the huge nonproducing welfare constituency and the liberal elite (media, intelligentsia and bureaucracy) that sustains it."[31] While conservatives awaited this sunrise on the Right, liberals hoped to assemble a "new populism" based on an alliance of

[30]Kevin Phillips, *The Emerging Republican Majority* (New Rochelle, N.Y.: Arlington House, 1969).
[31]William Rusher, *San Francisco Chronicle*, 24 March 1975, p. 32.

racial minorities with low- or moderate-income whites against the entrenched power and privilege of the business-industrial establishment.[32]

These various scenarios of the political future may not seem to have much in common, but they all stand together on the same piece of the American dominant social paradigm. They operate on the assumption that politics is essentially a competition among members of different groups for a larger piece of the pie — meaning more material goods — and that the alternative strategies offered by the two parties will be different ways of managing the system so as to offer more goods to certain groups. If it is possible to suggest that the party's strategy will offer more for everybody, so much the better. Amid all the vagueness of politics, competing sides retain a remarkably clear fix on the central belief that the American is first of all a consumer.

The party system structures controversy, and also avoids it; there is a powerful tendency toward the middle of the road in American politics, born of the recognition that the surest way to achieve a large majority is to capture the massive center, the voters whose political stance reflects the culture's basic values. I quote here two points from Dye and Zeigler's analysis of the American party system:

1. *American parties share consensus both in basic democratic values and on major directions of American policy. They believe in the sanctity of private property, the free enterprise economy, individual liberty, and limited government. Moreover both parties have supported the same general domestic and foreign policy — including social security, a graduated income tax, counter-cyclical fiscal and monetary policies, anti-communism, the Cold War, and the Korean and Vietnamese wars.*
2. *The American parties do not present clear ideological alternatives to the American voter. Both American parties are overwhelmingly middle class in organization, values, and goals. Deviation from the shared consensus by either party ("a choice not an echo") is more likely to lose than attract voters.*[33]

The parties' conflict-structuring function is also diluted by the ever-present tendency to state policy proposals in vague and misleading terms. To assemble and maintain a broad-based coalition it is necessary to appeal to as many people as possible and alienate as few as possible. The result of this tactic is

220

---

[32]Newfield and Greenfield, *A Populist Manifesto.*
[33]Dye and Zeigler, *The Irony of Democracy*, p. 330.

obscure political language and campaigns based on the symbolic "image" of the candidate or the party — not a clear presentation of alternatives.

The presentation of alternatives is the single most important function the parties are supposed to perform. They are characterized as links between the individual voter and the government; in systems analyses of politics, the parties are assigned the role of monitors of the "input" that determines the general direction of the system's action. But this responsibility is precisely the one that critics of the parties see as the parties' greatest failure. The parties, it is often said, are Tweedledum and Tweedledee; the differences they offer are meaningless.

You are most likely to hear this criticism from those whose opinions are the most energetically held and most distinct from the political middle of the road. Strong conservatives and strong radicals are the people who often become dissatisfied with the usual party vagueness and struggle for more emphatic positions on issues. Thus when the Goldwater conservatives won control of the Republican party in 1964, the motto they broadcast to the public was, "A choice, not an echo" — communicating their conviction that their party had formerly been offering nothing more than watered-down Democratic policies.

The result in that particular presidential campaign was that the Democrats leaped on Goldwater's more controversial positions, especially his enthusiasm for aggressive anticommunist military action and changes in Social Security, and used them in a dazzling anti-Goldwater media campaign. One TV spot showed a Social Security card being torn in half, thereby conveying graphically (if not accurately) that Goldwater planned to do away with Social Security entirely. Actually Goldwater had only suggested (in a primary campaign) that Social Security might be made voluntary — a position he edged away from as election time drew closer. Goldwater began to move toward the center, repudiating positions that might be called "extreme" and consequently sounding more and more like an echo. Meanwhile his opponent confused the public about the nature of the choice. The same pressures and tactics emerged in 1972 when a strongly liberal candidate was nominated by the Democratic party and proceeded to lose even more decisively than Goldwater had in 1964.

I have offered examples of two candidates who tried (to some extent) to communicate their positions on issues and to present real alternatives. I could have offered many more examples of candidates whose campaign strategy was to discuss as few issues as possible and avoid presenting any alternative that

> Conservatives think government interferes too much in business; liberals think business interferes too much in government. The truth is that the two are not really divisible except conceptually; their existence is as interdependent as the two sides of an arch.

221

might jeopardize their claim to middle-of-the-road solidarity. This is the direction that party politics in America generally takes; political campaigns rarely bear any resemblance to public debates on issues, in which candidates take clearly different stands.

It may well be that the system works better this way; perhaps it is the only way the system can work. Many serious observers of American politics believe this to be true, and offer the historical reminder that a notable instance when the choices and issues became clear ended in a civil war. D. W. Brogan summarized this idea in his suggestion that it might be "possible that the American shrinking from doctrinaire parties, from people who knew their own minds, who would not compromise, who had a social theory to defend or attack, owed something to the recollection of the time when America *had* such parties, when, to the astonishment of each side, North and South found themselves at war."[34] This remark speaks for the fear that a political system based on clear alternatives might become deeply embroiled in conflict. Another argument buttressed by a good deal of research and the consistently low turnout of American voters is that the voting public is neither informed enough nor interested enough to respond to a campaign structured as a detailed deliberation of major policy alternatives.

222

In the first election after the ratification of the United States Constitution, a few hundred thousand white male property owners voted. Since then the nation, struggling to become more democratic ("A complex society is under constant pressure to adjust its institutions to its central value system"[35]) has extended the franchise to more and more people: the propertyless, the freed slaves, women, everybody over eighteen. Meanwhile population growth swelled the total number of eligible voters. The system grew and it differentiated; decision making, as we have seen, separated into areas of specialization tended by experts and interested parties.

America has become both a mass democracy and a technocracy. In some ways these two developments are compatible, and in some ways they are not. Certainly the inner workings of specialized policy areas do not readily open themselves to deliberation in national election campaigns; at best the parties frame general policy guidelines that might, with luck, have some influence in the committee rooms and executive offices where decisions are made. But along the way campaigning has grown its own breed of technicians, specialists in mass media

[34]D. W. Brogan, *Politics in America* (New York: Harper, 1954), p. 5.
[35]See p. 44.

In the first election
after the ratification
of the United States
Constitution, a few
hundred thousand
white male property
owners voted. Since
then the nation has
extended the fran-
chise to more and
more people.

Candidates and their beliefs are shaped, polished, tested against the market, and merchandised at election time.

and public opinion, whose skills derive not so much from traditional party politics as from advertising and public relations. Candidates and their beliefs are shaped, polished, tested against the market, and merchandised at election time. This new breed of campaign experts understands even better than old-time machine politicians that elections should not be cluttered up with too many issues.

It appears that, as the American public becomes more mobile and standardized, as regional distinctions fade and the power of the national media grows, the nature of party politics is changing: coalition building has given way to image building as the key to campaign success; the parties are becoming more ephemeral and ad hoc than ever, to the point that they can barely be called organizations at all. There are many indicators that changes of this sort are taking place. In any case, neither traditional party politics nor modern electioneering bears much resemblance to the ideal model of democracy in which an informed electorate scrutinizes the candidates, weighs the issues, and thereby issues its commands. In this respect the society has had a hard time adjusting its institutions to its central value system.

My purpose here is not to moralize about the gap between politics as we celebrate it and politics as we practice it, but rather to raise the question of whether politics as we practice it is conducive to the survival of the species. Clearly our electoral system is strongly attracted toward the middle of the road, and the alternatives we are offered are really only minor variations on the DSP. Most of the major decisions that we have made about how to manage our environment have never even come up as political issues because they have operated from commonly held attitudes and because it was assumed that they would bring more prosperity and not do anyone serious harm. If these assumptions were true and continue to be true, then we may proceed as usual: the system may continue to move in its fixed course along the groove of the DSP. But if the DSP is in some way *not* an adequate guide to the kinds of decisions the system should make in order to deal with its evolutionary responsibilities, then we may be in trouble — because it has never been the function of party politics to question basic cultural values. This is an issue I will return to in the final chapter, after we look at another segment of our institutional power structure.

Government by the Private Sector
A favorite myth of American politics is the separation between

the "public sector," which is government, and the "private sector," which is business. People of different political persuasions keep the myth alive by stating it according to their particular bias: conservatives think government interferes too much in business; liberals think business interferes too much in government. The truth is that the two are not really divisible except conceptually; their existence is as interdependent as the two sides of an arch. Our political system is understandable only as an interaction of public and private institutions. Galbraith, in *The New Industrial State*, is lucid on this point:

The industrial system, in fact, is inextricably associated with the state. In notable respects the mature corporation is an arm of the state. And the state, in important matters, is an instrument of the industrial system. This runs strongly counter to the accepted doctrine. That assumes a clear line between government and private business enterprise. The position of this line — what is given to the state and what is accorded to private enterprise — tells whether the society is socialist or non-socialist. Nothing is so important. Any union between public and private organization is held, by liberal and conservative alike, to be deviant sin. To the liberal it means that public power has been captured for private advantage and profit. To the conservative it means that high private prerogative, the right to act without government interference, has been lost to the state. In fact, the line between public and private authority in the industrial system is indistinct and in large measure imaginary, and the abhorrent association of public and private organizatons is normal. When this is perceived, the central trends in American economic and political life become clear. On few matters is an effort to free the mind more rewarding.[36]

225

Although historical accounts of the transplantation of Western civilization to the New World have focused on public institution building and government, private institutional arrangements were an equally essential part of the operation. The British government did not, after all, undertake the project of colonization itself, but entrusted that task to corporations created specifically for the purpose, notably the Virginia Company and the Massachusetts Bay Company.

Throughout the colonial era there were few corporations formed for strictly commercial purposes — the crown was reluctant to permit any arrangements that might encourage colo-

[36]John Kenneth Galbraith, *The New Industrial State* (Boston: Houghton Mifflin, 1971), pp. 298-99.

Blow some my way"

Ch

Advertising saturates the culture with its images and values. The advertisement has become much more than just a device for serving the marketing needs of corporations. The true function of advertising in our system is to _create_ demand, not merely respond to it.

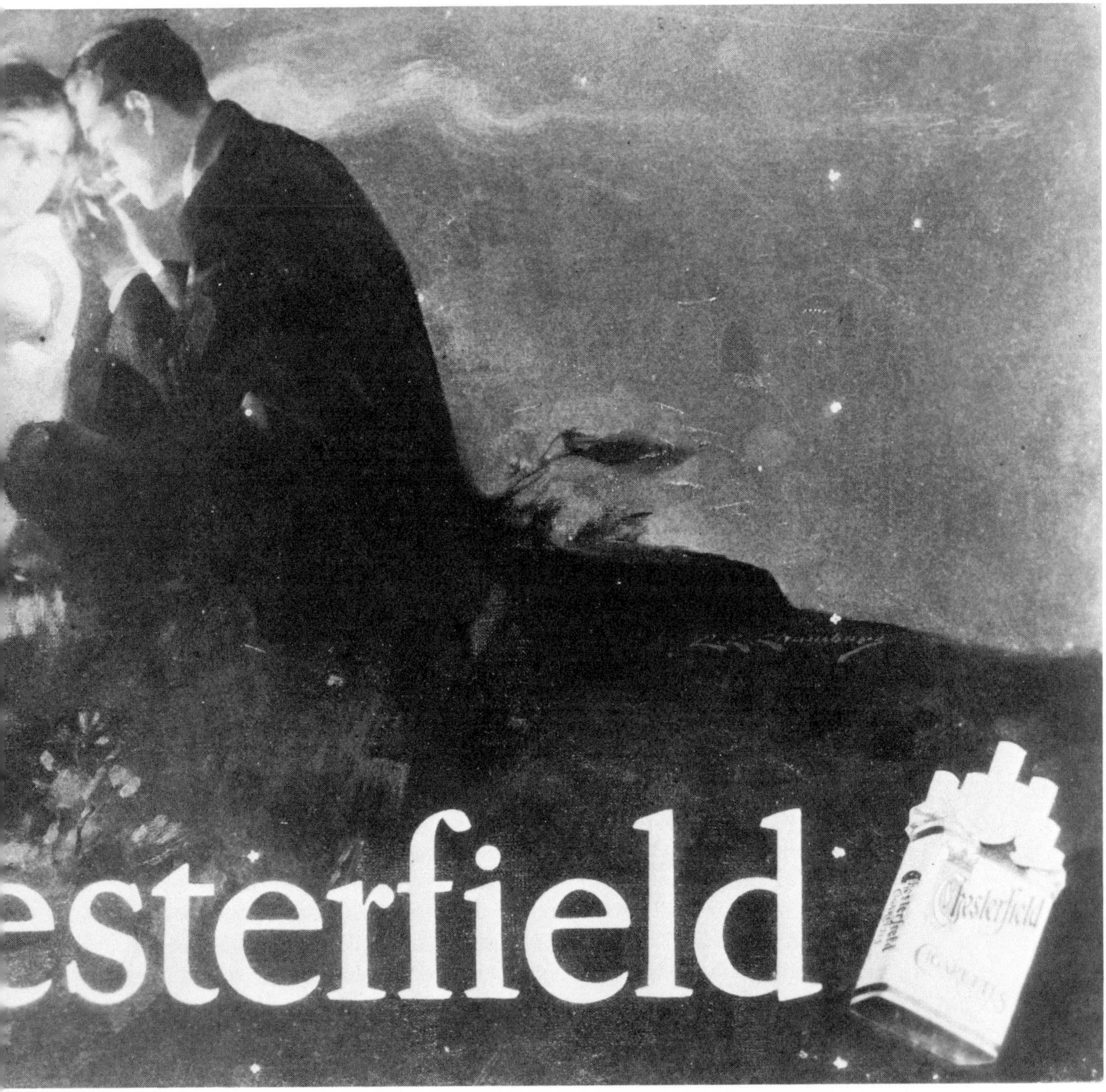
esterfield
Chesterfield
Cigarettes

nial self-sufficiency — but after independence business corporations proliferated. More than 300 were created in the first twenty years after the end of the Revolution. Most of these were for the purpose of building facilities for interstate commerce: canals, toll bridges, and turnpikes. As I have mentioned earlier, the internal improvement projects were part private business and part public policy.

In a time when capital was scarce and development of the environment was considered to be in the general interest, corporations were created to carry out specific projects and were granted such privileges as monopoly rights-of-way and tax exemptions. There were some manufacturing corporations, but most industry relied on simpler institutional arrangements such as private proprietorships and partnerships.

During the nineteenth century, as the consuming population increased and mass-manufacturing technology was developed, the nature and purpose of corporations changed. Both the number of corporations engaged in manufacturing and the size of these corporations increased. This trend accelerated in the post-Civil War era, when the modern corporation as we know it — with many stockholders, many employees, diversified operations, and massive marketing efforts — appeared on the American scene. Although these giant organizations employed an institutional form that had been available for centuries, they were in truth a new and immensely powerful force for mobilizing human energies and transforming the land.

In their early stages the great corporations were, like the great nations that struggled into being on the decline of feudalism, heavily dependent on charismatic leadership — the "captains of industry" such as Rockefeller and Carnegie and Ford. They also needed ideological support for their claims to power and autonomy. They found the ideology in several packages. For the pious there was still the Protestant ethic, God smiling down upon the successful businessman. Riches, J. D. Rockefeller once said, came as "a gift from Heaven, signifying, 'This is my beloved son, in whom I am well pleased.' "[37] For those who preferred a quasi-scientific view there was social Darwinism, picturing all life as a brutal conflict in which the survival of the fittest led inevitably to the improvement of the species. For economists and politicians there was laissez-faire theory, with its "hidden hand" that guided the economy and needed only to proceed free of undue interference from government. The government was not to meddle in the growth or trusts or monopolies, but laissez-faire theory allowed room for

[37]Edward Ziegler, *The Vested Interests* (New York: Macmillan, 1964), p. 6.

it to meddle in international trade by creating high tariffs to protect American industry from foreign competition and by using military force to protect American interests abroad.

Late in the nineteenth century supporters of the new industrial philosophy became a majority on the United States Supreme Court, and their decisions aided the development of corporate institutions. The corporations were given the legal status of "corporate persons," which thus brought them under the Fourteenth Amendment's provision that no person might be deprived of property without due process of law.[38] The concept of personal freedom became increasingly tied to an emphasis on "freedom of contract," which stood as a legal wall of opposition to governmental efforts to improve the conditions of the powerless and poor. In the case of *Lochner* v. *New York* the court ruled that a state law limiting bakers' working time to sixty hours a week (one of many attempts the states were making to end oppressive work conditions for children and adults) was unconstitutional. "The statute," said the opinion, "necessarily interferes with the right of contract between the employer and employee, concerning the number of hours in which the latter may labor in the bakery of the employer. The general right to make a contract in relation to his business is part of the liberty of the individual."[39]

The trouble with this point of view, its critics said, was that times had changed; the institutional arrangements which the concept of "freedom of contract" was meant to serve had changed. Economic relationships were no longer agreements between individuals but between people and corporations. Woodrow Wilson represented this argument when he wrote: "Today, the everyday relationships of men are largely with great impersonal concerns, with organizations, not with other individual men. . . . The truth is, we are all caught up in a great economic system which is heartless. The modern corporation is not engaged in business as an individual."[40]

Wilson and others recognized in the industrial corporation a concentration of power that rendered obsolete much of the traditional idealism of American commerce: individual enterprise, personal freedom, competition. One of the most disturbing characteristics of the industrial corporations was their tendency to grow and keep growing. In many industries such as oil, steel, and copper, leading corporations eliminated their small competitors and monopolized their field of operation.

---

[38]*San Mateo County* v. *Southern Pacific Railroad Co.* 116 U.S. 138 (1885); and *Santa Clara County* v. *Southern Pacific Railroad Co.* 118 U.S. 394, 396 (1886).
[39]198 U.S. 45 (1905).
[40]Woodrow Wilson, *The New Freedom* (New York: Doubleday, 1913), pp. 4-5.

Other forms of corporate organization — trusts, holding companies, interlocking directorates — were further experiments in institution building that expanded the power of business entrepreneurs and for a time confounded all efforts at regulation or control. They were in many ways larger than the political institutions that were supposed to regulate them. The capital used to organize the steel trust, for example, was about twice the contemporary federal budget for a year's operations.[41] Richard Hofstadter summarizes the findings of a congressional investigating committee in 1912:

The Morgan interests at the peak of the financial system held 341 directorships in 112 corporations (insurance companies, transportation systems, manufacturing and trading corporations, and public utilities) with aggregate resources or capitalization of $22,245,000,000. This inventory — an incomplete one — thus showed a single network of interests commanding more than three times the assessed value of all the real and personal property in the thirteen Southern states; or more than all the property in the twenty-two states west of the Mississippi.[42]

230

As the corporations grew they began to develop marketing methods that were still another reach for power (although this was not recognized at the time). By aiming aggressive advertising at the consuming public, manufacturers of retail goods were attempting to revolutionize the market economy. Galbraith has suggested that "The general effect of sales effort, defined in the broadest terms, is to shift the focus of decision in the purchase of goods from the consumer where it is beyond control to the firm where it is subject to control."[43] He further notes that the transfer is by no means complete — but although the control may not be perfect, it is still a control. As another writer described it, the "general rule with fewer exceptions than we would like to think, is that if they make it we will buy it."[44]

Economists generally have described advertising as a new kind of (or a replacement for) competition. Instead of resorting to the most primitive kind of competition — price cutting — which is incompatible with the needs for operational stability and long-range planning, firms seek their share of the market by attempting to persuade the customer to buy their product instead of somebody else's. This in itself is a major departure

[41]Richard Hofstadter, *The Age of Reform* (New York: Vintage, 1955), p. 232.
[42]Ibid., pp. 232-33.
[43]Galbraith, *The New Industrial State*, p. 206.
[44]Andrew Hacker, "A Country Called Corporate America," *New York Times Magazine*, 3 July 1966.

Upton Sinclair, one of the "muckraking" reformers, wrote a scathing indictment of the meat-packing industry in *The Jungle*.

232

In the factories, where the operations of human beings were made ever more routine and repetitive in the service of greater efficiency, the image of the human individual as a cog in a vast impersonal machinery was simply a description of the obvious.

233

from earlier business practices, but it is not the most significant aspect of advertising. The idea of competition implies that firms are advertising in order to appeal to the consumer who wants or needs a certain item and has only to decide which brand to buy; but the true function of advertising in our system is to *create* demand, not merely respond to it. New products are continually introduced into the market and launched with intensive advertising campaigns to convince the consumer — who was never previously aware of a need for the item — that it is desirable. Underarm deodorants, for example, were not brought forth in response to any public clamor for such a product; their salability is dependent on continual advertising to persuade people that they need it. This is what Jules Henry, in the passages quoted in Chapter One, meant by the absence of "production-needs complementarity." Demand stimulation relates to one of the basic realities of our system: the constant increase in rates of consumption.

Advertising is a much-maligned part of our social system, criticized (deservedly, in my opinion) for its tastelessness, its insistence on offering some kind of purchase as the solution to every problem, its distortions of reality, and its demeaning portrayals of human life. But it refuses to disappear. If it were to vanish, our system would be totally different. Not only our economy but our culture, our ways of thinking about life, are intimately connected to it.

The advertising industry occupies a central position in American life. Radio and television are financed through advertising revenue, and the content of popular entertainment is shaped to serve advertising policies. Newspapers and magazines also depend on advertising. And although advertising may not directly control the content of the media, the culture is pervaded with its images and values. It has become much more than a device for serving the marketing needs of mass corporate structures.

Another by-product of the giant industrial corporations, closely related to advertising, is public relations. PR emerged as a profession in the latter part of the nineteenth century in response to the growing public distrust of big business. This protest movement, stimulated by the "muckraking" journalism of Ida Tarbell, Lincoln Steffens, and Upton Sinclair, threatened to provoke meaningful political reforms to place limits on corporate power. To counter this threat, the major corporations reversed their earlier policy of releasing as little information as possible and began to employ professional publicists whose job was to tell the business side of the story by making information available and encouraging the press to print material favorable to industry. Public relations quickly became a major industry in its own right; today every large corporation has a public relations departmnnt, and most find occasion to employ special consultants from independent PR firms as well.

The corporation was not only a concentration of economic and political power but also a new social form with the ability to mobilize many thousands of people in the service of its goals, and thus to shape and direct their individual lives. Whole new systems of roles were created; with them came new life styles and new expectations. For the ambitious young American success was now to be achieved not by clearing a plot of land for a farm or by starting an individual business enterprise but by moving upward through the hierarchy of a massive institution.

It is easy to see how so many observers of this social transformation saw the new organizations that were developing as human machines, different only in minor characteristics from the factories. And certainly in the factories, where the operations of human beings were made ever more routine and repetitive in the service of greater efficiency, the image of the human individual as a cog in a vast impersonal machinery was simply a description of the obvious. The concept of time as money had always been part of the Protestant ethic, but in the industrial era it took on a whole new meaning, as efficiency became more and more a predominant cultural value.

The corporate structure built a powerful new system of living that harnessed together the long-stored energies of fossil fuels — unleashed after millennia of gestation beneath the surface of the American continent — and the energies of millions of human beings transported from Europe and the Orient.

The corportions expanded vertically and horizontally, absorbing and merging, taking in competitors and suppliers and distributors. In simple economic terms the Darwinist ethic provided a blessing for the growth of these powerful new economic beings and the extinction of less efficient forms. Profits and productivity grew. Enormous personal fortunes were amassed, and an unprecedented volume of consumer goods poured into the marketplace. At a rather early stage in their development the leading industrial corporations seized much of the initiative for directing the course of society as a whole. The chief focus of governmental planning had been internal improvements to create a system of transportation and communications that would facilitate interstate commerce; this provided a suitable foundation for private business and industry to take over and make even greater changes.

The great size of the modern corporation requires long-range planning, and its power makes planning possible. The elements of planning that Galbraith cites — control of supply, control of demand, provision of capital, minimization of risk[45] — all involve attempts to manipulate the system of which the corporation is a part. The thrust of growth is to overcome the vagaries of the marketplace and create an environment in which the coroporation can build, plan, and invest with some confidence that a profit will be returned. There is a great deal of rhetoric about risk and daring in the business world, concealing the ever-present effort to reduce uncertainty wherever possible.

The corporations' need to plan, to guarantee profit and productivity over a long period of time, naturally calls for efforts to direct the course of the system. Although government engages in planning in many ways, in many ways it is merely reactive to corporate initiative. For corporate planning there is no natural limit to the desirable size: monopoly, from the entrepreneur's point of view, was the ideal arrangement for rational planning and minimizing of risk. The federal government has taken steps over the years to limit monopoly — again, a reaction to corporate initiative — but corporate growth continues in new ways. The new manifestations of corporate growth are not the monopolies and trusts of the turn of the century but conglomerates and multinationals. The conglomerates, overleaping the old ideas of vertical and horizontal expansion, grow by combining operations that have no necessary relation to one another. Thus International Telephone and Telegraph combines under a single corporate structure such diverse activities as hotel management (Sheraton), baking (Wonder Bread), home building (Levitt), car rental (Avis), and several more industries, including data processing, insurance, loans, and book publishing. The multinationals, many of which are also conglomerates, are worldwide firms whose operations are carried out in a number of countries.

Most of the major multinational corporations are of American origin, but it is no longer precisely correct to say that they are American. Multinationals are sometimes described as stateless entities or even as superstates or empires. I think it would be more accurate to describe them as global systems. They move goods and people and money around the world, and in the process transform regional environments and individual lives. Multinational firms set up plants in Taiwan (where cheap labor will permit goods to be manufactured for sale at low prices in the U.S.) and the result is a new way of life for the Taiwanese

[45]Galbraith, *The New Industrial State*, p. 76.

laborer and pollution for the Taiwanese air. Without ever having to leave home, peasants around the world are making the same abrupt transition from agricultural employment to industrial employment that was experienced by American immigrants. And sometimes, when the multinational finds it convenient to set up shop elsewhere, they are making the transition back again.

Part of the rationale of multinational corporate organization is to find the optimum materials and conditions: convenient resources, cheap labor, a friendly political climate. If the government sets up too many demands concerning, say, work conditions or pollution controls, the corporation may take its operations elsewhere. The world corporations influence national governments (large and small), in addition to having many tactics for manipulating national currencies and avoiding excessive regulation. Multinational corporations have a national identity, but that is not the same thing as patriotism. They are motivated by corporate, not national, interests.

Although the corporations' power to make decisions and form policies that influence the course of our lives and the condition of the natural environment is enormous, and although these institutions function as an integral part of a system that calls itself democratic, the corporations do not themselves operate democratically. The closest thing to a democratic mechanism in the corporate structure is the voting power of stockholders, but stockholders normally relinquish this through proxies. There is no more meaningless and totally ceremonial gathering than the stockholders' meeting of a large corporation, in which a few hundred people — mostly small investors — assemble for their annual glimpse of the management. In reality even major stockholders have little to do with real corporate decision making. Many major stockholders are trusts, foundations, educational institutions, investment funds of various kinds, with no interest in the corporation beyond its function as a source of revenue. The real power is vested in a fairly small number of top-level executives, who guide corporate policy with little threat of interference so long as the firm makes a profit. The corporation is not a democracy, but neither is it the oligarchy it is sometimes pictured to be; actually it is a technocracy, a relatively impersonal social machine run by professional managers, whose decision making is carried out on the basis of expert information provided by staffs of planners, designers, and marketing specialists.

The corporation as an institutional form has shown itself to be capable of great flexibility in organization, but it has no

238

Most of the major
multinational corpo-
rations are of
American origin, but
it is no longer pre-
cisely correct to say
that they are Ameri-
can. Multinationals
are sometimes de-
scribed as stateless
entities or even as
superstates or em-
pires. I think it
would be more accu-
rate to describe
them as global sys-
tems.

239

flexibility whatever in its basic purposes. So long as it produces goods and services and returns a profit to investors, its management may continue in office and internal upheavals are likely to be minimal. Battles for control of large corporations have generally arisen only when the firms were not doing well. Some well-meaning institutions have sought to use the leverage of their investment holdings to steer corporations in the direction of greater "social responsibility," only to find that they were required by law to invest for profit and nothing else. For all its power, the corporation has even less opportunity than the "public" segments of the system to evaluate and change its basic goals: it is fixed by its own structure on a course of profit and growth, and its influences are applied toward directing the entire system along the same path.

Occasionally we hear that all this is no longer true, that the corporations now operate on the basis of motives other than mere profit. If so, this change in course opens up serious questions and inner contradictions, as E. F. Schumacher points out:

The capitalist today wishes to deny that the one final aim of all his activities is profit. He says: "Oh no, we do a lot for our employees which we do not really have to do; we try to preserve the beauty of the countryside; we engage in research that may not pay off," etc., etc. All these claims are very familiar; sometimes they are justified, sometimes not.

What concerns us here is this: private enterprise "old style," let us say, goes simply for profits; it thereby achieves a most powerful simplification of objectives and gains a perfect measuring rod of success or failure. Private enterprise "new style," on the other hand (let us assume), pursues a great variety of objectives; it tries to consider the whole fullness of life and not merely the money-making aspect; it therefore achieves no powerful simplification of objectives and possesses no reliable measuring rod of success or failure. If this is so, private enterprise "new style," as organized in large joint-stock companies, differs from public enterprise only in one respect; namely that it provides an unearned income to its shareholders.

Clearly, the protagonists of capitalism cannot have it both ways. They cannot say "We are all socialists now" and maintain at the same time that socialism cannot possibly work. If they themselves pursue objectives other than that of profit-making, then they cannot very well argue that it becomes impossible to administer the nation's means of production efficiently as soon as considerations other than those of profit-making are allowed to enter.[46]

240

[46]E. F. Schumacher, *Small Is Beautiful* (New York: Harper & Row, 1973), pp. 256-57.

The fact of the matter is, however, that profit has not been deposed from its position as the main rationale and purpose of the corporate institution. Most nonprofit activities turn out to be public relations, aimed at improving the corporate image or cooling down the opposition — in other words, creating a climate in which the corporation can safely pursue its profit-making purposes.

This basic single-mindedness of the corporate structure creates some serious problems because corporations play an extremely large and important part in the system's environmental management, and the profit motive is a seriously deficient basis for such responsibility; it leads to many shortsighted and destructive policies. Other writers have made this abundantly clear in relation to corporate responsibility (or lack of it) in air and water pollution and resource management generally. Less has been said about how the profit rationale contributes to some of our current social woes in regard to energy use and employment. It is now beginning to appear that these two are not separate items after all, but that both are consequences of a mode of production that has become increasingly automated and, in the process, has frequently replaced human laborers with fuel-consuming machines. This is a "rational" and "progressive" change from the profit-making point of view, but it ignores other important considerations such as the need of human beings to work — even if they are less efficient — and the wider social and ecological problems that we get ourselves into in a continual pursuit of new energy sources.

I have come to the conclusion that (1) the corporate structure and the profit-making function are inseparable; (2) the "private sector" makes decisions that influence the whole system; and (3) the imperatives of profit making are so narrow and shortsighted that it is virtually impossible for a system operating on such a basis to carry out wisely the things that we now must do: managing the environment and determining the course of evolution. I realize that in stating these conclusions I am challenging a belief that is most cherished by the American DSP, namely, the inherent wisdom of free enterprise. But the more I observe the actions of American business, the less confident I feel about entrusting the board of directors of a corporation with the future of anything.

Free enterprise may yet save the day, but I suspect that if it does it will be in a somewhat different package from the modern giant corporation. Schumacher argues persuasively in *Small Is Beautiful* that free enterprise *on a human scale* can be an important part of the kind of life style we must create. We may well find, as many people already strongly suspect, that neither the multinational corporation nor the socialized nation-state is the ideal institutional tool for the task of creating a humane and ecologically responsible social order. In any case we can be sure that the forms we now have will change; institutions may seem to be above the law, but they are not above the fundamental law of evolution, which is that everything changes.

Institutional Evolution

The American Bicentennial is an event (or nonevent) that rests on the belief that the institutions we have today are in some meaningful sense the ones created by the men who wrote the Declaration of Independence and the United States Constitution. In certain ways they are; we retain enough basic structures and basic values (and certainly enough symbolic superstructure) to justify a sense of continuity. It may also be that a society changing as rapidly as ours needs to establish this kind of connection to its past, an opportunity to put out a hand and rest against a solid piece of history that has a connection to the bewildering present. Yet the truth is that the Revolution and the establishment of a federal government were only elements in a long line of innovation that is still unfolding. We would have much more to celebrate if we concentrated on the changes that have taken place *since* 1776, on the ways that the system then and the system now differ from each other.

There has been an amazing amount of evolutionary change in the nation's two centuries. More species of plant and animal life have become extinct during this time than in all the continent's previous existence; new species have been introduced and new strains developed through artificial breeding; a new human population has occupied the land, bringing together a variety of biological and cultural heritages into something that, despite its diversity and changeability, we recognize as a distinctly American civilization; the land itself has changed, and so have the institutions by which people organize themselves to live on the land.

I have spoken of institutions as patterns of adaptation, as arrangements created by human beings for the sake of living optimally within the environment. In creating a federal republic people worked out the basic arrangement for building a prosperous commercial society on the eastern seaboard. In extending their institutional forms westward they provided for the establishment of a similar kind of society all across the continent. Along the way new institutional forms evolved: corporations, regional governments, regulatory agencies. If we look more closely at such institutional innovations we can see that they are responses to environmental conditions, and that they are mainly responses to environmental conditions *that were created by human action*. Such man-made developments as urbanization, industrialization, new communications technology, and population growth present the environmental challenges to which the system must respond.

We will encounter many more such challenges as we awaken to an understanding of what our system is and what it has done; and we will be called on to respond with not only new policies and programs but also new institutional structures. This will undoubtedly require abandoning some of the old institutional forms familiar to us. I believe that our present arrangement of city and county governments is already obsolete, and I also doubt that the nation-state will endure much longer as the basic unit of political organization. This is a perilous subject to raise, since we invest our emotions heavily in institutional structures and seem to believe that, once created, they have some transcendent call to exist forever. But they never do last forever, and those that manage to span a long stretch of history — consider the Roman Catholic church or the British Empire — pass through numerous metamorphoses.

Human cultural evolution has witnessed the birth and death of many institutional structures and will undoubtedly witness more. As we look through history at the particular flurry of institution building that took place on the American continent in the late eighteenth century, it should not be with a sense of contemplating some monumental era when a task was undertaken and then finished for good. The Founding Fathers were simply doing what human beings have done since the beginning of civilization, and probably always will do: they discarded old structures and created new ones, using whatever building materials the cultural heritage contained.

243

5

Power
and
Awareness

You can search the *Congressional Record* for speeches which show awareness that the problems of government are biological problems, and you will find very, very few that apply biological insight. Extraordinary!

In general, governmental decisions are made by persons who are as ignorant of these matters as pigeons. Like the famous Dr. Skinner, in *The Way of All Flesh*, they "combine the wisdom of the dove with the harmlessness of the serpent."

GREGORY BATESON, *Steps to an Ecology of Mind*

In this final chapter I would like to examine further how we now control the course of evolution, and also pay attention to the remarkable fact that we do this without quite knowing we do it. The control is something essentially human. Our species has been variously described as the political animal, as the symbolic animal, and as *homo faber*, the tool maker. We can as accurately, without discarding any of the above, define the human species as the one that creates its own environment.

With the first extensions of human skill and knowledge, at the very point when cultural evolution began, people were gaining control over the environment and winning freedom from the old rule of evolutionary survival. By developing clothing and shelter and mastering fire, they became capable of surviving in different climates. Inventing tools for hunting, learning to domesticate animals, and acquiring the technology for agriculture brought power over other living species and also amended the laws of survival generally, since animals were now bred and protected because of their usefulness to people. Evolution evolved. With weapons, shelter, and fire human beings learned to hold off predators. Eventually as medical skills developed, human beings learned also to lessen the probability of death from accident or disease.

From the beginning the struggle to control the conditions of evolution must have been a social activity; certainly all the evidence of recorded history points that way. The ancient city, the first true artificial environment, was not only a monumental achievement of technology but also a monumental effort of

Gregory Bateson, *Steps to an Ecology of Mind* (New York: Ballantine, 1972), p. 437.

American history has
been a steady march
in the direction of
creating an artificial
life system on this
continent.

human cooperation. Today our social network stretches around the world; we modify our environments by moving resources and life forms and manufactured products from continent to continent.

Artificial systems of one kind or another now cover most of the inhabited portions of the earth. Even in the countries we call "underdeveloped" the land is planted with monocultures, worked with domesticated animals, and watered by irrigation systems. Our intervention has changed the composition of the atmosphere and altered the balance of life in the oceans to the extent that there hardly remains a life form totally untouched by human hands.

American history has been a steady march in the direction of creating an artificial life system on this continent. All of the events I have dealt with in this book — immigration, importation of plants and animals, alteration of the land, industrialization, development of institutions — fit together as parts of that massive achievement in environmental engineering. Our cultural values, old and new, also fit the pattern: the myth of the pioneer's struggle against nature, the Protestant ethic, consumerism. The energies of millions of people have been expended for centuries in this cooperative effort, and the vast, forbidding space the explorers discovered a few centuries ago has now been remodeled to suit our commercial purposes.

Yet here is where we bump up against our present political situation, because human ingenuity cannot yet create *permanent* artificial systems. In fact the most common characteristic of the systems we set up is their fragility. Our food supply depends on plant monocultures that are supported by pesticides, chemical fertilizers, and irrigation; dairy animals, poultry, and meat animals are also artificial life systems that must be protected from predators and disease, fed, and maintained through selective breeding. The water for our cities and farms is processed through complex artificial arrangements — reservoirs, canals, pumping systems. All this huge apparatus that we have built to keep our bodies alive requires our constant attention. We must forever battle the predators and weeds and diseases, manufacture the chemicals, mine for the fertilizers, find fuel for the pumps. Fuel. This system, like all life processes, needs energy, and because it is an energy-intensive system we must work hard to keep it running. Because it is an enormously complex social enterprise it requires us to organize ourselves into systems of production and consumption and management that have the power to influence the way we live our individual lives.

Thus we find ourselves endlessly searching for energy sources — oil, coal, nuclear fission. At the same time we see all around us huge concentrations of power in the forms of corporations and fedeal bureaucracies. Neither of these developments is accidental, although we sometimes seem to be rather surprised by them. Our reluctance to confront the obvious realities of our evolutionary condition is truly remarkable. In spite of the fact that American history has been a single-minded pursuit to achieve power over the environment, there is a national shyness about admitting that such power is ours and confronting its logical consequences.

Avoidance, American Style

In a psychological study of American foreign policy William Blanchard argues that its most pervasive characteristic is self-deception: aggression masked by idealism. I wish to examine his thesis at length here, because there are distinct similarities between our behavior as a force in world politics and our behavior as a force in evolution. Blanchard writes:

The American style of aggression is similar in some respects to the British, from whom we derive the notion that a world empire is (and should be) a burden and not a source of pleasure. However, the major part of the British Empire was created during the period of a genuine monarchy and its development was deliberate. It was achieved through the conquest of territory in a conscious motive of acquisition and growth. In the growth of the American Empire, a different process is apparent. Even the early conquest and settlement of the American continent was conceived, not so much in terms of a quest for power, but as part of a "Manifest Destiny," a sense of mission through which we would set an example of our goodness for the rest of the world. American annexation of territory would proceed not by wars, but simply by consenting to the requests of other republics for annexation. William H. Seward at one time believed that the United States would embrace the entire continent through such a peaceful process. However, with the growing power of the United States, the urge to thrust "democracy" upon the other nations of the world has grown accordingly. We began with a desire to protect South America from the European powers. Later we determined to "open up" Japan to the influence of the Western World. Today we have a policy, not yet disavowed, of coming to the aid of "free people" everywhere in the world. . . . In the more recent expansion of American power, there is an effort to continue the early myth of Manifest Destiny. The chief characteris-

tic of this myth was that things happened to us because of our essential goodness. Others wanted to be like us, to join us, to submit to our gentle dominion. We did not seek power. If we became powerful, it happened to us without any conscious intent on our part.[1]

Blanchard mentioned a 1969 speech by Richard Nixon as an expression of this attitude. Nixon spoke of "the role of leadership which is ours, one that we accept, one that we did not ask for.... We are the first power to be the major power in the world that did not ask for it."[2] This attitude, suggests Blanchard, is not peculiar to Nixon but rather a general reflection of American consciousness: "The notion of a deliberate, conscious struggle to dominate others is foreign to our national ethos. We do it, of course, in both our domestic and foreign policy. But it is part of the American style that it must happen without conscious intent."[3]

The expansion of American power in world affairs and the expansion of our power over nature were concurrent, in many ways identical, processes. I have noted, for example, that acquiring new territory was often justified in terms of our ability to make better use of it. In many other ways acquiring political power abroad — through using food supplies as an instrument of foreign policy, selling weapons manufactured from American resources, and expanding into world trade generally — necessitated acquiring power over the native environment. Conversely it would never have been possible to develop American resources, at least in the manner in which our civilization chose to do it, without becoming a world power by entering into complex exchanges of goods and money that would have to be protected by political policies, either diplomatic or military.

There is a common and tragically misled view of American history which holds that the United States was, over a long period of time, isolated — buffered by the wide oceans from the politics of the rest of the world and turned inward upon itself, preoccupied with its internal politics and internal economics and its march across the continent. This notion rests on such historical evidence as Washington's famous farewell address cautioning against "entangling alliances," the avoidance of permanent military treaties from that time until the post-World War II era, the generally small size of the peacetime military establishment (again, until the post-World War II pe-

---

[1]William Blanchard, *Aggression – American Style: A Psychological Study of American Foreign Policy* (unpublished manuscript).
[2]Ibid.
[3]Ibid.

riod), the successful struggle by avowed isolationists against American membership in the League of Nations, and the nature of the events (the explosion of the *Maine*, the sinking of the *Lusitania*, the attack on Pearl Harbor) that seemed to precipitate America against its will into international conflict.

Actually isolationism was always a fantasy and an avoidance of reality. It is true that for a long time military expenditures were kept reasonably low and permanent military alliances were avoided. But during all the years that isolationism was being preached, American ships were plying the oceans of the world and tying the people living on this continent into inextricable networks of exchange with people in other parts of the world who produced goods used here, or who used goods produced here. For a long time America managed to survive in the crevices of power, buying and selling without making a commitment to the ponderous military/diplomatic interactions that occupied the other world-trading societies. But in the long run John Jay's foresight, when he warned in *Federalist* No. 4 that America's commercial energies would inevitably propel the nation into military conflicts, proved sounder than Washington's advice against "entangling alliances."

The early Yankee traders that set out to "try all ports" were taking the first steps on a course of action that led to a position of world leadership. This position was not acquired by accident, by events beyond American control. We were not, as one political scientist put it, simply "catapulted into an hegemonial position as a result of worldwide political and international forces."[4] Rather, when American policy took a turn in the post-World War II years toward permanent military alliance and a massive standing military establishment, it was because it had finally become apparent that a society not economically isolated from the rest of the world cannot be militarily and diplomatically isolated either. The forces that "catapulted" America into this position were in large part American forces; there may have been a sincere desire to avoid the responsibilities of economic empire, but this is not quite the same thing as acquiring power without having sought it.

The drive for power over nature has been similarly disguised: aggressive actions are magically transformed into defensive ones, abroad or at home. Abroad we set up military and economic establishments in foreign countries and then regard attacks on them as acts of war or terrorism. At home we build towns in flood plains and then when the inevitable floods come they are "mad rampages of nature." Massive assaults on

251

---

[4]Kenneth W. Thompson, *American Political Science Review*, December 1971, p. 1259.

Millions of Americans living in highly artificial environments and remote from the sources of their own biological sustenance actually do not know how they are kept alive or understand the extent and costs of the environmental manipulations of which they are a part.

ecosystems are unfailingly described as "internal improvements," and the destruction of entire species for the shallowest of human purposes is justified as economic necessity. There is also the simple absence of knowledge of how nature is managed and used. Millions of Americans living in highly artificial environments and remote from the sources of their own biological sustenance actually do not know how they are kept alive or understand the extent and costs of the environmental manipulations of which they are a part.

I have already touched on several of these issues, but I have not yet discussed the economics of environmental management. It is time to take a look at this subject because our economic concepts are an important part of how we think about (or refuse to think about) our interactions with the natural environment.

The Economics of Unawareness
Economics textbooks have traditionally mentioned a class of commodities called "free goods," which are believed to be apart from the marketplace, not calculable in economic terms. Air is the good most frequently assigned to this class. It is literally free and can be used by anyone, supposedly without any cost to anyone ("free as the air"). The concept of a free good carries the assumption that the commodity is either not damaged by being used or exists in such abundance that its use creates no shortage for anyone else.

However, it now begins to appear that the free goods are not really free. The air may have qualified for that category so long as it was only used for breathing, but technological change creates new uses: the air receives automobile exhaust and the smoke from houses and factories. These uses tend to remove air from the free goods category because they create costs. If a house's paint is soiled by smoke, if an agricultural crop or a human being's health is harmed by smog, the use of the air is no longer free.

Two different ways of dealing with this problem have emerged. One way is to pass laws against air pollution and fine offenders. The trouble with this is that it frequently turns out to be cheaper for the offender to pay the fine than to make the expensive alterations in equipment that would stop pollution. This problem is cited as an argument in favor of the second alternative, whch is to recognize that air is no longer a free good and opt for a user-charge strategy that would permit pollution but require the polluter to "pay by the pound" for whatever is dumped into the air. (The same solution is often proposed for water use.) The two approaches come from different ideological wellsprings: the first is standard liberalism, the second is beloved of conservatives who like "economic realities" and distrust excessive governmental activity. But both approaches run up against similar problems. First, political opposition is frequently strong enough to prevent either alternative from being put into actual practice. Second, considerable public expense in monitoring discharge and developing technology for cleaning up pollution is still involved.

The debates on this issue overlook a most significant point, which is that the air itself is now an artificial environment that must be maintained as a matter of public policy and at public expense. Air was a free good only until population and technology reached a certain level; now it is a public trust.

We are also beginning to discover that the things we *know* we pay for — the products of our consumer economy — cost us more than the apparent market price. There are additional costs that have been "externalized" by the market system. This is a disturbing discovery to economists, as Robert Heilbroner explains:

By externalities *we mean effects exerted by the process of producing or consuming goods that bypass the price system. For example, ordinarily when we consider the price of a good — say an automobile — we assume that this price fully reflects all its costs of manufacturing. But suppose that the auto factory emits smoke that lowers local real estate values or multiplies local cleaning bills. These are costs that are not included in the price of autos. Or suppose that the* use *of automobiles requires the installation of traffic lights or expensive throughways. These are consumption externalities that will impose costs (taxes) on users and nonusers alike. Or suppose the consumption or production of a product has* beneficial *externalities, such as the construction of a new school that greatly improves the value of a neighborhood. One would think that these benefits would be credited against the cost of the school, but they are not.*

We used to believe that externalities were mere curiosities of the economic process — that the prices of a perfectly competitive market system fully reflected all *costs of outputs or* all *benefits that buyers expected to obtain from them. But we have begun to recognize that* externalities are a pervasive and inescapable attribute of nearly all economic processes, and that one of the problems of even a perfect market system is that it fails to take into account their benefits or costs. *Thus the new, environment-threatening technologies constitute a special case of the ecologi-*

255

cal crisis only because they point up more sharply the failure of the market system to deal with a well-nigh universal, but previously ignored problem.[5]

Although the problem is now receiving closer attention in light of the growing interest in ecology, economists have generally recognized for some time that production usually involves costs not reflected in market prices; they have also frequently pointed out that these costs are likely to be borne by the public. This problem gets the most attention from socialist writers, but it can even be found in the works of classical economists, from Adam Smith in the eighteenth century on.[6] Economists have pointed out that production activities result in such externalities as occupational accidents and diseases, water and air pollution, wasteful exploitation of natural resources, invisible costs involved in distribution and transportation of goods, limits on scientific research, deterioration of residential areas as a result of factory construction, military costs in the protection of foreign investment, public programs ("internal improvements") carried out mainly for the benefit of commerce and industry, and many governmental policies at all levels aimed to create favorable conditions for commercial enterprise.

256

The list of these externalities is both partial and fragmentary. It does not quite communicate the basic point, which is that a society such as ours, with its industry, commerce, urbanization, and large consumer population, can exist only in an artificial environment; further, the creation and maintenance of such an environment tends to become a matter of public expense. These costs may be external to the market system but they are not external to the general adaptive enterprise that has been underway on this continent for several centuries.

Since this adaptive activity has been so strongly motivated by economic drives, it makes sense to begin by developing some concepts capable of helping us understand the economics of evolution. First, notice the close connection between the words *economics* and *ecology*. Both contain the Greek root *oikos*, meaning "house"; *economics* means "the management of the house" and *ecology* means "the science or study of the house." In spite of their natural unity, the two have been allowed to separate into different lines of study that pay precious little attention to each other. Most economic theory concerns itself with the transfer of money and, despite much talk of resources,

[5]Robert Heilbroner, *The Economic Problem* (Englewood Cliffs, N.J.: Prentice-Hall, 1972), pp. 570-71. Reprinted by permission. Italics in original.
[6]This subject is treated extensively in K. William Kapp, *The Social Costs of Private Enterprise* (Cambridge, Mass.: Harvard University Press, 1950).

shows little awareness of economic activity as a life force that alters the world ecosystem and is also a part of it. For all its professed realism, economics often seems curiously cut off from reality. To quote Schumacher:

Economics . . . deals with goods in accordance with their market value and not in accordance with what they really are. The same rules are applied to primary goods, which man has to win from nature, and secondary goods, which presuppose the existence of primary goods and are manufactured from them. All goods are created the same, because the point of view is fundamentally that of private profit-making, and this means that it is inherent in the methodology of economics to ignore man's dependence on the natural world.[7]

There are a few economists who recognize the evolutionary/ ecological nature of commercial activity: Heilbroner, Boulding, Schumacher, and Georgescu-Roegen (who looks at economics in terms of energy and the laws of thermodynamics).[8] These signs that economics may be discovering the natural world are encouraging, because our house — the living piece of the world that we inhabit — is in serious disorder, and we desperately need economic wisdom to help us manage it.

Taking Responsibility for Evolution

So far in this chapter I have been talking about the public conspiracy to avoid taking responsibility for the power we have gained over our environment and the processes of evolution; now I would like to pay closer attention to what these processes are. We should keep in mind along the way that the human species is not just now reaching the point of being able to control the course of evolution; rather it is reaching the point of realizing that this is what we have done all along. Obviously our impact is now greater and still growing, but the basic situation is an integral part of human civilization.

As a result we now begin to see what we do; we finally get the message about the role of human civilization and political power in the evolutionary scheme of things. The main bearer of this message is the environmental crisis — pollution, resource depletion, energy shortage, and all the other signs of malfunction in the system. Most of us have reacted to environmental crises the way people are proverbially supposed to react to a

---

[7]E. F. Schumacher, *Small Is Beautiful* (New York: Harper & Row, 1973), pp. 43-44.
[8]Nicholas Georgescu-Roegen, *The Entropy Law and the Economic Process* (Cambridge, Mass.: Harvard University Press, 1971).

bearer of bad news, that is, with resentment and hostility. We have tried to ignore it, misread its message, reject it violently as a conspirator against the American Dream, or at the very least hope it would soon go away. But it hasn't disappeared, and neither will the message it brings us, which is simply that we are in power, that evolutionary change is now determined by human action.

I have discussed this mainly in terms of how we alter the environment and control the survival of other life forms. But that is only part of it. We also have the ability to control the genetic and the cultural evolution of the human species.

As we turn now to some of the technology of genetic evolution, we are entering an area that may seem out of place in a book about American politics, or at least vaguely irrelevant to the various ecological, economic, and political issues we have explored thus far. I hope I will be able to convince the reader that some of the discoveries now being made by geneticists are part of the same picture, merely another dimension of the astounding capacity of the human species to guide its own evolution.

The Politics of Genetic Evolution

Most biologists believe that the genetic evolution of the species is still going on and that cultural evolution and genetic evolution are now inseparable. George Gaylord Simpson summarizes the prevailing opinion:

The consensus ... is that the bodily — somatic — evolution of Homo sapiens *is continuing for better or for worse, and will continue.... human populations have biological aspects that are known to lead eventually to marked evolutionary change in other species and must almost inevitably do so also in this one. Furthermore biology and culture are not two quite independent things such that one can, like a relay runner, pass on the torch of progress — or simply of change — to the other. They are parts of an interacting system, in which cultural change will certainly affect the nature and rate of somatic change and may well accelerate it. And cultural accomplishment has already reached the point where men could deliberately accelerate the evolution of the species and influence its direction.*[9]

One way to influence the rate and direction of evolution is by directly manipulating genetic material: "genetic engineering." Technology in this field is developing rapidly along several lines, all of which lead eventually to areas of public concern.

[9]George Gaylord Simpson, *Biology and Man* (New York: Harcourt Brace, 1969), p. 131.

The image shows a baby sitting inside a glass Erlenmeyer flask, with a tag reading "ENGINEER MALE/I.Q. 160 #79314B"

James Watson, a Nobel Prize-winning biochemist, says that if the technology "proceeds in its current nondirected fashion, a human being born of clonal reproduction most likely will appear on earth within the next twenty to fifty years."

259

Cloning is a process whereby scientists can precisely reproduce either a single copy or infinite copies of a living individual. This has been done successfully with frogs by replacing the nucleus from an egg cell with the nucleus of a body cell from an adult frog. The result is a young frog that is not the offspring of the cell donor but an exact replica of it. Cloning has not yet been accomplished with mammals, but scientists expect that it will soon be possible to produce entire herds of livestock with the characteristics of the most outstanding individual member of the species — a giant step forward in the already highly sophisticated technology of selective breeding. The prospect of cloned human beings follows naturally from this and is taken seriously by scientists. James Watson, a Nobel Prize-winning biochemist, says that if the technology "proceeds in its current nondirected fashion, a human being born of clonal reproduction most likely will appear on earth within the next twenty to fifty years, and even sooner if some nation actively promotes the venture."[10]

Genetic transplanting is a manipulation of genetic material to introduce a genetic characteristic, either from another individual of the same species or from a member of another species. There have been successful transplant experiments with the genes of frogs, mice, and fruit flies. A 1974 *Science News* article suggests some of the future research possibilities:

> *The gene for insulin production ... could theorteically be removed from human DNA, placed in bacterial DNA, and start producing the insulin molecule in the new system. It could then be harvested and used for cheap, efficient drug production. The gene for nitrogen-fixation could be added to nonnitrogen-fixing bacteria or plants, and of course, genetic manipulation could conceivably correct human genetic disorders.*[11]

So far this kind of research has been successful only with single-gene traits and has not effectively proceeded to the much more complex realm of polygenic traits — such features as size, intelligence, strength, or temperament — which are the products of many different genes and environmental factors as well.[12] But even at its limited level of progess genetic transplant research has created a profound uneasiness in the scientific community. In 1974 a group of leading molecular biologists backed by the National Academy of Sciences took the

[10]James Watson, "Moving Toward the Clonal Man," *Atlantic Monthly*, May 1971, p. 52.
[11]"Geneticists and Gene Transplants: A Historic Call for a Ban on Research," *Science News*, 27 July 1974, p. 52.
[12]Bernard D. Davis, "Genetic Engineering: How Great Is the Danger?" *Science*, 25 October 1974, p. 186.

260

unprecedented step of calling for a self-imposed ban on genetic transplant research, mainly because of its potential for creating new technologies of biological warfare. The issue was aired in the scientific journals, and concerned scientists are now attempting to enforce a moratorium on this kind of work.

Amniocentesis is a mature, reliable technique that needs no further development to reach the point of being capable of influencing the course of human evolution. It is a procedure in which a doctor can remove a small quantity of fluid from the amniotic sac containing an unborn human fetus and have it analyzed to determine whether the fetus has any genetic abnormality such as mongolism. If the test is positive, parents normally choose to abort.

Amniocentesis carries its own load of biological/political issues. Its proponents argue that it will reduce the proportion of defective human beings — who frequently become dependent on public institutions for existence — and that it will improve the human gene pool. Others believe that it will have precisely the opposite effect, for the following reason. Children with genetic afflictions do not usually reach reproductive age and therefore do not pass their defect on to the next generation. But if parents who have conceived one child with a genetic defect abort it and then have a "normal" child, the normal child will pass the defective genes on to future generations and eventually the number of defective genes in the human gene pool will multiply enormously. There is also the problem of precisely defining a "genetic defect." Diabetes is ordinarily so classified but it may, as one argument holds, well have survival value in a situation of limited food supply and be "deleterious only in the context of the grossly excessive and unbalanced diets which characterize our civilization."[13] Sickle-cell anemia is also classed as a genetic defect, but it is linked to resistance to malaria. These are two cases of defects that might become advantages in a different environment. It is also frequently pointed out that many of the greatest human beings in history came into the world with some sort of genetic affliction.

These are not hypothetical questions to be debated at leisure; they are real issues that already affect lives of human beings living and yet unborn. What is more, such questions have a powerful tendency to become public issues. As Amitai Etzioni noted, questions that might seem capable of being determined by either the expertise of medical science or the personal preference of individuals are never really made in a political vacuum: laws concerning abortion, social pressures, medical costs,

261

---

[13]Amitai Etzioni, "Biomedicine and Ethics," *Current*, January 1974, p. 43.

The growth of larger political systems seems to proceed at the expense of certain human needs that are better met by smaller political units.

and the availability of medical care are all ways that the society's values and institutions intervene: "In short, what we can do as citizens in regard to our bodies, is, unfortunately, not just a personal question between us and our families, us and our physicians. The whole legal, economic, political, institutional continuum has to be dealt with. And whether we like it or not, the road to personal liberties passes through many civic intersections."[14]

The political dimension becomes more visible as we consider traits that might be not only defective but also socially undesirable. At the present time nearly all states have legal and, in most cases, compulsory screening programs for detecting genetic defects.[15] Mostly these are for the purpose of providing medical care, but such programs are capable of expanding into other concerns. In many states the list of genetic defects now includes the presence of the extra Y chromosome in males, which is believed to be connected with a tendency toward criminal violence. It has been proposed (a logical extension) that such children be registered at birth so they can be observed for the rest of their lives by the appropriate public agencies; at least one prominent biologist, Bentley Glass, believes that amniocentesis and abortion should be employed to eliminate the extra Y chromosome from the human strain entirely.[16]

The old debate of heredity versus environment becomes politics, not just biological theory, whenever an attempt is made to deal with a behavioral trait as though it were genetically inherited. This issue arises periodically over concerns about violence, sexual deviancy, and mental defectiveness of any kind. In 1971, twenty-one states had laws authorizing sterilization of "mentally defective" individuals, and the laws have been applied. Between 1960 and 1968 North Carolina's eugenics board sterilized 1,620 persons; most of them were young black women.[17]

It is generally assumed that the purpose and the result of human tinkering with genetic evolution is to improve the species through eliminating defective characteristics in the gene pool. But many biologists suspect that the actual progress may well be in the opposite direction. Julian Huxley, for example, has written that "The general quality of the world's population . . . is deteriorating, thanks to genetic defectives who would

[14]Ibid., p. 49.
[15]Frederick Ausubel, Jon Beckwith, and Kaaren Janssen, "The Politics of Genetic Engineering: Who Decides Who's Defective,"*Psychology Today*, June 1974, pp. 30-43.
[16]Bentley Glass, in Ausubel et al., "The Politics of Genetic Engineering: Who Decides Who's Defective," p. 37.
[17]Robert Williams, "Scientific Racism and IQ," *Psychology Today*, May 1974.

otherwise have died being kept alive, and thanks to the crop of new mutations due to fallout. In modern man the direction of genetic evolution has started to change its sign, from positive to negative, from advance to retreat."[18] And Bentley Glass, affirming this opinion, has said: "By surrounding ourselves with an ever more artificial environment, we unwittingly modify the rigor of natural selection in many ways. The price we must pay, in the end, for the mercies of medical care and surgical aid is a dysgenic increase in the frequencies of certain detrimental genes the effects of which we have learned to ameliorate."[19]

Both of these statements, Glass's explicitly, raise the point that medical science generally tends to create an artificial environment, to shift determination of the course of human genetic change from the laws of evolution to the laws and policies of human societies. Medical science developed out of straightforward survival needs and has been strongly supported by society on the basis of the understandable belief that the preservation and protection of human life is among the highest social goals. But evolutionary developments are now calling for a reappraisal of those assumptions, which may well prove to be one of the most difficult tasks ever undertaken by human civilization. The question raised by Huxley, Glass, and other biologists — that is, whether medicine results in a deterioration of the genetic quality of the human population — is one such reappraisal. This is an unpopular issue because it seems to call for measures that are contrary to the most basic human values. It is also a debatable issue; we don't have actual data telling us that the number of genetic defects in the total human gene pool is increasing, or if such an increase presents any problems that cannot be dealt with by future medical or genetic technology.

The evidence is considerably clearer in another closely related genetic-evolutionary issue: population. There is no doubt that improvements in medical technology, especially immunization, have contributed greatly to the remarkable increase in the number of living human beings. There has been a steady increase in the birthrate and a corresponding decline in the death rate, to the point that overpopulation is a major world crisis. Efforts to meet this crisis by reducing the birthrate are underway — for example, improving birth-control technologies, investing in the widespread distribution of contraceptive materials, making abortions available on demand, and aiming

[18]Julian Huxley, in Etzioni, "Biomedicine and Ethics," p. 42.
[19]Bentley Glass, in Etzioni, "Biomedicine and Ethics," p. 42.

programs toward changing cultural attitudes regarding family size. Yet the efforts directed at increasing the size of world population by reducing death rates still have a much higher social priority. In the United States, as in all other countries, far more public money is spent on research to eliminate fatal diseases than on reducing birthrates. It is difficult (and certainly not politically opportune) to argue that the priorities should be reversed, but there is a serious question about whether our emphasis on medicine has the survival value for the species that we once assumed it did.

Population growth is an obvious example of evolutionary change caused by socially created environmental conditions; we should also note that present worldwide patterns of population growth are causing major changes in the racial composition of the human species. Rates of growth are leveling off in the more industrially developed nations with predominantly white populations and continuing to increase in third-world nations, thus causing a much smaller proportion of whites in the species as a whole. The implications for survival are alarming when we consider that the less densely populated nations continue to consume disproportionately large amounts of the world's resources.

These problems become serious because we avoid confronting them, and we avoid confronting them because they are so serious. It is rarely pleasant to bring into full consciousness the evolutionary impacts of our political policies, and more often than not officials would rather operate under the pretense that the acts of governments have either a beneficial effect on evolution or no effect at all.

Another reason that issues bearing on genetic evolution are not adequately aired in public discussion is that they have a tendency to be explosive. Population control is denounced as genocide; abortion and birth control get into trouble with organized religion. It probably does not help, either, that the best-known historical example of a political leader who took an active interest in controlled genetic evolution was Adolph Hitler. Even among scientists debates on these issues are often bitter and emotional, and when the discussion gets into the public arena it frequently polarizes opposing groups and makes politicians run for cover. It is understandable, considering the aura of ideology and emotionalism surrounding matters of genetics, that these issues are often avoided.

Yet these are momentous decisions concerning the future of the human race that must be widely discussed if democracy means anything at all. We need a much higher level of public awareness of explicitly genetic issues such as those mentioned here and also a better understanding that other political acts — every war, every migration of people, every redrawing of a national boundary — are alterations of social settings that will have direct or indirect effects on genetic evolution. Genetic evolution is the compounded effect of the basic realities of human existence — who lives, who dies, who marries whom, and whose children survive — and anything a political system does (or doesn't do) in regard to those realities has an evolutionary consequence.

Cultural Evolution
Even if the genetic condition of the human species should remain the same in the coming centuries, there would still be cultural change. There is no sign of a leveling off of cultural evolution; on the contrary, it appears to be proceeding more rapidly. A woman born in a European village a few centuries ago could expect to stay in the same place, occupy the same social stratum, participate in the same rituals, and occupy her time in the same way as her great-grandmother; she could expect also that her great-granddaughter would live out approximately the same life pattern. A ruler would die and a new ruler would take his place but the monarchy would still exist. Tools, houses, means of transportation would remain the same. Religion would be the same.

265

Today we expect that the world will change during our own lifetime: that new revolutions and new inventions are somewhere around the corner, and that the basic conditions of our existence will probably, for better or for worse, be different from what they are today. Few of us pursue the same life's work as our parents did, and more and more Americans find it possible to change careers once (or more than once) along the way, either because their preferences change or because the social environment changes. Cultural change becomes an integral part of the course of every individual's life.

Institutional Change One kind of change we can expect is change in the nature of our political institutions. There will be new policies, new programs, new laws, and undoubtedly structural changes through the formal process for modification. In the sixties and seventies there were several important changes of this kind: the Supreme Court's "one man, one vote" decision in the 1962 case of *Baker* v. *Carr*, which forced reapportionment of most state legislatures; the 1965 Voting Rights Act, which helped blacks gain political power in the South; the Twenty-

Fifth Amendment permitting the appointment of a vice-president, which proved crucial during the Watergate upheavals; and the various state and federal laws regulating campaign practices. The changes came into being through different parts of the political system: the Supreme Court, Congress, the amendment process, the state legislatures. Each of these can be expected to produce further major adjustments in the political decision-making process.

There may well be more momentous rearrangements in the offing, in the form of new institutions, large or small. There are forces pushing toward larger organizational systems and others striving for greater differentiation within the system, diffusion of power into smaller and more manageable local units. This division creates some odd political configurations. Among those favoring larger, worldwide forms of organization are environmentalists, world federalists, Communists, pacifists, and executives of multinational corporations. Among those favoring more decentralization are radical community organizers, conservative "states' rights" defenders, opponents of school integration, some ethnic and religious minority groups, and participatory-democracy adherents of all varieties.

Clearly there is a need for world organization. One of the first things that becomes apparent as we recognize our government's role in management of the American environment is that this enormous space is still only a subsystem in a worldwide ecological unit. Each extension of commerce and each development in communications or transportation technology knits together the world system. And whenever such connections are established, formal organizational arrangements tend to develop.

We already have many kinds of international institutions: remnants of empire, military alliances, political blocs, religious organizations, the United Nations, societies and associations of all sorts, and of course the multinational corporations. Some of these may have the potential to evolve into new supranational institutional forms. Most of the betting right now seems to be on the multinational corporations, which are showing a remarkable capacity to manipulate international politics, control resources, and make basic decisions about how people in many parts of the world will live and work. And, for precisely the same reasons that corporations grew when they were mainly continental U.S. organizations, the multinationals seek to expand. "To talk about global corporations that do not grow or that voluntarily limit their growth," one recent study said, "is to talk about a fundamental transformation of that institution which defies both its own basic ideology and the laws of oligopolistic competition."[20]

The growth of the multinational corporations is one good argument for creating *other* international organizations (or expanding the power of existing ones) to regulate them and guide international development on some other basis than corporate profit. There are further reasons why we will probably need more effective international organization — such problems as worldwide air and water pollution, depletion of marine species — all of which boil down to the fact that environmental management at our present level of technology inescapably becomes worldwide environmental management.

But to return to the case for decentralization, the growth of larger political systems seems to proceed at the expense of certain human needs that are better met by smaller political units. Our political wisdom so far has been rather slow to recognize that efficient programs and policies are not the only measures of the worth of a political system; the experiential quality of the political process and its ability to allow satisfying human participation in decision making must also be judged.

Nor can we yet conclude that all issues of environmental management are best decided at the level of international organizations. It may turn out that as we learn more about the art of relating human societies to their physical environments, natural ecosystem boundaries make sense as the legal limits of political subsystems. We already have some experience with governmental units shaped in recognition of the ecological unity of a region — for example, the Tennessee Valley Authority and the air-basin approach to pollution control. This could become a model for new forms of regional government with some degree of regional autonomy.

I say "some degree" because it seems unlikely, given the world's present headlong rush toward more industrialization and more population, that local or regional units of any kind can function except as subsystems in a world system. This is the central point of Garrett Hardin's celebrated essay on "The Tragedy of the Commons," which states that the exercise of certain traditional human freedoms — to reproduce, to maximize personal gain — tends to create situations that call for those freedoms to be restricted.[21] True autonomy is possible only where there is no pollution and no dependence on scarce resources — a condition that would be hard to find in any

267

[20]Richard J. Barnet and Ronald E. Muller, *Global Reach* (New York: Simon & Schuster, 1974), p. 337.
[21]Garrett Hardin, "The Tragedy of the Commons," *Science*, 13 December 1968, pp. 1243-48.

The kind of technological change we have been undergoing in the past few decades has been rapid and spectacular. But we should not assume that it has produced an across-the-board improvement in the human condition.

269

270

populated region in the world, especially in the United States.

Actually, the era of the world system has already arrived, and institutional forms to guide it are emerging. The question is whether we can have worldwide organization that is more than a huge bureaucracy or a cluster of corporate giants, something that retains or, better yet, *increases* opportunities for self-government, cultural variety, and community.

Technological Change   A conspicuous feature of the American episode in human evolution has been an abundance of technological developments. Building a new civilization on the American continent was a great stimulus to inventiveness, which became a quality much prized in our value system. I doubt that any other society has placed so high a premium on this particular human trait. Our patriotic literature extols "Yankee ingenuity"; our more successful inventors — Alexander Graham Bell, Thomas Edison — are great national heroes; the public has generally equated invention with progress, and progress with betterment. "America," Tocqueville observed, "is a land of wonders, in which everything is in constant motion and every change seems an improvement. The idea of novelty is there indissolubly connected with the idea of amelioration."[22]

This attitude may be changing. Recent opinion polls reveal that the American public is less optimistic about the future, which has to do with the realization that new technology sometimes causes problems instead of solving them. Discussion of environmental issues has given rise to a certain amount of hostility toward the traditional hopefulness that some new invention will come along to avert every crisis, for example, that new agricultural technology to increase food production will deal effectively with the population problem.

Debates of this sort are sometimes described as pro- and antitechnology, which is not precisely correct. In the case of the population debate the antipopulation-growth side is also interested in new technology such as birth-control devices. The argument is not for or against technology but rather about what kind of a world we want and, more specifically, what lines of technological progress are most desirable to follow. The argument has to do with priorities and with understanding that technological change always has multiple consequences.

In the past we did not know how to think holistically about

[22]Alexis de Tocqueville, *Democracy in America*, Part I, Chapter 18, trans. Henry Reeve (New Rochelle, N.Y.: Arlington House, 1966).

technological change — we did not know how to and did not want to. We did not understand that major new technologies do more than simply improve the functioning of one part of a system — instead they change the whole system. In the matter of transportation, for example, the construction of the transcontinental railroad had an incredibly complex and far-reaching set of repercussions that are still echoing through the nation. The railroad resulted in the building of cities and the rise of economic empires; the alteration of land spaces and the creation of political boundaries; it influenced the use of resources and the patterns of life for millions of people. The emergence of the automobile as a mode of transportation, again, did much more than merely provide a new way of moving people and goods: it truly changed the entire social, economic, and ecological structure of the nation.

To return to the problem of overpopulation (which is itself a product of technological change), we must understand that either alternative, growth or no growth, will necessitate other adjustments in society. Growth requires more schools, jobs, houses, and food; no growth requires new guarantees of old-age security for people who have traditionally bred large families to ensure for that eventuality, and also new social roles for women. If new land is to be converted to agricultural productivity, or if high-yield crops are to be grown, then there will have to be more irrigation systems (more dams, more canals) and greater use of artificial fertilizers and pesticides (resulting in more water pollution).

One way or another there will be technological change. Just what kind of change is the real issue, and certainly a political one in the fullest sense. Thus if we consider the political agenda offered by Barry Commoner, a prominent environmentalist, we find merely a different set of priorities. What we need, he says, are:

major new technologies, including: systems to return sewage and garbage directly to the soil; the replacement of many synthetic materials by natural ones; the reversal of the present trend to retire land from cultivation and to elevate the yield per acre by heavy fertilization; replacement of synthetic pesticides, as rapidly as possible, by biological ones; the discouragement of power-consuming industries; the development of land transport that operates with maximal fuel efficiency at low combustion temperatures and with minimal land use; essentially complete containment and reclamation of wastes from combustion pro-

271

cesses, smelting, and chemical operations (smokestacks must become rarities); essentially complete recycling of all reusable metal, glass, and paper products.[23]

It is important that we not be confused here by the use of such words as *natural* and *biological* in place of *synthetic*; we are talking about different kinds of technology, not a choice between technology and no technology. We are not "returning to nature" when we use reclaimed wastes for fertilizer or send one species of insect in against another as a form of pesticide. True, we may find it necessary to reexamine some forms of technology that have been around for a long time, such as the use of animal wastes as fertilizer, but the reality is that nature is still being manipulated for human purposes. Evolution does not go in reverse. What Commoner and others of his general persuasion advocate is not no technology but rather a more sophisticated and, one hopes, less wasteful technology that might emerge from a better understanding of biological processes and the by-products of certain lines of change.

272

The kind of technological change we have been undergoing in the past few decades has been rapid and spectacular. But we should not assume that it has produced an across-the-board improvement in the human condition. In most parts of the world, per capita housing and food supplies are worse than they were twenty years ago; moreover, with populations doubling every twenty to thirty years these conditions are likely to continue to deteriorate. Technological progress in the United States when examined closely does not turn out to equate with better living. Commoner and his associates reviewed the statistics on American industrial progress since World War II and found that:

While production for most basic needs —food, clothing, housing, has just about kept up with the 40 to 50 percent or so increase in population (that is, production per capita has been essentially constant), the kinds of goods produced to meet these needs have changed drastically. New production technologies have displaced old ones. Soap powder has been displaced by synthetic detergents; natural fibers (cotton and wool) have been displaced by synthetic ones; steel and lumber have been displaced by aluminum, plastics, and concrete; returnable bottles have been displaced by nonreturnable ones. On the road, the low-powered automobile engines of the 1920s and 1930s have been displaced by high-powered ones. On the farm, while per capita production has

[23]Barry Commoner, *The Closing Circle* (New York: Alfred Knopf, 1972), pp. 283-84.

remained about constant, the amount of harvested acreage has decreased; in effect, fertilizer has displaced land. Older methods of insect control have been displaced by synthetic insecticides . . . and for controlling weeds the cultivator has been displaced by the herbicide spray. Range-feeding of livestock has been displaced by feedlots.[24]

The greatest single growth commodity in the post-World War II years was non-returnable soda bottles: up 53,000 percent.

The reasons for the kinds of technological change we have had are mainly short-range economic ones. The automobile industry and related industries had huge profits during the lengthy big-car binges; whole new industries grew up around the manufacture of different kinds of synthetics. The costs, which were externalized onto the society as a whole and to future generations, were not readily apparent; we saw the gross national product grow each year and called it prosperity, without thinking about the whole-system impacts of the kind of growth that was taking place.

Perhaps I can make this point more clearly by pointing out that the greatest single growth commodity in the post-World War II years was nonreturnable soda bottles: up 53,000 percent. A bit farther down on the list were plastics, up 19,689 percent; and electric household appliances, up 1,040 percent.[25] All of these, admittedly, swelled the GNP; they also made their contributions to the solid waste problem and the energy crisis.

We need not simply more technology (or less, either) but rather a higher and wiser technology, a better understanding of the costs and effects. We need an expanded capacity to forecast probable consequences of different lines of development; this capacity is especially ugent whenever we are dealing with exponential rates of change. We are caught off base by environmental crises and energy crises because we set processes in motion without having developed a way of predicting their outcomes. Advanced technological capacities have rendered obsolete our ways of predicting and observing their effects. By the time a problem becomes obvious, it is already too late to solve it except at great cost.

For example, it is already too late to solve the population problem painlessly because millions of people who are starving or living barely marginal existences are already experiencing its effects. To give an example closer to home, it is already too late to clean up Lake Erie painlessly because it is polluted to a level that would call for a massive technological effort, and meanwhile many people have an economic interest in polluting

273

---

[24]Ibid., p. 144.
[25]Ibid., p. 143.

it still more. The time when these crises could have been easily averted has already come and gone.

If we look again at the agenda for technological change proposed by Commoner, we can see that many of its items are simply remedies for problems produced by earlier technological changes. This is an inescapable part of anybody's agenda; even people who staunchly defend the whole production-consumption system and hope for infinite industrial growth include pollution-control technology somewhere among their priorities. Actually pollution-control technology is already a sizable growth industry; ironically several of the major corporations most heavily involved in it are also among the greatest polluters.

But there is a difference between a commitment to increasing industrial growth supported by the conviction that all problems will eventually be solved by new technology, and a commitment to searching for different *kinds* of technology that might have fewer and less serious secondary impacts (such as pollution, heavy energy use, heavy dependency on scarce resources) and thus create fewer crises.

Commoner and many other ecologists believe that the most likely alternative technology will rely more than we have in the recent past on natural processes and natural materials. As I have mentioned, change in the post-World War II era has been strongly in the direction of an increased dependency on synthetic materials such as plastics and chemicals, which tend to be higher in unanticipated secondary impacts. The "natural" technology being advocated to replace this would revive some old and familiar practices, and would also involve inventions and innovations: using plants such as water hyacinths to purify water for reuse, generating power from controlled decomposition processes (methane power plants). Some agriculturalists have suggested that instead of concentrating on developing chemical pesticides we could emphasize research in developing disease-resistant crop varieties and in using microbial agents, parasites, and predators against pests. The technology of genetic engineering opens up whole new approaches to plant nutrition and disease and pest control.

When we consider possible alternative courses of technological development we are dealing with *political* choices. We are not merely speculating about what kinds of discoveries the scientists may come up with in the future; we are talking about what kind of a social order we want and what price we are prepared to pay for it. There will, of course, be discoveries by lonely scientists in their laboratories, but the decisions about how the society produces its energy and its food and housing and clothes, what it does with the land and with other living species, are social decisions. For some time to come they will be made (as they have been in the past) in the public and private institutions to which we entrust such power, and they will have the active or passive consent of most of us.

The conversion to automobile transportation, to return to our example of how a society can launch itself into a new technological phase, was not simply a product of Henry Ford's imagination or the result of a conspiracy of automobile manufacturers. It proceeded from a social consensus that was expressed in the policies of all levels of government and in the actions of millions of Americans who worked in the factories, built the freeways, pumped the gasoline, and — most important of all — bought the cars. It grew out of our social values and our images of what we wanted our society to be.

Two related points to be made here are that technological change is not accidental but the product of social choice, and that technological change is always social change as well — which may be a bit harder to accept. When a system changes, it changes. Put that way the matter sounds simple enough. Yet there is a great deal of resistance to understanding that whenever a society embarks on a course of technological change it is choosing to be a different society. This is an axiom yet to be learned by American policy makers, most of whom seem to believe that it is possible to be technologically progressive and politically conservative at the same time.

Paradigm Change In his book *The End of the Modern Age,* Allen Wheelis gives a useful summary of social paradigm change:

Since man became a historical being each age has been able to recognize the certainties of the past as mistaken, often as absurd. Eternal verities prove both transient and untrue. We look back and see that they were held by a particular people with unique mores living on a limited segment of earth during a certain period of time, and that whatever apparent validity they had was bound to those circumstances. What was self-evident truth to them is seen by us to be arbitrary, culturally relative, derived from needs and fears.

As historical consciousness lengthens, more layers of the past can be examined and compared. It becomes possible for a certain age, A, to look back to an earlier age, B, and to observe that B, in writing the history of a still earlier age, C, recognizes (correctly, we believe) the cherished beliefs of C as primitive superstitions,

Politics is not merely
a conflict between
economic factions
but a dialogue — a
rather murky and
strident one, but a
dialogue neverthe-
less — about cultural
change.

Taking on responsibility for cultural evolution is admittedly a rather tall order for a species that has only rather recently in its historical past realized that there *is* such a thing as cultural evolution or, for that matter, any evolution at all.

278

whereas B's cherished beliefs are seen by B as enlightened and rational, indeed not as beliefs at all, but as objective findings, self-evident truths. But A, in considering B's beliefs, alleged to be so rational and enlightened, find them just as mistaken, though perhaps in a different direction, as C's.

Such findings pose a special problem: If at every level of the past, eternal verities are found to be culturally relative, must we not infer likewise for our own? [26]

Wheelis is touching on one of the most interesting aspects of cultural evolution, which is that beliefs periodically become obsolete; they are shed like a snake's skin by the human species in its developmental process and replaced by new ones. And it appears that this kind of change, like other aspects of cultural evolution we have considered, is altering its rate of change: the life expectancy of eternal verities is getting progressively shorter, as new revolutions in thought succeed old ones with accelerating rapidity.

In the distant past the human species had long, comfortable stretches of time in which to assimilate new inventions and discoveries, to alter basic ideas about the nature of the world, to make the necessary social adjustments to new views of reality. The Western world lived for well over a thousand years with the Ptolemaic image of the earth-centered solar system and the Christian view of the Great Ladder of Being, in which each species had its fixed and unchanging place. Then came a series of scientific discoveries, each of which demanded that people let go of their basic ideas of what was real. Nicholas Copernicus and Giordano Bruno showed a new solar system, in which the sun no longer rotated around the earth; Isaac Newton showed the universe operating according to laws that could be discovered by scientific observation; Charles Darwin showed the human species as an evolving animal distantly related to the apes. Early in the twentieth century Albert Einstein sketched a new image of the universe, rendering obsolete a good portion of the eternal verities we had inherited from Copernicus and Newton. Sigmund Freud, updating Darwin, held up to the human race a new view of itself in which the animal past still lived on in the depths of the unconscious mind.

In our time much of Einstein's and Freud's work is already showing signs of age, and in several fields — astronomy, biology, nuclear physics — fundamental realities change every few years.

---

[26] Allen Wheelis, *The End of the Modern Age* (New York: Basic Books, 1971), p. 83.

As our beliefs change, so do our values; we experience the world differently and form different ideas about what is good and bad, what is desirable for a society or an individual. Consider, for example, the contrast between Europe of a few centuries ago, when the existence of distinct social classes was seen as an expression of divine will, and an individual's duty was to occupy his or her station contentedly, and contemporary America, where the best society is seen as the one with the greatest freedom of opportunity, and the individual's duty is to rise as far as his or her talents (or luck) permit. (I write this with some hesitance because our values are in motion and even that most sacred of all American cows, personal achievement, seems to be losing its foothold a bit.)

Politics is not merely a conflict between economic factions but a dialogue (albeit rather murky and strident) about cultural change. This was evident in the protest movements of the mid-1960s, when political activism came equipped with a new morality and a new life style, and again in the elections of the late 1960s when such candidates as Ronald Reagan and Richard Nixon came to power as defenders of the American DSP. The dialogue in the 1970s turns to the reexamination of the social roles of men and women, and the discussion of such political issues as honesty in government, personal privacy, and sexual freedom. This dialogue has appropriately produced some change in the way we talk about cultural change. New words have been introduced into our vocabulary, as observers have attempted to comprehend the nature of the change. *Futureshock.* Alvin Toffler spoke of the effect of cultural change on individuals, the "shattering stress and disorientation" that comes with the attempt to handle cultural transition; he argued that human life has become fundamentally different from what it was:

We have in our time released a totally new social force — a stream of change so accelerated that it influences our sense of time, revolutionizes the tempo of daily life, and affects the very way we "feel' the world around us. We no longer "feel" life as men did in the past. And this is the ultimate difference, the distinction that separates the truly contemporary man from all others. For this acceleration lies behind the impermanence — the transcience — that penetrates and tinctures our consciousness, radically affecting the way we relate to other people, to things, to the entire universe of ideas, art and values.[27]

---

[27]Alvin Toffler, *Futureshock* (New York: Random House, 1970), p. 18.

Counterculture. Theodore Roszak, focusing on rebellious American youth, offered the idea that the transition was not so much a giving way (slowly or rapidly) of an old set of values to a new set, but rather that the new set had already flowered into something resembling a culture even while the old culture still survived. The America he showed was a schizoid society in which the old DSP — what he called "technocratic values" — continued to run the system, while at the same time the young and their mentors erected about themselves a cultural milieu as different from it as possible: "For better or worse," said Roszak, "most of what is presently happening that is new, provocative and engaging in politics, education, the arts, social relations (love, courtship, family, community), is the creation either of youth who are profoundly, even fanatically, alienated from the parental generation, or of those who address themselves primarily to the young."[28]

Consciousness III. Charles Reich constructed a model of American cultural evolution (and revolution) that focused, as Roszak had, on youth as the bearers of an emerging value system. In Reich's analysis, each stage of American history had been dominated by a different kind of consciousness. Consciousness I was the mind set of the pioneer, the rugged individualist, the self-guided and independent farmer, worker, or small businessman. Consciousness II was created by the needs of an organizational society dominated by big business and big government; it was the mentality of the organization man, the bureaucrat, the professional, the team player. Each of these mind sets represents a historical period, a specific set of circumstances to which they were an adaptive response, and each, said Reich, continues anachronistically in modern society. At the same time there is appearing within the society a new way of being in the world, Consciousness III. This is roughly the same phenomenon as Roszak's counterculture, a couple of years farther along. Reich saw it as a new kind of revolution that would change the political order, even without being in itself explicitly political:

It is now spreading with amazing rapidity, and already our laws, institutions and social structure are changing in consequence. It promises a higher reason, a more human community, and a new and liberated individual. Its ultimate creation will be a new and

280

---

[28]Theodore Roszak, *The Making of a Counter-Culture* (New York: Doubleday, 1969), p. 1.

enduring wholeness and beauty — a renewed relationship of man to himself, to other men, to society, to nature, and to the land.[29]

The New Morality. Throughout the late 1960s and early 1970s Daniel Yankelovich and his associates conducted a series of nationwide surveys that confirmed (and also gave the blessing of legitimate sociological research methodology to) some of the findings of Roszak and Reich. A different value system, which Yankelovich called the "New Morality," had indeed made its appearance within American society. The most striking thing shown by the Yankelovich findings was the speed with which the new value system had spread from a narrow enclave of student radicals to American youth generally (including non-college youth) and, to a lesser degree, older Americans as well. The transition he documented — a far more momentous one than the explosion of the 1960s, which had briefly caught the fickle attention of the mass media — was a process of cultural diffusion taking place *since* that time:

Indeed, so startling are the shifts in values and beliefs between the late 1960s, when our youth studies were first launched, and the present time that social historians of the future should have little difficulty in identifying the end of one era and the beginning of a new one. Rarely has a transition between one decade and the next seemed so abrupt.[30]

Some of the specifics of the shift included a massive change in sexual morality (judging from responses to several survey questions dealing with premarital sex, homosexuality, and abortion), a general agreement with many of the goals of the women's movement, and a declining attachment to traditional values of patriotism and religion. There was also a decline in political activism and a separation of radical life style from radical politics. However, I do not think we have seen the last of the new morality's impact on the political system, especially if we accept the wider view of "politics-as-adaptation," which I have been advocating. In fact Yankelovich in another work described the emerging value system as a "new naturalism," and mentioned these among its components:

To push the Darwinian version of nature as "survival of the fittest" into the background, and to emphasize instead the interdependence of all things and species in nature.

> When society goes through major cultural changes each person within it experiences (perhaps more than once) a personal *metanoia,* in which many values are changed, beliefs rethought, and life styles reorganized.

281

---

[29]Charles Reich, *The Greening of America* (New York: Random House, 1970), p. 2.
[30]Daniel Yankelovich, *The New Morality* (New York: McGraw-Hill, 1974), p. 3.

To stress cooperation rather than competition.

To reject "official" and hence artificial forms of authority.

To preserve the environment at the expense of economic growth and technology.[31]

Obviously such values as these cannot spread very far within a society without altering its political institutions and public policies, as Yankelovich recognized. "Just when the students have abandoned their evangelism and activism," he concluded, "the seeds of the idea that now flourishes on campus have taken root in the larger culture. Before the decade of the 1970s has passed, the new naturalism will become a powerful force, nationwide in scope."[32]

At several points we have already touched on the evolutionary meaning of change in social values, and now I want to consider that matter more explicitly. One way of looking at it is to ask the question: does a society's survival depend on its values and beliefs? To put it another way, is a dominant social paradigm itself an adaptive mechanism, evolved to help the society deal with its environment? This is a subject that historians of culture have not yet undertaken to clarify for us, but I do not think it is going too far to suggest it as a working hypothesis. Taking Reich's model, for example, we could say that Consciousness I was the perfect value system for a society out to conquer and dominate a continent, that Consciousness II worked for a new mode of social adaptation stressing industry and mass organization, and that Consciousness III is a way of dealing with some of the problems created by I and II.

Waddington was getting at this same idea when he first advanced his theory of the biological basis of ethics. He argued that, "Observation of the world of living things reveals a general evolutionary direction, which has a philosophical status similar to that of healthy growth," and concluded that "Any particular set of ethical beliefs . . . can be meaningfully judged according to their efficacy in furthering this general evolutionary direction."[33]

Thus we might roughly compare the values of a society to the genetically inherited traits of an animal species. The giraffe's long neck, for example, enables it to function well in a suitable environment by feeding on the leaves of tall trees; the self-reliance of a Yankee pioneer evolved, similarly, in response to certain environmental conditions and functioned well within

282

---

[31]Daniel Yankelovich, "The New Naturalism," *Saturday Review*, 1 April 1972, p. 35.
[32]Ibid., p. 37.
[33]C. H. Waddington, *The Ethical Animal* (London: George Allen and Unwin, 1960), p. 7.

them. But the parallel only goes so far: cultural evolution plays according to a different set of rules. There can be rapid change from one generation to the next or within the life span of a single generation; in addition, there is the phenomenon of cultural diffusion, whereby one society can learn from another and thus in some measure become like another, and one person or group can change within a society in response to another person or group. Cultural diffusion may explain what appears to be happening as some of the values of the college youth culture of the 1960s become diffused through American society. Furthermore, cultural evolution creates the environmental circumstances that permit or require still further cultural evolution. This is the basic premise of the Marxist dialectic of history, which holds that a given social arrangement, such as capitalism, creates the conditions for the emergence of the opposite arrangement that will replace it.

In spite of the need for care in not confusing cultural values with genetic traits, we can still — and I think we had better — evaluate our social values and beliefs according to their ability to help us meet the challenges of our present evolutionary condition.

This raises another interesting question, one that the human species has never had to think about before: can we deliberately remake culture to suit present needs? Pirages and Ehrlich, the authors of *Ark II*, say we can and we must: "The task before us . . . is one of accelerating this movement toward a new DSP to replace the one that has been shaped by the industrial revolution and that is now leading inexorably toward the destruction of industrial society. Industrial mankind must remake its culture and direct future cultural evolution."[34]

Taking on responsibility for cultural evolution is admittedly a rather tall order for a species that has only rather recently in its historical past realized that there *is* such a thing as cultural evolution or, for that matter, any evolution at all.

Yet I rather suspect that we have already begun to do this and even to know that we are doing it. Certainly the American conservative's powerful reaction against "permissive" child-rearing has to do with the belief (probably correct) that such attitudes helped to produce the kinds of people we have discussed here under such rubrics as "counterculture" and "Consciousness III." Another sign of public awareness of our responsibility for cultural evolution is the politically charged interest in education; all this ferment about the content of textbooks and the presence or absence of discipline stems from

283

---
[34]Dennis C. Pirages and Paul R. Ehrlich, *Ark II* (New York: Viking, 1974), p. 61.

the conviction that what we do now will influence and shape the future.

Determining just what form this responsibility should take is difficult because we don't really know what the future will be like; we know only that it will be different from the present. Actually, human civilization has always been concerned with directing the course of cultural evolution, with shaping the future, but by far the greatest amount of effort has been committed to the perennially frustrated aim of perpetuating the past.

One thing our culture lacks at this point is a clear understanding of how much change is possible in a given time. In Chapter One I discussed some of the prevalent ideas on the subject of internalization, or the notion that a social paradigm becomes truly a part of each of us. This means that when society goes through major cultural changes each person within it experiences (perhaps more than once) a personal *metanoia* in which many values are changed, beliefs rethought, and life styles reorganized. We have never undergone cultural change at this rate before (I often wonder what time scale is being used by disillusioned radicals who think nothing much has happened in the past decade), and we do not have anything in our accumulated storehouse of experience to tell us what happens when a society is confronted with such changes. Yet such transformations are now part of the life experience of all of us. We can, of course, embrace the changes or resist them, but in either case we are caught up in a personal struggle to deal with the unfamiliar challenge of living out a human life span in the midst of a rapidly changing society. The most curious thing of all is that, even as we stand at the center of this whirlwind of change, we hold onto the belief that the "real" changes are going on in other parts of the world.

America as a Developing Nation

For several decades world politics has been torn by an ideological conflict over alternative courses of cultural evolution — essentially capitalist versus socialist. The socialist side had the advantage of starting with an explicitly evolutionary concept of politics: Marxist theory is structured on a timetable, a program for change. The capitalist nations, struggling to become something more than merely anti-Marxist, have had to create their own model of how societies should develop.

In America this grew rather naturally out of the dominant social paradigm and its reverence for economic progress, industry, and democratic institutions, and flowered into a sizable

I am truly amazed that sane men and women could look at American foreign policy and think their country had outgrown its "missionary fervor."

body of theoretical work.[35] The capitalist version of developmental theory is characterized by a conviction that the future of the so-called underdeveloped countries will resemble the past of the United States: "development," "modernization," and "Americanization" become more or less interchangeable terms. Here, for example, is a summary of current thinking on developmental theory by American political scientists:

Most commonly political scientists studying the phenomenon of modernization have treated what they call political development as a dependent variable, using other facets of modernization as independent variables. Accordingly, broad-gauged changes occurring in the political realm are usually regarded as subordinate to the general processes of (1) industrialization, (2) urbanization, (3) the spread of education and literacy, (4) increasing exposure to the mass media, and (5) the expansion of a secular culture. These independent factors are said to account for a variety of more strictly political developments such as (1) the growth of modern bureaucracies, (2) the development of a sense of nationhood, (3) the advent of political parties, (4) the expansion of popular political participation, (5) the increased capacity of the political system to mobilize resources for the accomplishment of its ends, and in the most modern politics, (6) the decline in the missionary fervor of political movements.[36]

These concepts of modernization are obviously inspired by America's availability as an example of what the successfully developed political system looks like. Furthermore, and here again we see that curious blocking of awareness, this summary is marked by an unwillingness to recognize the rather heavy American investment in *guiding* the development of the rest of the world along certain lines. I am truly amazed that sane men and women could look at American foreign policy and think their country had outgrown its "missionary fervor," but that was a common belief during the time American developmental theory was taking shape. Social scientists in the 1950s and 1960s talked about "the end of ideology" and tended to agree that, although there was much work left to be done in allocating the values of modern society, the kind of organization suitable to this task had been achieved. There was no longer any need

[35]Some examples of this genre include Gabriel Almond and James S. Coleman (eds.), *The Politics of Developing Areas* (Princeton, N.J.: Princeton University Press 1960); Gabriel Almond and G. Bingham Powell, Jr., *Comparative Politics: A Developmental Approach* (Boston: Little, Brown, 1966); Lucian W. Pye, *Aspects of Political Development* (Boston: Little, Brown, 1966); W. W. Rostow, *The Stages of Economic Growth* (London: Cambridge University Press, 1960).
[36]Stephen L. Wasby, *Political Science: The Discipline and Its Dimensions* (New York: Scribner's, 1970), p. 504.

for ideology if that meant raising basic questions about what the values should be (that is, what human beings *need*) or how the society should be organized. Seymour Lipset expressed this well:

The fundamental political problems of the industrial revolution have been solved: the workers have achieved industrial and political citizenship; the conservatives have accepted the welfare state; and the democratic left has recognized that an increase in over-all state power carries with it more dangers to freedom than solutions for economic problems. This very triumph of the democratic social revolution in the West ends domestic politics for those intellectuals who must have ideologies or utopias to motivate them to political action.[37]

The job, in short, had been done. Humanity's long quest for the good society had reached its goal. Democracy, said Lipset (clearly meaning "democracy" as it is practiced in Western industrialized nations), is "not only or even primarily a means through which different groups can attain their ends or seek the good society; it is the good society itself in operation."[38]

This complacency about the achievements of Western civilization was the solid ground from which America could look at the rest of the world — particularly at the peoples who had only recently been set free from colonial status — and discern some pattern in their ordeal. The United States had emerged from colonialism, consolidated its factions and regions into a nation-state, utilized its resources, and turned itself into a rich and relatively stable society. It seemed reasonable to expect that something similar might happen, or might be made to happen, elsewhere. There was an urgency in this program for development, since socialism was the obvious and persistent alternative.

Nobody was quite so naïve as to believe that other nations would proceed *precisely* as America had; developmental theorists granted that it might take a good long while, given the cultural differences, for fully democratic political institutions to evolve. There might even be a need for a certain amount of authoritarianism to build nations out of tribal societies, to convert simple agricultural economies into complex industrial ones. When stability and prosperity had been established, democracy would in time make its appearance. This slightly modified developmental theory legitimized our support of any

287

---

[37]Seymour Martin Lipset, *Political Man* (New York: Doubleday, 1960), p. 442.
[38]Ibid., p. 439.

number of autocratic, but at least noncommunist, rulers.

Theories of political development and the political acts they expressed — and I am talking now about a solid thirty years of American foreign policy, from the Truman Doctrine down through Kissinger diplomacy — were preoccupied with change *in certain parts of the world*. There were developed nations and developing nations, and that was that.

From this perspective it was clear that the *developing* nations would have to modify their values and beliefs. An economist noted that in India, for example, "Agricultural practices are controlled by custom and tradition. A villager is fearful of science. For many villagers, insecticide is taboo because all life is sacred."[39]

Obviously, for the sake of progress toward a better life the villagers would have to give up their archaic notions about the sacredness of all life and learn to perceive the world through the window of Western science. A UNESCO report reacting in a similar way to the discovery of different attitudes toward work stated: "In the least developed areas, the worker's attitude toward labour may entirely lack time perspective, let alone the concept of productive investment. For example, the day labourer in a rural area on his way to work, who finds a fish in the net he placed in the river the night before, is observed to return home, his needs being met."[40]

288

Another case of obsolete consciousness. Observations of this sort, noting the "backwardness" of cultural value systems in the developing areas, are commonplace. What I find particularly interesting is that they reveal a total acceptance of some of the notions about cultural evolution I have been offering here: that cultural values and beliefs are adaptive mechanisms by which a society functions (or fails to function) in its environment, and that they can be deliberately changed. I suspect the latter might have struck many readers as new and strange (it seemed so to me when I ran across the idea in *Ark II*), and yet its strangeness has to do only with applying it to our own culture. What else, after all, have we been trying to do with all our aid and assistance and advice to developing nations except deliberately change their values and beliefs, coax them into another mode of experiencing the world? And we have done this because we saw their values and beliefs as maladaptive, because (having, of course, abandoned our missionary fervor) we believed that they would not survive unless they embraced the American DSP.

[39]Alvin Hansen, *Economic Issues of the 1960's* (New York: McGraw-Hill, 1960), p. 157.
[40]UNESCO, *Report on the World Social Situation*, 9 March 1961, p. 69.

While we were so
energetically in-
volved in working
out an agenda for
the cultural evolution
of other people we
neglected to think
about our own de-
velopment.

289

While we were so energetically involved in working out an agenda for the cultural evolution of other people we neglected to think about our own development. We were prepared for incremental changes — adjustments, reforms, improvements — but not transformations; that was to be done elsewhere. The only concept we had of transformation was revolution, violent political upheaval followed by socialism or anarchy or perhaps both. Most Americans rejected this idea and in the process rejected the possibility of major change altogether. We had no other way of thinking about it.

The demand for change was there: the protests against our immense military involvements; the increasing restiveness of minority groups; the environmental movement; the various social critiques claiming that even those who enjoyed a piece of the pie were dehumanized, alienated, cut off from one another and from their deepest needs. All these seemed to add up to some kind of a demand that America *go* somewhere, but we had a hard time conceptualizing American development with anything like the Promethean vigor with which we mapped out evolutionary futures for other societies.

As a way of exploring the possibilities of change beyond our present "developed" state, let us take another look at the political developmental theory I have berated in the foregoing pages.

Writers in this field have generally divided themselves into two camps, depending on how they look at the changes that go on in developing countries. One group has searched for *continuum* patterns of growth — development along certain quantifiable lines such as GNP, employment, or political participation. Another has stressed *stages* of development — major leaps or transitions that mark the change from one level of growth to another. The following is another textbook excerpt that gives a good summary of the "stages" model of development:

At least three stages are usually postulated whenever an attempt is made to develop a stages model for application to countries the world over: (1) the traditional stage, characterized by an overwhelmingly rural society and agrarian economy, with appropriate political forms; (2) the transitional stage, still with a rural society, but characterized by an economy embarking on the early stages of industrialization and a political system which is accordingly undergoing transformation; and (3) the modern stage, characterized by a largely urban society and a mature industrial economy, with the appropriate political forms. In a general sense, the political system moves from (1) the traditional focus upon local concentrations of power with little articulation between the center and the periphery to (2) the transitional stage in which structures are emerging to involve the increasingly available masses in the political system while improving upon the technical means of expanding the power of the center into the periphery, and from there to (3) the modern stage with its centrally engineered economy and its perfected institutional means of involving all of society in the daily affairs of the individual at the same time the individual becomes involved in the national endeavor through whatever official means of participation are available to him.[41]

To the extent that we have thought about our own development, it has been mainly on the continuum model: greater GNP, higher standard of living, more equitable distribution of goods and services. Even the "postindustrial society" suggested by Daniel Bell and enshrined in the projections of that most backward of futurologists, Herman Kahn, turns out to be not a qualitative change in the nature of American society but rather an extension of past development in which (while the rest of the world becomes more Westernized) Western civilization becomes more like itself.[42] In this vision more will be produced and more will be consumed. All Americans will live suburban lives of gadget-filled contentment, worried only about what to do with their surplus of leisure time.

This brand of futurology is marked by a capacity to project change (including exponential change) within a certain paradigm, but it cannot deal with paradigm change — and obviously a development to a new historical stage (such as from primitive to transitional, from transitional to modern) must be a whole-system evolution involving changes in social values and beliefs, technology, and institutional forms. I am suggesting, of course, a transition to the *next* stage beyond modern industrial civilization.

Kenneth Boulding wrote of such a transition in his book *The Meaning of the Twentieth Century:*

The twentieth century marks the middle period of a great transition in the state of the human race. It may properly be called the second great transition in the history of mankind.

The first transition was that from precivilized to civilized society.... This is a transition that is still going on in some parts

---

[41]Wasby, *Political Science: The Discipline*, pp. 505-6.
[42]See, for example, Herman Kahn and B. Bruce-Briggs, *Things to Come* (New York: Macmillan, 1972).

Any choice we make will be an affirmation of our responsibility and of our ability to build on the experiences of the past. Evolution has no reverse gear.

of the world, although it can be regarded as almost complete. Precivilized society can now be found only in small and rapidly diminishing pockets in remote areas. It is doubtful whether more than 5 percent of the world's population could now be classified as living in a genuinely precivilized society.

Even as the first great transition is approaching completion, however, a second great transition is treading on its heels. It may be called the transition from civilized to post-civilized society.[43]

Boulding did not speculate about the possible characteristics of a postcivilization stage, but he did note that it might produce societies "quite different not only in the political and social institutions but in the value systems and the nature and quality of human life which they support."[44] Other writers, agreeing with Boulding that we are in the midst of a qualitative transition to a new stage of social revolution, have tried to discern some of the outlines of the emerging order of things.

Toffler in *Futureshock* predicts an "ad-hocracy" in which institutional forms become more flexible and impermanent, a collapse of hierarchical bureaucratic structures, increasing personal mobility, different property arrangements (the "rental revolution"), and a technology oriented more toward refining and enriching human life than merely producing objects.[45] George Leonard in *The Transformation* talks of fundamental alterations in our experience of such things as politics, war, race, sexuality, energy, information.[46] And Robin Clarke offers the following, admittedly utopian, program for change (see table following).

Programs and analyses of this sort are significant in that they deal with the question of the development of "developed" industrial societies, and they also deal with a stage model of development. They may use extrapolations of future development along present lines — such as the projections of resource depletion in *The Limits to Growth*[47] — but this is usually with the intention of proving the necessity for complete change into a new kind of social system with a different technology and economy. Usually in place of the assumptions about growth, which have been cherished in traditional visions of the American future, there is talk about "steady-state" or "no-growth" economy, about zero or negative population growth.

292

---

[43]Kenneth E. Boulding, *The Meaning of the Twentieth Century: The Great Transition* (New York: Harper & Row, 1965). Volume 34 of World Perspectives Series, planned and edited by Ruth Nanda Anshen.
[44]Ibid., p. 19.
[45]Toffler, *Futureshock*.
[46]George Leonard, *The Transformation* (New York: Delacorte, 1972).
[47]Donella H. Meadows et al., *The Limits to Growth* (New York: Universe Books, 1972).

Some Utopian Characteristics of Soft Technology

"HARD" TECHNOLOGY SOCIETY	"SOFT" TECHNOLOGY SOCIETY
1. Ecologically unsound	Ecologically sound
2. Large energy input	Small energy input
3. High pollution rate	Low or no pollution rate
4. Nonreversible use of materials and energy sources	Reversible materials and energy sources only
5. Functional for limited time only	Functional for all time
6. Mass production	Craft industry
7. High specialization	Low specialization
8. Nuclear family	Communal units
9. City emphasis	Village emphasis
10. Alienation from nature	Integration with nature
11. Consensus politics	Democratic politics
12. Technical boundaries set by wealth	Technical boundaries set by nature
13. Worldwide trade	Local bartering
14. Destructive of local culture	Compatible with local culture
15. Technology liable to misuse	Safeguards against misuse
16. Highly destructive to other species	Dependent on well-being of other species
17. Innovation regulated by profit and war	Innovation regulated by need
18. Growth-oriented economy	Steady-state economy
19. Capital intensive	Labor intensive
20. Alienates young and old	Integrates young and old
21. Centralist	Decentralist
22. General efficiency increases with size	General efficiency increases with smallness
23. Operating modes too complicated for general comprehension	Operating modes understandable by all
24. Technological accidents frequent and serious	Technological accidents few and unimportant
25. Singular solutions to technical and social problems	Diverse solutions to technical and social problems
26. Agricultural emphasis on monoculture	Agricultural emphasis on diversity
27. Quantity criteria highly valued	Quality criteria highly valued
28. Food production specialized industry	Food production shared by all
29. Work undertaken primarily for income	Work undertaken primarily for satisfaction
30. Small units totally dependent on others	Small units self-sufficient
31. Science and technology alienated from culture	Science and technology integrated with culture
32. Science and technology performed by specialist elites	Science and technology performed by all
33. Strong work/leisure distinction	Weak or nonexistent work/leisure distinction
34. High unemployment	(Concept not valid)
35. Technical goals valid for only a small proportion of the globe for a finite time	Technical goals valid "for all men for all time"

Source: Robin Clarke, *The Co-Evolution Quarterly*, Winter Solstice 1974, p. 59.

Beginning to take shape out of such works as those I have just cited, out of our changing cultural values, out of our various urges to close the glaring ideal/reality gaps in the workings of government and of our dawning sense of environmental responsibility is a vision of an alternative future, a possible evolution toward a different kind of society. This could be called a new "political development" theory; it is often described by those who are striving actively to bring it into being as a new paradigm. For the moment I would like to call it an ideology, a body of ideas capable of being stated in *political* terms for the purpose of articulating alternative lines of evolutionary change.

Of course the question of how we choose to develop is a political question; it has not quite matured to the status of a political issue. Although there are many conflicts that have to do with what kind of future society we are creating (most environmental conflicts are in this category), for the most part these seem to be unrelated skirmishes rather than what they are — preludes to an opening dialogue about what kind of species we want to be, how we shall choose to organize in relation to each other and to the natural environment that we inhabit and are learning to control. Its appearance as an issue is obscured by the popularity of the idea that we have reached an "end of ideology," that there are no basic choices to be made, that all our political and economic decisions are merely minor adjustments in the onward-and-upward course toward a more efficiently productive technocracy.

It will take us a while to get the feel of evolutionary politics, to admit to our awareness that the decisions made by human institutions shape the course of our own cultural *and* genetic evolution, the survival of species, the face of the planet. Since we are already engaged in shaping evolution, it seems to me that the very least we can do is to recognize it and think about the incredible array of options we have about *how* to do it.

I am speaking primarily of American politics, since we are the society farthest along the road of "modernization" and most in need of some dialogues about what comes next. Moreover we exert a tremendous influence over the rest of the world. There is scarcely a corner of the planet that does not feel the impact of American technology, American business, American politics, American culture. Even the Communist world, so resolutely embarked on its own course of cultural evolution, appears to be powerfully affected by our gross success in the production of goods. We need to pay more attention than we have in the past to our own development, but whatever happens here will undoubtedly be part of the evolution of the species — and the world as a whole.

I hope I have made clear that there is no going back, that *any* choice we make will be an affirmation of our responsibility and of our ability to build on the experiences of the past. Evolution has no reverse gear. If we should choose in the future to develop simpler and smaller technologies and communities, we will still not be going back to the Middle Ages; we will merely be using what we have learned from the experience of the modern era. If we should choose to protect endangered species and areas of wilderness, we will be doing so by deliberate action and under conditions far removed from the old "survival-of-the-fittest" rules of evolution. We left that garden long ago. Whatever happens next will be what we, as a society, decide to make happen.

I realize that this is a rather awesome responsibility to load on our system of institutions, and I would not be proposing to make us responsible for the course of evolution unless we had already taken on that responsibility. Athough I am not overwhelmed by the wisdom of democratic policy making, it seems to me that this is a reasonable place for the responsibility to lie. We have had our day with kings, and the current choice is whether the course of human evolution will be charted by small groups of experts or by large numbers of people working within the institutions we have evolved for the purpose of articulating alternatives and making choices.

This particular mission may not have been what the Founding Fathers had in mind. But for better or for worse, the living planet will have to take its chances on democracy.

Epilogue:

Humanism and Human Chauvinism

We take a tiny colony of soft corals
from a rock in a little water world. And
that isn't terribly important to the tide
pool. Fifty miles away the Japanese shrimp
boats are dredging with overlapping scoops,
bringing up tons of shrimps, rapidly
destroying the ecological balance of the
whole region. That isn't very important in
the world. And six thousand miles away the
great bombs are falling on London and the
stars are not moved thereby. None of it is
important or all of it is.

JOHN STEINBECK AND EDWARD F. RICKETTS, *Sea of Cortez*

All thoughts about politics, whether they go by the name of theory, ideology, or paradigm, rest on some assumptions about human needs. We do not begin to build a new social order or evaluate the one we have now except by asking questions about what human beings need to live satisfying and fulfilling lives. Different political viewpoints give different answers. A social libertarian will tell you that people need freedom; a Marxist will say they need control over the means of production; a fascist will say they need order and national pride. Democratic theory, especially alert to the threat of tyranny, elevated certain needs to the status of inalienable rights, God-given, which were the duty of governments to guarantee and protect.

In Chapter One I mentioned Abraham Maslow's humanistic theory of needs, which was constructed on a hierarchical model. At the bottom are certain physiological needs that always claim first priority, and as these are met other needs — for belongingness and love, self-respect and self-actualization — tend to emerge into consciousness and claim the attention of the growing person. Maslow believed (and so do I) that these needs are genetically inherited and specieswide. Nevertheless they can be modified by cultural conditioning: different people in different societies have different senses of what they need. We can learn to repress our sexual needs, for example (that is what

John Steinbeck and Edward F. Ricketts, *Sea of Cortez* (New York: Viking, 1941), pp. 3-4.

Freudian psychoanalysis is about), and we can also learn to want things we don't really need (that is what advertising is about).

Human beings create social organizations because most needs can be better met by cooperative effort and, I suspect, because cooperative effort itself meets a need. The evolution of societies should be in the direction of creating a greater understanding of what human needs are and creating greater opportunities for these needs to be met. Most change is not a direct onward-and-upward march along all fronts but an uncertain advance, with many losses among the gains. I doubt, for example, that belongingness and love needs are more adequately taken care of in modern New York City than they were in a medieval village.

The special genius of the American system is producing goods, but goods take care of only the basic needs for food and shelter. The higher needs — for love and belongingness, self-respect and respect from others, actualization of latent talents and abilities — must be satisfied in less tangible ways, through experiences and relationships, in that realm of human interaction the economists unromantically call "services." The system has tried hard to perpetuate the myth that objects could do it all, that belongingness comes free with a better mouthwash, and self-respect is synonymous with pride of ownership. The myth is, to put it more bluntly and accurately, a lie: the higher human needs are not satisfied by manufactured goods, and the attempt to do so is incredibly wasteful of energy and resources. We look behind the proud statistic of a 53,000 percent increase in disposable soda bottles and find no commensurate improvement in the human condition; we find nothing at all except broken glass.

The shift in cultural values that I have been discussing in this epilogue has to do with a perhaps dim recognition of this truth by a relatively large segment of the American population. There is just the possibility that we may now be starting to develop a better understanding of what human beings need so we can create social arrangements more enriching to human life. It is appropriate and probably not accidental that we turn to this emerging consciousness at the same time that we confront some of the ecological consequences of our past over-emphasis on production and consumption of material goods.

American history has been pervaded by a sense of limitlessness: first limitless expanses of land and then, as the frontiers ran out, limitless possibilities of urban growth, productivity, technology, and energy. The lesson we are being forced to learn

The living things that coexist with us on the American space and the space itself — the land and water and air — are all parts of the same living system. They are inseparable parts.

299

The species we save
(or destroy) will be
our own.

from ecological crisis is that there are limits: limits to how much the human population can increase, limits to the manageability of urban growth, limits on converting new land to agricultural use, limits to the quantities of waste that can be dumped into the air and water and onto the land, limits to resources, limits to energy.

This is sobering news, and it is not surprising that the environmentalists are most unpopular in some circles. Yet it may turn out that the news is not all bad. If we can back away slightly from our infatuation with plastic wrappers and pocket calculators and take another look at what we know about human needs, we see abundant — perhaps limitless — possibilities for creating humanistic social arrangements to satisfy them. We may well have to deal with a real scarcity of commodities such as fossil fuels, but we do not have to assume that self-respect and love must always be regarded as scarce and parceled out so frugally. (Although I am using Maslow's need hierarchy as a frame of reference here, humanistic psychology is only a recent embellishment on the vast amount of evidence that human societies can produce great quantities of joy and dignity out of a limited supply of material goods.)

300

Let me make it clear that I am not suggesting we counsel the poor to be happy with their lot. We cannot deny the preeminence of simple physiological needs: the hungry need food and the homeless need shelter. I am saying that our overstuffed society would do well to reconsider its priorities and pay more attention to politics as a way of creating, or allowing to come into being, social arrangements aimed directly at satisfying higher human needs. If we can do so our sudden encounter with natural limits becomes not the end of the world but the beginning of a new phase of cultural evolution.

I have been talking about people, and like any humanist I can easily get caught up with thoughts of how to enrich the quality of life for many people, how to search out new directions for human evolution. But politics is not an exclusively human enterprise. Surely we can see from the record of American history that the system includes all the species whose lives are affected by it. Our government may be of the people and by the people, but it is not for the people only; it is also for billions of other living creatures.

Our culture has endowed us with a limited perspective on that subject. Generally we think of life processes only in relation to human purposes. You can hear this in the words we use. A swamp or a desert teeming with life is "useless." Plants and animals are either "useful to man" and hence "good," or "harmful to man" and consequently out of luck. Animals that threaten domestic species are "pests" or "predators," and plants we don't like are "weeds." There is no precise botanical definition of a weed; it is merely a name for whatever flora get in our way.

Our political heritage reflects this human-centered view of nature. It tells us that all men are endowed by their creator with inalienable rights, and that among these are the right to life, liberty, and the pursuit of happiness; further it suggests by its silence on the subject that the endowing went no further, that other beings have no rights whatever. We have no place in our legal system for other life forms except the status of property.

Can we think about such things some other way? Undoubtedly we can; some people are already doing so. In 1972 the University of Southern California Law Review published an essay entitled "Should Trees Have Standing? Toward Legal Rights for Natural Objects."[1] The essay, written by Christopher D. Stone, professor at the USC law school, proposed that natural objects such as trees be recognized as having rights and be protected by law against wanton destruction, even by their legal owners. Stone's argument was cited by Justice William O. Douglas in his dissenting opinion in the case of *Sierra Club* v. *Morton:* "Contemporary public concern for protecting nature's ecological equilibrium should lead to the conferral of standing upon environmental objects to sue for their own protection."[2] Justices Blackmun and Brennan agreed.

Stone pointed out in support of this idea that there is ample precedent for recognizing the legal rights of mute, even nonhuman, entities: "It is no answer to say that streams and forests cannot have standing because streams and forests cannot speak. Corporations cannot speak either; nor can states, estates, infants, incompetents, municipalities or universities. Lawyers speak for them, as they customarily do for the ordinary citizen with legal problems."[3]

The gist of Stone's argument is that the courts should allow organizations such as the Sierra Club to be given a legal status similar to guardianship, which would permit them to bring suits on behalf of threatened nonhuman entities. Thus what seems at first glance to be weird and unthinkable turns out to be quite thinkable after all. "The fact is," writes Stone, "that each

301

[1]Stone, 45 S. Cal. L. Rev. 450 (1972).
[2]401 U.S. 907 (1971).
[3]Christopher D. Stone, *Should Trees Have Standing?* (Los Altos, Calif.: William Kaufmann, 1974), p. 17. This book includes the essay and opinions in *Sierra Club* v. *Morton.*

time there is a movement to confer rights onto some new 'entity,' the proposal is bound to sound odd or frightening or laughable. This is partly because until the rightless thing receives its rights, we cannot see it as anything but a *thing* for the use of 'us' — those who are holding rights at the time."[4] The rights of trees are, given the appropriate stage of cultural evolution, as thinkable as the rights of women or children or slaves.

The living things that coexist with us on the American space and the space itself — the land and water and air — are all parts of the same living system. They are inseparable parts. We can separate the economy or the political system *conceptually*, for whatever intellectual gratification that may give us, but no economic or political power — no human life, in fact — exists apart from its support system. This is true even though the wealth extracted from the ecosystem is applied to human purposes, and of course the decisions about how it is to be managed are made by human beings.

I do not propose that the human species abdicate this role; the question is whether we recognize the full extent of the responsibility we have acquired along with our power, and whether we at least consider whether the entities that make up the other 99-plus percent of the ecosystem have any rights. It should be made clear that the only right under discussion is the right to exist, and also that we are in many cases dealing with the question of the existence of species, not merely the lives of individual beings. At the level of power that we have now reached, and with our ability to guide the course of the evolution of species, it is reasonable that the question of criteria be raised. In other words, it is time to ask whether other elements in the system are to be recognized as having any function except in relation to human purposes. This does not mean completely abandoning our human-centered perspective, because there is also the fact of interdependence: over the long haul of environmental management it may turn out that, to paraphrase an old safety slogan, the species we save (or destroy) will be our own.

To deal with these questions we will have to rethink or refeel some of our deepest beliefs about the role of the human species in the world and in the cosmos. This will mean creating a new paradigm, but in the process of doing so we may find to our surprise that we can dust off and reuse some of the old, neglected pieces of our Western heritage. Although the book of Genesis is frequently cited as the fountainhead of our belief in

302

---

[4]Ibid., p. 8.

the rightness of manipulating nature (which in a sense it is), Genesis also contains an idea of stewardship, a mandate to replenish the earth as well as subdue it. We could do worse than use that as a cornerstone for a new paradigm.

The political power I have been writing about here, the human power over the course of evolution, is greater now than it has ever been, but it is not exactly new: human beings since before recorded history have altered landscapes and climates, perpetuated the existence of some species and hastened the extinction of others. We are at a place where we must recognize that we have such power and have had it all along. We must recognize also that there are limits, laws we do not yet fully understand; we can see that we are powerful, though not yet omnipotent. We must become aware that evolution has changed its course and that the human species is the agent of change. We can do whatever we want to do with that knowledge except the one thing we have tried hardest to do: avoid it. That knowledge, once gained, will not go away, and it will probably change us.

Index

304

306

Art & Photography Credits

Cover: left to right
Culver Pictures, Inc.
Jean-Claude LeJeune, The Stockmarket, L.A.
Baker and Johnston, The Smithsonian Institution
Brown Brothers
Library of Congress
Jean-Claude LeJeune, The Stockmarket, L.A.

  1 Burk Uzzle, Magnum
  7 Glade Walker, U.S. Department of the Interior
  9 Jean-Claude LeJeune, The Stockmarket, L.A.
 14 George Tooker, The Metropolitan Museum of Art
 23 Bruce Davidson, Magnum
 25 Bob Fitch, Black Star
 29 Bill Owens
 34 Eddie Adams, Wide World Photos
 42 Denver Public Library, Western Collection
 45 Library of Congress
 49 Brown Brothers
 52 Library of Congress
 59 Historical Pictures Service, Inc.
 64 Brown Brothers
 72 Arnold Genthe, The Museum of Modern Art
 75 Brown Brothers
 80 Brown Brothers
 87 Brown Brothers
 92 Solomon D. Butcher Collection, Nebraska State Historical Society
 98 Library of Congress
101 Charles Marut, The Stockmarket, L.A.
105 The Bettmann Archive
107 Brown Brothers
111 Brown Brothers
113 U.S. Department of Agriculture
116 Jean-Claude LeJeune, The Stockmarket, L.A.
119 The Washington State Historical Society
121 The Burton Holmes Collection, The Stockmarket, L.A.
125 The Library of Congress
128 John Launois, Black Star
133 Leo Choplin, Black Star
136 The Burton Holmes Collection, The Stockmarket, L.A.
137 Charles Moore, Black Star
141 Walker Evans, The Library of Congress
145 Los Angeles County Flood Control District
151 Jean-Claude LeJeune, The Stockmarket, L.A.
157 Brown Brothers
161 Brown Brothers
165 Bruce Davidson, Magnum
170 Declan Haun, Black Star
176 Fred Ward, Black Star
181 Library of Congress
190 Brown Brothers
199 Dan McCoy, Black Star
202 Marshall Licht, The Stockmarket, L.A.
213 Mark Godfrey, Magnum
216 Brown Brothers
223 Historical Pictures Service, Inc.
226 Courtesy of Liggett & Meyers
231 Brown Brothers
232 Lewis Hine, Library of Congress
238 Jean-Claude LeJeune, The Stockmarket, L.A.
244 Jean-Claude LeJeune, The Stockmarket, L.A.
247 Daniel S. Brody, Stock, Boston
252 John Launois, Black Star
259 Ken Kay
268 Jean-Claude LeJeune, The Stockmarket, L.A.
276 Jean-Claude LeJeune, The Stockmarket, L.A.
285 Jean-Claude LeJeune, The Stockmarket, L.A.
289 Dennis Brack, Black Star
296 Redwood Empire Association
303 Jean-Claude LeJeune, The Stockmarket, L.A.